The Rise and Fall of the Sideshow Geek

Snake Eaters, Human Ostriches, & Other Extreme Entertainments

Nathan Wakefield

IMPRINTS

Outside Talker Press (an imprint of Vaudevisuals Press) in partnership with

Shocked and Amazed! Imprints (A Subsidiary of Dolphin-Moon Press)

Layout by Nathan Wakefield
Edited by James Taylor
Illustrations by Peter Striffolino
Cover Design by Lisa Marie Pompilio

ISBN: 978-1-7372036-4-3

Library of Congress Control Number: 2023910643

Published by Outside Talker Press (an imprint of Vaudevisuals Press) in partnership with Shocked and Amazed! Imprints (A Subsidiary of Dolphin-Moon Press).
www.outsidetalkerpress.com
www.shockedandamazed.com

When you feel like giving up, go lie down with the geek.

- Unknown

Contents

Foreword: "It's Common"

Not to be a heretic about the showbiz, but maybe some shows were almost designed "to be missed": geek shows, for example. Shows so extreme, so "other," that, though they attracted huge numbers (and money) in their day, they also drove huge numbers away. Let me explain by way of a jackpot (a showman's tale). My first mentor in this end of the business – the outdoor end, including circus and carnival – was my ma's boyfriend, Jerry Farrow, himself more a ride guy, a jointee, so called, a concessionaire, who was never a hardcore showman. Except when he almost was.

Jerry's first season on the road may not have been on Prell's Broadway Shows, but he always talked as though it were; certainly, that show and old man Prell – whom Jerry called Pop – were instrumental in making him the outdoor carnival man he became. He had the first and likely only pony ride that ever played Prell's (Jerry loved his ponies), but he just couldn't do any time on the midway and not be lured to the shows, a distinct – and distinctly different – end of the outdoor business that could be an expensive end to maintain: Shows carried large numbers of staff & talent (money) and were large-scale affairs (time & logistics) that could draw as much heat (read: law enforcement) as any game, certainly as any mere concession. So any show that was an almost-guaranteed money-maker, Jerry and any other showman would likely jump at that chance.

Which gets us to Jerry in "Pop" Prell's office, his trailer on the lot. And Jerry's been made an offer that he could hardly refuse. As Prell told it to Jerry (and Jerry to me, as I remember it), there was a showman on the carnival who was also quite the gambler, meaning, his luck was crap. And what did the showman lose in that gambling he'd gone up against? His show. His GEEK show. Which, of course, included his talent and staff on the show, all of whose contracts would transfer to the new owner. Yeah, you see where this is going: The show was offered to – and accepted by – the newly minted showman, Jerry Farrow. And a week goes by. And Jerry's making so much money off the show, it's stunning to him, a pony guy, a ride guy, a jointee. But Pop Prell also knew the rest of the story. "So, Jerry, you been in your show yet?" asks the old man.

"No, Pop, haven't."

"You need to go into your show, Jerry. It's common."

"Swallows Living Animals" attraction. Image courtesy of the Shocked and Amazed! archive.

This was the geek show Jerry now owned: On the bally platform in front of the show sat the attractant, what got your attention, and she sat in front of the midway crowd doing her bit, chain smoking cigarettes, popping mice into her mouth from a little box she had beside her, belching the mice back up after "swallowing" them (which she really wasn't), smoking some more, then repeat. All day, every day of the fair when the show was running. Inside, the true geek made the real show. Calling himself the English Subject (Jerry never got his birth name), his was a "pit" show, as most geek shows were: him standing in the middle of a canvas enclosure about waist high, a cloth wall to hold back the crowd, and, in his act, a crap-load of snakes doing their business at, over and around his feet. And, reaching down to pick one up, he'd glare maniacally at the crowd... and swallow the snake, tail first, down & down, a sword swallowing act perpetrated with a living reptile. Pulled back up – the snake unharmed, as much as – the English Subject would cackle, glare at the crowd, and shout out, "Ooooo, tickled my gizzard! Felt so good, I gotta do it again!" And true to his geekish word, that he would. Dropping that snake, he'd reach down, pick up "another snake," glare and cackle at the crowd, then into his mouth with it. Pulling it out, though, led to the geek whirling it around his head, its black whip winging overhead the English Subject. And then he'd hurl it into the crowd. Exit crowd: screaming. Which got the complete attention of everyone on the midway. Hell, it got the attention of everybody at the fair. Of course, that's that show's express purpose: get 'em in, get 'em out; never let anything stand in the way of your money. That's the showbiz.

Jerry finally did go into and witness "his" geek show. And he ran out and lost his lunch. It really was that kind of show. It was *supposed* to be that kind of show in effect. The reality, the behind the scenes, the framing of the show, of course, was not what it appeared, not even to Jerry at first: No show was going to carry the amount of livestock – be it snakes or the more "literary" chickens or piglets – that would have been needed to have a geek chow down on a life form every show. A dozen shows or more a day? Doubtful. Besides, who in the biz wants to put out all that money to buy all that livestock, even if you are making back the investment on the front of the show? No, the simplest and easiest was to gaff the act, use misdirection and sleight of hand, fake it. Sometimes – maybe – the last show of the last night would be "real," but what would that matter as long as the show was worth the admission? For that matter, what does it say about the audience which's paying good money to watch a fellow human being as he "swallows living animals"? Or seem to: That snake whirled overhead, tossed frighteningly into the crowd? A piece of black rope the English Subject had lying amidst the true snakes. The savageness of the English Subject himself? He was a degreed herpetologist with a bank account in every town they played, where – week's end – he'd deposit his sizeable end of the gross (which eventually turned into a piece of property to which he retired, thank you very much).

But at week's end, Jerry having sent to his bank account and then-living wife an amount of money equal to a month's take otherwise, she asked the logical question: "What's goin' on, Jerry? This is an awful lot of money."

"I got a show, hon'. It's goin' great!"

"What kind of show, Jerry?"

"Uh, it's a geek show."

"Don't come home with no geek show, Jerry."

And that was the end of Jerry's geek show days. Such is also the show biz. But who knows, for some things – these shows included, apparently – the stories and history lessons are more profound, perhaps, than the shows themselves.

James Taylor

Introduction

Why write a book about a single sideshow act, especially one as vile as the Geek act? It's a logical question – one that I have asked myself many times, in fact. A short answer would be simple: intrigue. But that doesn't really do the subject at hand justice, so I shall expand upon my motivations further before taking you on this dark and bizarre journey.

The variety arts have always interested me, particularly sideshow. I remember hearing about all of the various acts and performers when I was younger and being completely amazed by the idea of this sort of spectacle. As I became older, I began reading about them in detail, going to modern sideshow performances, and eventually performing sideshow-style acts myself. Reading old books about the various types of sideshow acts and then comparing them to their contemporary counterparts fascinated me. I enjoyed the information I found about fakirs jabbing themselves with needles, people with physical abnormalities being put on display for public viewing, and human marvels subjecting themselves to fire in ways that you wouldn't think possible. But one act always stood out to me the most as I studied sideshow – the geek act.

Something about the geek act really stuck with me. The extreme nature and macabre element of it all fascinated me to no end – particularly that it was widespread enough at one point in history to have become a standardized type of act with its own verbiage and performance expectations. However, it also brought up many questions: How did something this weird start? How widespread was it? Were there any famous geeks? Thus began my early research.

The biggest point of frustration I had initially when I began to seek out resources specifically on the subject was that, while there are no shortages of literary sources that reference the existence of the geek act, finding detailed information is difficult. Most works I'd read were content to simply mention in a small section that a geek show was a vile and macabre performance. Usually, this would entail an author casually referencing the common trope of the geek show centering around a performer biting the head off a living creature and offer no other context or information. However, the rest of the book would then contain in-depth information about specific historical figures within other subgenres of sideshow and cover various other working acts at great length, relegating the geeks to the margins. Although they acknowledged the geek and touched upon it slightly, they rarely provided other insights about this particular facet of sideshow history. Most works seem to barely scratch the surface of geek. They provide an alluring hook with the general description but no payoff once they have the reader's attention. The act seemed so gruesome but profound on a primal level, so I wanted to find out more; I was interested in a deep exploration of the subject.

Even more frustrating is the lack of media that relates to geek shows specifically. There are many vintage and widely circulated photos of sword swallowers, fire eaters, and born oddities, even video in some cases. These bits of media provide valuable historical context and give a stunning visual to match specific performers to known act types. But the same resources aren't available when it comes to geek shows, thus making vague descriptions found in widely circulated texts the primary sources of information. This leaves those interested in the subject disappointed and yearning for a better picture. What did an actual, true-blue sideshow geek look like? What techniques did they use? Further, are these performances as interesting as they sound, or is it simply a case of mystique fueling fascination?

The paltry amount of historic geek show media is due not only to the violent nature of the act but also to the fact that the geeks worked in carnivals. Itinerate performers working in "lowbrow" establishments were hardly a priority for historical preservation, particularly in the context of what recording devices were available at the time period in which geek shows peaked in popularity. Given some of the questionable conditions surrounding many geek shows, it is unlikely that some showmen would have been welcoming toward open documentation anyway. Going further, sideshows themselves have long been known for their use of extreme puffery as a means to promote their attractions. Most was good-natured in the name of entertainment, but in cases of shows that have very little recorded history of credible nature and rely instead on hearsay, it becomes difficult to separate fact from fiction.

Many traditional sideshow acts have evolved and are performed to this day. The venues have changed but the acts themselves have been preserved. Instead of seeing sword swallowers, human pincushions, and little people at the fairgrounds under a tent, you are more likely to see their shows today at a rock music club or tattoo convention, with updated presentations for contemporary audiences.

This is not true for the geek act, at least not in the traditional sense. Due to animal and human rights laws as well as changing social perspectives, the geek act is largely a thing of the past as it relates to commonplace entertainment and will likely never be revived in an open public setting. Like many elements of history that are put under a microscope, the geek act is not morally pristine, especially when viewed through the lens of contemporary social perspectives. There are absolutely elements of physical abuse and racism found in the history of the geek act. These aspects are referenced herein to provide an authentic historical picture, not as a means of endorsement.

What this all comes down to ultimately is that the geek show is a traditional circus and carnival sideshow act that is widely referenced but poorly documented, probably exaggerated, historically controversial, and will likely never be repeated. Much of the information that existed about it has been largely forgotten. Not only that, but due to the evolution of the word *geek* both in popular culture and in performance, the word is often misused and misunderstood.

Although this work started out as late-night research and rage-writing sessions, it slowly evolved into something much more substantial. I began digging deeper and deeper into the subject, uncovering interesting information and piecing it together into a formatted piece of history. Over the next few years, I found myself scouring through newspaper articles, visiting library archives, having old texts translated, and interviewing show people, hoping they could answer some of the many questions that arose from my research. Soon, I found myself deep down the rabbit hole of all things geek and I became obsessed with finding out as much as I could. I became determined to put everything together into a work of my own. If I could not find a good resource to read about geeks, then I would create my own comprehensive source on the subject. You could say that I eventually found myself geeking out over geeks.

A challenge that I found after this work evolved into a serious project was that I was several decades too late in my research in one regard: Most showmen who were actively running geek shows have since passed on. Many of the old-timers in carnival and circus now still possess a wealth of knowledge on the subject but it is, with a few exceptions, largely a result of secondhand information passed down to them rather than from firsthand experience working in actual geek shows. Nonetheless, I am still very pleased at the hundreds of sources I was able to locate and utilize on this subject. Many books on the variety arts unfortunately lack proper source citations (even today). To help aid in proper historical preservation and provide ease of use for researchers interested in the original source material, I have listed all of my sources in the back of this work and provided in-text citations as well. I am a firm believer in hearing history in the intended form when applicable, so where I was able, I made a point to include long-form quotes and historical texts so that the historical value is in the original words.

In an effort to be as complete as possible, I've attempted to profile as many relevant historical figures as I could. However, this is by no means a complete representation as there are always going to be additional biographies that readers may feel could have been included. I have also included several well-known historical figures for context but have kept their biographies brief, as there are so many other works currently available that document their lives in detail. I have made a point to try to expand upon their lives with additional information I was able to uncover, but I have tried to focus on including more detailed and longer bios on the more obscure performers where less had been written about them previously. I am very pleased that much of the information included has not been widely published before, and some of the findings contained here actually dispel and correct erroneous information contained in other publications.

To help tell the story of the geek show as well as I am able, I've also made a point to include as many pictures as I could to help provide the reader with better visual context. There are numerous images I was able to uncover from old archives and images I obtained personally that have not (to my knowledge) been widely circulated prior to this publication, at least not in over a century.

I am not sure a work that covers such an unusual and somewhat historically scattered piece of live entertainment can ever truly be considered a complete history. However, I am very pleased with how it came out and am grateful for everyone's cooperation who helped me uncover the history of the geek show as it is presented here. It is my hope that by compiling information, uncovering obscure references, gaining insight from those with expertise on the subject, and providing personal commentary, I can help preserve the past and present a greater understanding of this strange element of sideshow history from years gone by.

So sit back, dim the lights, and refrain from eating anything anytime soon. Things are about to get real weird.

Nathan Wakefield

Ypsilanti, MI, USA

May 2023

Chapter 1

Defining Geek

P icture this, if you will. It's a warm summer day in the 1930s. The local carnival is in town at the county fairgrounds in a middle-American town. Thousands of community members of all ages are out in full force to enjoy the festivities.

The farmers have their animals on display, and local vendors are out promoting their goods and services. Children nibble on sweet treats from the concession stands and young adults try their hand at the carnival games, many of them getting in line to ride the Ferris wheel later on. The carnival has a little something for everyone in the family to enjoy.

There's even some live entertainment over at the midway.[1] One tent has a banner painting that shows a man eating fire. Another depicts a very overweight man, claiming that he is the heaviest in the world. One attraction, however, seems oddly darker than the rest. Rather than conveying a sense of joy or amazement, the banner outside this tent is a painting of a maniacal person holding up a snake, with a murderous glare painted onto their face. Screams periodically emanate from within this tent as paying customers flee from it in terror. Between shows, one of the men working the attraction stands outside the tent, encouraging fair-goers to purchase a ticket to see the performer "eat 'em alive." This is the tent that houses the geek show. But just what exactly is a geek?

Like many words, *geek* can mean different things and have different definitions depending on the context. These days, many people relate the word to be largely synonymous with *nerd*, as that has become the most common usage. This book focuses on geek as it relates to one particular usage of the word – that which relates to the circus or carnival sideshow act.

In regards to raw terminology, the word *geek* is most likely an evolved variant of the word *geck*, defined as "A fool, simpleton; one who is befooled or derided, a dupe." It's German origin dates to the 1500s, where it began as *Geke*. In the 1600s it was seen as *Gecke*, then finally *Geck* starting in the mid-1800s ("geck, n.1." OED Online). By the late 1800s, the spelling of it began to show up occasionally as *geek*, with it retaining the same general definition and usage. However, it wasn't until a number of years into the 20th century that the word would be used to describe a particular type of live performance.

Though the sideshow geek act does, in fact, refer to a very specific type of act, there are some challenges when it comes to outlining exactly what elements must be in place in order for the performance to qualify as a true "geek show." This is due to the ever-changing nature of language as well as a grey area existing in terms of how geek acts were presented. The threshold to qualify being a "full-blown geek show" as opposed to an act of similar nature can be one of ambiguity and debate. Naturally, there is bound to be some disagreement over a pure definition from both academics and subject authorities alike. In an effort to give the best overall approach to defining what the geek act is, let's examine

---

1. The midway is the amusement area just after the main entrance (Keyser). In a traditional carnival setting, sideshow attractions are set up at the "backend" of the carnival midway and are referred to as "backend shows" by carnival show folk.

definitions from authoritative academic resources on language as well as resources dealing directly with the sideshow.

Academic Definitions and Sideshow Industry Perspectives

The Oxford English Dictionary offers this definition of *geek*:

> *A performer at a carnival or circus whose show consists of bizarre or grotesque acts, such as biting the head off a live animal* ("geek, n." OED Online).

Merriam-Webster defines *geek* as:

> *A carnival performer often billed as a wild man whose act usually includes biting the head off a live chicken or snake* ("geek." Merriam-Webster).

Dictionary.com states:

> *A carnival performer who performs sensationally morbid or disgusting acts, as biting off the head of a live chicken* ("geek" Dictionary.com).

Others in the business have their own definitions.

Historical author and former sideshow performer Daniel P. Mannix wrote this about the geek act in 1976:

> *A geek sits in a pit wearing some outlandish costume and kills chickens and snakes with his teeth, afterwards eating them raw* (Mannix, *Freaks* 90).

In his 1980 publication *Circus Lingo*, circus and carnival trouper/historian Joe McKennon gives this simple definition:

(Mostly Carnival) A person working, mostly sitting, in a den of snakes (McKennon, *Circus Lingo* 38).

When asked about the subject in 2019, variety performer and geek aficionado Magic Brian defined a sideshow geek as follows:

For a traditional geek act, you'd need a drunk or someone with low morals, desperate for money or booze (or both), who is willing to pretend to be a crazy person or some kind of primitive human and can physically bite the heads off of chickens, mice, snakes, etc. (Brian).

Sideshow performer Reggie Bügmüncher, who started out in show business with an insectivore (bug-eating) act, provides this perspective on defining geek:

It's a gross-out act specifically involving live animals. You might not have to necessarily eat them; you could regurgitate them...

Expanding upon the elements needed for a geek act, she says:

Historically, I would say that it would involve eating one live animal in an entertaining way to gross people out (Bügmüncher).

Painter, actor, and former geek performance artist Joe Coleman offers this definition:

I think that the taking of a live animal's life with your own teeth does qualify as a geek.

On if any additional elements are needed to constitute a geek act, he says:

There are geek acts that don't involve the killing of an animal; it has happened before. But there has to be something that crosses a border (Coleman).

During a 2023 interview, Professor of Theater Arts and geek researcher, Rhett Bryson provided this definition:

> *It's a person who performs in a pit show at the carnival or event. He is presented either as a wild man or a feral creature of some kind and he is poorly dressed – maybe dressed as a native of some foreign country of far away and he's in the pit. He is prodded by the talker of the show and he may bite the head off chickens or rats, drink their blood, and snakes as well, and do those disgusting kind of things, sort of proving that he is a wild man, untamed by culture.* (Bryson, Interview).

Two Geek Classifications: Ordinary and Glomming

Intriguingly, when we dig deeper into the niche of defining geek and begin to look at carnival resources that discuss the definition, a two-tiered hierarchy emerges in the form of ordinary geeks vs. glomming geeks.

A very early example of this distinction is found in the September 24, 1936 edition of the *Richmond Times-Dispatch*, where they profile showman Max Linderman, who discusses with the paper the carnival lingo of the times. On the subject of geeks, the *Times-Dispatch* states:

> *Take it from Linderman, a "geek" is not necessarily a "glom" - no matter how you've always felt about it. A "geek," as any sideshow man will tell you, is the wild man of a carnival jungle show.*

On "glom" acts, the article reads:[2]

---

2. The term "glom" or "glomming" is a US slang word that arose in the early 1900s and means "To steal; to grab, snatch" ("glom, v." OED Online).

Now, a "glom" is a "geek" too, but he's a specialized "geek." He spices his show by biting off the head of a live chicken before your astonished eyes ("Harry Tucker On Main Street").

Author Leslie Fiedler also notes this distinction in his 1978 historical work *Freaks: Myths and Images of the Secret Self*, as he states that:

The title "Geek" was originally given to any side show "Wild Man," presented in a cage with snakes; while those who chewed and swallowed down living animals with real relish were known as "glomming Geeks" (Fiedler 162).

Wayne N. Keyser also references the distinction in his *Carny Lingo Dictionary* from his 2008 eBook *On The Midway*, when he defines *geek* as:

An unskilled performer whose performance consists of shocking, repulsive and repugnant acts. This "lowest of the low" member of the carny trade would commonly bite the head off a living chicken or snake. Some distinguish between "ordinary geeks" who pretend to be wild men or drug burnouts, and "glomming geeks" who actually bite the heads off live chickens and the like (Keyser).

In his aforementioned 1980 *Circus Lingo* book, Joe McKennon wrote this regarding glomming geeks:[3]

A 'Geek' who ate live chickens, rats or snakes (McKennon, *Circus Lingo* 39-40).

Daniel P. Mannix offers a slightly different interpretation between the two, writing in 1976:

---

3. McKennon uses the "gloamer" spelling in his definition.

A "glomming geek" seizes his prey with his hands and tears it apart. An ordinary geek is so drunk or feeble-minded that the animals have to be put into his mouth (Mannix, *Freaks* 91).

Showman Lou Pease indicates something similar in an interview published in 1970:

An ordinary geek doesn't actually eat the snakes, just bites off chunks of 'em, chicken heads and rats. And most of the time the geek'd be so drunk or hopped up you had to wake 'em and shake 'em, then shove the 'food' into their mouths (Lewis 298).

Pease says that, compared to ordinary geeks, there were considerably fewer glomming geek acts that worked in show business. Expanding on the differentiating factor of a glomming geek, he further says:

A glommin' geek used his hands to 'glom' the thing he was gonna eat instead of havin' it pushed in his face. And he liked it, too, and chewed it up good. He really ate it; not pretended to and then spit it out like an ordinary geek (Lewis 298).

Rhett Bryson concurs with the notion of the glomming geek possessing greater enthusiasm for their profession:

The glomming geek is one who really enjoys it. They spend a lot of time doing it. They see that as their lot in life, their profession. They are probably proud of that. They've done that for a long time. The other geeks are kind of geeks in waiting, they've been impressed into service in the locality where the show comes...every now and then, the ones that ran the show would recruit some wino, down-and-out, disabled person and kind of teach them the act and tell them what to do. But they are less purposeful about their performance as a geek and maybe didn't last a long time (Bryson, Interview).

When asked about this difference between glomming geeks and a standard geek show, career sideshow entertainer John "Red" Stuart had this to say during a 2019 interview:

A Glommer actually eats the animal or attacks the animal. That's the difference between a glomming geek and a geek...You don't have to eat it; you can just tear the animal apart. Some would just bite the heads off. Some, maybe possibly even a few, would actually eat like the snake or whatever, or start eating part of the chicken or the pig once they tear it apart. With the snake it was fairly easy because after the head is gone, the snake can't do nothing to you, you can just turn around and start eating the damn thing. With the pig or whatever you have to make sure it's good and dead before you start eating, but you have to worry about salmonella and things of that nature, same thing with eating raw meat. Thing is, with the glomming it is the act of you tearing into a live animal and making it suffer or run around, and the show is how long that animal can run around fatally injured before it finally keels over. Once he keels over, you start acting like the wild and insane man that you are, start picking up and spinning the animal parts around and people leave. That's it. That's the show (Stuart).

By searching for commonalities among these definitions and commentaries, we arrive at several generally agreed upon factors that constitute a true geek show:

- They are in the context of some form of organized performance.

- The intent is to illicit feelings of shock and disgust from the audience.

- Live vertebrate animals are utilized.

- There is typically an oral execution or implication, whereas something is placed into the mouth, bitten, or swallowed.

In short, ordinary geeks may sit in a pit of live animals and behave oddly with them in an effort to shock the audience. Those that were called glomming (sometimes spelled gloming, gloaming, or glooming) geeks were much rarer than ordinary geeks and were regarded as more hardcore. Glomming geeks are sometimes simply referred to as "glommers" and utilize the animals in a way that results in the fatalities of the creatures through an oral means. To some purists, a true glommer would have to actually consume pieces of the live animal, but to others, simply killing the animal with the mouth was enough to constitute being a glomming geek. In any event, glomming geek shows were of the far more extreme variety.

Given the less-than-flattering descriptions of geek performers in these definitions, it is perhaps rather fitting that this act and word evolved from the German *Geck*, which refers to a fool or simpleton.

Though the word *geek* in this context is typically used as a noun describing the person playing the role of the geek, in some historical instances the word is used as a verb instead to describe the action of performing as a geek rather than the physical geek itself. For example, "He'll work as the geek" can be simply shortened to "He'll geek" ("geek, v." OED Online).[4]

There are several types of performances that are similar to geek acts but have their own defining characteristics. For example, some of the aforementioned descriptions make reference to geeks as "wild men." This is not simply a matter of description, as acts known as "wild man shows" were common around the traveling carnival circuit and were often attributed as geek shows. These performances played into the public fascination with "primitive" cultures that were especially prevalent in the 1800s and early 1900s and were quite popular. Wild man shows often featured a performer dressed up as a "jungle native" or feral creature that was contained in a captive environment. They would behave wildly, running around snarling and exciting customers who paid to see the attraction. Sometimes geeks were portrayed as wild men sitting in their pit with snakes or chickens; other times, wild man acts were simply caged alone and would rattle the cage as people passed by. Due to this, there was a strong overlap between geek shows and wild men. The primary factor of distinction seems to be if they were working from within a pit of live animals. Wild men were often geeks but not always, just as geeks were often given wild men backstories and costumes to fit the nature of their performance. Geeks could be wild men and wild men could be geeks, but they were not always one and the same.

There were also wild woman shows, though some showmen went a less geek-oriented direction with these types of shows. For some of these attractions, rather than focusing on ugly and disturbing shock imagery found in a traditional geek show, they went the

---

4. This phenomenon of a noun being converted to a verb is sometimes known as denominalization.

route of sex appeal and would feature an attractive, scantily clad woman. Inside, the female performer would sit among snakes and play with them while interacting with the audience. These snake acts would not constitute a geek show because the intent was not to shock but rather to titillate the audience. Walter Hudson wrote about his experiences with such an attraction in his sideshow memoirs, *I Was a Teenage Blockhead!* When encountering one during his time on the midway, he noted that the showman promoting the attraction was adamant that it was absolutely not a geek show (Hudson). During the performance, the woman in the show could often be persuaded to remove additional clothing among the snakes as a ding.[5]

There were other acts at this time that combined serpents with exotic dancing in the form of belly dancers or snake charmers who would frequently perform with large live snakes during their shows at carnivals. In these shows, the snake is wrapped around the performer's body while the dancer moves skillfully about. With instances like this, the snake is not used for shock but rather sensuality. In some performances along these lines, the snake may even be seen as a representation of a phallus to further the erotic theme. Violence and shock may be alluring to audiences, but for some show people, the old adage of "sex sells" was often the best formula for profitability.

Another type of act that was akin to a geek act but not always the same was the "human ostrich" act. Those that performed as human ostriches would base their acts on eating non-food household objects rather than living things. Ostriches have a reputation for eating nearly anything they can find, so human ostrich performers would frequently eat things like nails, glass, and pocket watches. Some of those billed as human ostriches were also regurgitators, who were capable of bringing these items back up at will, though most simply ate and digested the objects.

---

5. A ding is an offer, to those customers already inside your show, of the chance to see a really special added attraction, not advertised on the outside, for an additional fee (Keyser).

Chapter 2

The Operation of a Geek Show

Historically, geeks were most often found on a traditional carnival midway, though they were also occasionally seen in circuses and festivals across the United States.[1] The goal of the geek show was to use curiosity, fright, and disgust as a means of entertainment. Nearly everyone can recall a time in their life when they saw something completely repulsive yet found it hard to look away, transfixed with intrigue and shock. In some instances, we may have even heard about something completely appalling but felt compelled to go examine the peculiarity firsthand, our morbid curiosities getting the best

---

1. Fittingly, the word "carnival" is derived from a medieval Latin term which refers to "the putting away or removal of flesh (as food)" ("carnival, n." OED Online).

of us. A traditional geek show exploited this human condition and used it as a means for financial gain by showmen.

Captain Jim Moore's Famous Shows, 1910s. A classic carnival sideshow exterior with banners, including one illustrating a "Snake Enchantress." From the author's private collection.

Theater professor Rhett Bryson witnessed a geek show as a child in the mid-1950s in Dothan, AL. It left an impression on him, one that he carried into adulthood. Decades later, he began earnestly researching the subject, even presenting a formal lecture on the sideshow geek to students, faculty, and staff in 1989 at Furman University. Rhett has faint memories of the experience from his childhood and shares his perspective on sideshow geeks as performers:

> *I remember it was startling and repulsive at the same time, which made it fascinating to a young mind. As I became an adult and got involved even more deeply in the theatrical world, I began to reflect on that experience with seeing the geek and thinking of that as a performer, maybe on the low end of the totem pole, where somebody like Laurence Olivier, the great Shakespearian British actor, might be at the top end of the scale of performer and then everything in between. I feel like anybody who is a performer*

that presents themselves in front of the public has a kind of dignity and
importance no matter what level of performance it is.

On the public's fascination with the geek and the theatrics involved in a geek show:

I think a reason for the fascination for freaks in general and geeks in specific
is that they are so different from the public and the public is in a superior
position intellectually, culturally, and they are fascinated with something
very different from themselves. They want to see about it, to see something
that is so forbidden or unusual... the theatrics of it, overdoing the wildness,
the rushing the audience and yelling and that kind of stuff would be part of
the theatrics of playing the character. And they were playing a character just
like any actor does. They are just simply playing the character of this geek
persona and I think that theatrics is exciting. It's something you've never
seen before. It's a thing you are going to be able to tell family and friends
who weren't there, and it takes you away from your ordinary plain life into
a world that is somehow forbidden, but you get to participate in it briefly
(Bryson, Interview).

While there are numerous historical accounts of performers eating live animals that date back centuries, geek shows as an organized form of widespread entertainment did not become common until the early 20th century, peaking in popularity around the mid-20th century.

Geek shows were more common in the midwestern and southern states of America. The South in particular was more accepting of grittier forms of outdoor entertainment during that time period (Taylor, "(After Tonight's About) Geek Shows").

Most geek shows were set up and operated in a pit show format – that is, the attraction ran inside of a pit rather than on a stage. The term "pit show" typically does not refer to a hole in the ground, however. In some cases, literal pits were dug in the ground, though more often the pits were temporary show set-ups made aboveground, often constructed of canvas and wood. Sometimes pit shows would feature a raised walkway, which would allow customers to look down into the pit from above (Keyser). It's interesting to consider also that since geek shows were not typically on elevated stages like many variety acts, the result of the geeks being looked down upon in the realm of performance can be seen as both metaphorical and literal. This aboveground arrangement lent itself to efficient setup and teardown when traveling from carnival to carnival during fair season. The geek would sit inside the makeshift pit, which would also contain animals such as snakes, chickens, pigs, or rats. Snakes and chickens were the most common animals associated with the geek show. Venomous snakes were often turned into venomoids; that is, they had undergone a procedure to remove or inhibit their venom production. This was done to keep the geeks safe, though not all geek shows took these precautions.

On the outside of the tent, there would often be a banner depicting the wild geek, usually in a jungle setting. Someone would stand outside the tent, often on the bally stage, and promote the act within the tent, typically emphasizing that it was nearly time to feed the geek. Intrigued audience members would then pay admission at the ticket box at the door and enter the tent, which contained the pit where the geek was located.

The pit inside the tent was designed at a scale that would be large enough to allow spectators easy viewing access and for them to be moved in and out of the attraction quickly to maximize the number of shows that could be done. It also had to be large enough to allow the geek to move around among the animals. As an example of dimensions of the attraction, geek showman William T. Usher has stated that his family's operation consisted of an 8' by 16' pit inside of a 20' by 30' tent (Usher 26).

Showman Jon Friday once described his experiences and observations in terms of how geek shows were constructed and operated:

> The pit of a geek show was usually very simple – just about 5' x 10' with plywood construction & often a chicken wire top. The tent was small as it only contained the one attraction, say anywhere from 15' x 20' to 20' x 30'. Most geek shows were bust-out shows i. e. if the crowds hung around too long or started to be a physical threat to the attraction – the geek was trained to throw a snake or other unpleasant object at them or start to escape thu a side door.....the girls would scream & people would literally run outside onto the busy midway which would just build another tip for the operator (Friday).

Once inside, the geek, often disheveled in appearance, would roam around the pit acting wildly. Though their actions were often vile, their appearances and behavior were typically a result of character acting for the attraction. Geeks were nearly always male, but the allure of seeing a wild woman engaging in such vile acts was often provocative and more marketable to audiences. In these instances, the outside banner on the tent would depict an attractive, scantily clad woman posed in a state of wild savagery. Once the patron had paid admission and stepped inside, they would be met with a dirty male geek, poorly dressed to appear female (Boles 29).

Common Geek Show Practices and Elements

There were several standardized practices that were common operations and trademarks of most geek shows. One tool that some geek shows employed was a device known as a "squawker" or "grunt." This was a large bucket with a string pulled through a hole in the bottom (somewhat akin to the makeshift telephones that children make with two cans and string). The geek or show operator would rub a cloth with rosin up and down the string. This would make a scary roaring sound that would emanate from where the geek show was, which would in turn attract curious passersby. Typically, someone working the attraction operated the device before shows, though sometimes it was hidden from view and ran continuously even during the show (Usher 26-27; "Facts About Freaks and Fakes"). In other cases, the noisemakers were just simple percussive sounds with workers banging on available items like sticks, tins, drums, and cowbells to create a wild sound that would draw attention to their attraction (Boles 30).

Geek shows also occasionally employed props to enhance the experience. A common fake-out act in geek shows would be for the geek to go about their performance, interacting with snakes. After playing up the audience, the geek would then grab a nearby piece of rope or tubing that was made out to be the length and color of a snake. Then the geek would throw it into the audience, giving the crowd quite the scare. Geek shows would occasionally also use colored water and chocolate to simulate mud and feces, which some geeks would also eat and throw into the audience. As the audience would run from the tent in terror, people outside the tent would be compelled to buy a ticket just to see what was so shocking inside (Wilder 9).

Jeffrey Murray of Harmur Side Shows recalled one gross-out geek show tactic that featured a performer dressed as a wild man sitting in a snake pit with a hospital bowl containing a jar of peanut butter hidden inside next to him:

> *Every so often, he would sit on the bowl and pretend to have a "movement,"*
> *pulling down his ragged pants, but not exposing anything. After the sup-*

posed defecation, he would reach down behind himself...into the bowl and
get his fingers covered in the brown peanut butter and relish eating it. This
would really freak out the patrons...as you can imagine...almost got the show
closed at a couple of spots. There was usually a sign which said "throw in a
quarter and see what he does" (Murray).

One thing that made many geek acts so thrilling to watch was the audience interaction. Geeks would often lunge at those nearby, causing people to jump and run off, sometimes even going so far as to wipe real animal blood on them or tear at their clothing if they got too close (Wilder 9). Occasionally, blood was simulated with beet juice or other substances around the geek's mouth (Ballantine 9). In some instances, a person working inside the geek show would swat at the geek or use a weapon of sorts, such as a whip or a gun loaded with blanks, as a theatrical means to keep the geek under control. When a geek would lunge at the audience, it was known as a "roust" (Usher 27).

During the show, the geek would play with the animals, terrorize the onlookers, and shock the audience by putting the animals' heads into their mouth – if only for a moment. If it was a glomming geek, the climax of the performance would be the geek biting pieces (typically the heads) off of the animals in the pit. Some geeks went further by drinking the blood or eating the animal pieces while the onlookers stared in disgust.

Geek Technique

The method for a geek biting an animal's head off typically involves holding the animal steady with both hands, placing the head into the side of mouth near the premolars and biting down hard on the neck while pulling the animal's body away with the hands to help aid in the removal of the head.

An alternate way to geek with animals such as chickens or pigs that would not work with snakes and mice was to attack the midsection of the animal, biting with the incisors, to remove a chunk from the torso. This resulted in the entrails being exposed and the animal rushing about the pit, mortally wounded, causing a ruckus of a show (Stuart). After that, the geek would typically take a moment to throw the pieces around, spray or drink the blood, and play with the animal's carcass as a means to further shock the audience. Once done, the performance would end. Sometimes people would vomit or simply run out of the show in disgust. From the vantage point of those outside, seeing people running out of a tent in horror was enough to pique their curiosity.

Though the violence of the geek act was often very real, sometimes it was skewed to make it seem more extreme than it actually was. Often, simply putting an animal's head in the geek's mouth in front of a horrified audience was enough of an implication to convince those in attendance that the geek had bitten the head cleanly off.

Another practice that was used in some geek shows to make things easier for the performer was for the geek to secretly palm a razorblade while he was in the pit. Then, when the time came for him to bite the animal, he would simply pick up the animal and pantomime biting it while nicking its neck with the razor. That would cause the blood to flow quickly and freely without the geek having to actually bite through the animal's tissue. In some cases, the tool would work as an aid by making it easier for the geek to initially penetrate the flesh of the live animal (Thomas 109; Stuart).

There are some cases where geeks were also regurgitators. This was not common, as regurgitation is an obscure and carefully learned skill, as opposed to a glomming, which is based more on sheer willingness. Regurgitators were typically seen in dime museums and on vaudeville stages and favored inanimate objects over live animals. Though they tend to fall into their own category stylistically, there are a few recorded cases where traditional sideshow geeks working in carnival midways would actually regurgitate the small animals that they swallowed, returning them to the outside world unscathed (Stuart; "'SNAKEOID' IS READY TO QUIT").

A Typical Geek Show Profile

It could be said that the geek is a bit of an outcast even among sideshow performers, which are typically broken down into three types of acts. There are natural-born freak acts, who were born physically different (little people, conjoined twins, etc.) and displayed themselves in the show. There are the working acts, people who were born normally but performed learned skills for profit (sword swallowing, fire eating, etc.). Then there are the self-made freaks, who were also born physically normal, but then chose to alter their appearance in an extreme way (extensive tattooing, body modifications, etc.) While the geek leans more toward a working act, it doesn't really fall into any of these categories and is more of an everyman in many ways. The only real difference between the geek in the pit and those in the audience is the geek's willingness to subject themselves to such an extreme level of depravity for the profitability of the show.

This very concept was explored in great detail in William Lindsay Gresham's 1946 novel *Nightmare Alley* and its film adaptations. The original movie was a noir film released in 1947, just one year after the novel's publication. Edmund Goulding directed the film and Tyrone Power plays the title character. A darker and more violent telling of Gresham's novel came to screen with the 2021 adaptation of *Nightmare Alley*, directed by Guillermo del Toro and starring Bradley Cooper.

Nightmare Alley tells the story of an up-and-coming performer attempting to make it in show business as he transitions from small carnival entertainment to large-scale engagements. In the story, the geek is both a literal character and a symbol of personal failure – the message being that if your life really falls apart, *you* could be the one biting off chicken heads in the sideshow pit. *Nightmare Alley* is noteworthy not only for its lasting appeal but also because, unlike many books and films that would later feature a geek character, it was released when geek shows were still relatively common.

The appeal of seeing a geek show can be correlated to some degree to several modern scenarios. As children, many of us can recall a time where we saw a peer being dared to eat a bug or non-food item and were unable to look away. As adults, when we drive by car crashes, we sometimes find ourselves rubbernecking. We have all had moments where we hear about something so shocking in the news that we simply have to look it up ourselves to feed our fascination. In live entertainment, the value often comes from observing a skilled performance, a creative presentation, or witnessing something truly unique. The geek show is essentially the antithesis of these things. It is a raw and dirty act brought down to the most basic human level and largely void of artistic merit or skill. The audience interest is less about looking up to an artist in their field and more about the pure spectacle of someone willing to degrade themselves.

Another contemporary example of the appeal of a geek show is the modern haunted house attraction around Halloween. As of 2019, it is estimated that the haunted house industry generates between $300 and $500 million in ticket sales in America alone ("Haunted House Facts"). This small but profitable seasonal industry relies on the public's desire to pay money to see scary and disgusting things. Customers can see and experience horrific things for the thrill without actually being in danger. It is quite common for people to pay to see gory props and scenarios assembled and ultimately be chased to the exit by a chainsaw-wielding actor (a modern form of a roust) only to exclaim later on what a wonderful rush and fun time it was. Geek shows relied on this same morbid curiosity and interactive thrill, though in a less contrived manner.

In the early 1900s, the trade publication the *Billboard* was a common resource for carnival news and networking.[2] It was also convenient for those in the industry because the *Billboard* and *Variety* magazine offices used to hold mail for performers on the road. Each issue had an extensive classified ad section that made it easy for those in variety entertainment to connect. It was common to see ads specific to geek shows, with showmen looking for geeks and geek show operators. If a showman could not find a geek on the road, they could try placing a want ad in the publication. As a testament to the popularity of the attraction, a look through back issues of the *Billboard* from the 1920s through the 1960s yields hundreds of classified advertisements relating to geek shows. The verbiage of these classified ads provides a greater understanding of the business operations of seeking employment at a geek show. They read with text such as "Want Manager for Geek Show, will furnish complete outfit. Must be experienced Operator with Geek" (Southeast Missouri District Fair Advertisement) and "Want outstanding Geek for Geek Show. Must know snakes" (Johnny's United Shows Advertisement).

Being a sideshow geek was not regarded as a prestigious role in the carnival. Many geeks were locals with drug and alcohol problems that were coerced into the depravity of the role and often paid in alcohol for their performances (Boles 29). In some instances, geeks were handicapped individuals who were being taken advantage of (Antil 1). Volatility and short careers in the field were common. Geeks were also prone to broken teeth and animal-related sicknesses from the nature of the act and working conditions (Sabrina). As such, unlike many other acts found in sideshows, geeks generally did not achieve any notable degree of fame. Show producers often saw them as expendable but did value dependability and loyalty in the jobs. For many geeks, the role was an entry-level position in show business. If they were willing to perform such gross feats to establish themselves, perhaps they would be able to move up to more skillful roles after getting a foot in the door.

It was common to see geeks who were ethnic minorities, particularly of African American descent (Braden 9). Some showmen would take advantage of the unfortunate circumstance of the limited employment opportunities available to people of color by

---

2. Prior to becoming a magazine that focused on popular music, the "Billboard" was a weekly magazine that covered the outdoor entertainment industry.

bringing them in to perform in their geek shows. Darker-skinned performers also worked the angle of the geek playing the character of a wild man brought in from a jungle. In many ways, the rise of geek shows in the early to mid-1900s was a perfect storm of societal factors that contributed to its popularity. Coming off the heels of vaudeville, cheap live entertainment was in demand and television was not yet common in households. The civil rights movement had yet to begin, and the lack of commercially available alcohol during Prohibition opened the doors for bootleg booze to be used as a tool of persuasion or compensation. For some geeks, alcohol was also a form of self-medication and an enabler used to dissociate themselves from the level of depravity needed to work.

This isn't to say that all geeks were pressured into degrading performances and loathed their role in the circus or carnival. For some, it was an easy way to get a spot in show business and to make money. According to Reverend R.J. McCarthy, a showman who worked in the 1940s and became known as the "Carny Priest," geeks were often thankful to be able to participate. Reflecting on his experiences working with geeks, McCarthy once told the *Star Tribune* "the geek felt good about the fact that he was able to work. He had some dignity. If he was alive today, he'd be on welfare and miserable" (Grow 3B).

In any event, most geek shows had a certain homogeneity in terms of how they were set up and functioned, which eventually led to geek shows having their own discernible niche as a recognized form of live entertainment.

Chapter 3
Early Eaters

C uriosity about geek-like behavior existed long before geek shows became an established form of carnival and circus entertainment. The idea of eating seemingly inedible objects or still-living things in a shocking way has been around for centuries.

An early representation of such intrigue from ancient times can be seen in Greek mythology with the story of Cronus (sometimes identified as Saturn), the titan who, fearing that he would be overthrown by his progeny, ate his children after they were born. The gruesome act is depicted in graphic detail in several iconic works of art.

Two paintings of Cronus eating his offspring. (Left) Rubens, Peter Paul. Saturn.
1636-1638. https://upload.wikimedia.org/wikipedia/commons/d/dd/Rubens_saturn.jpg
(Right). Goya, Francisco. Saturn Devouring His Son.
1819-1823. https://upload.wikimedia.org/wikipedia/commons/8/82/Francisco_de_Goy
a%2C_Saturno_devorando_a_su_hijo_%281819-1823%29.jpg

There are also numerous documented cases of real-life bizarre eaters throughout history that pre-date the advent of organized geek shows. Many used their eating habits as a means for performance.

Stone Eaters

Some of the earliest accounts of real-life unusual dietary intake as a performance piece relate to stone eaters. Both Harry Houdini and Ricky Jay explored this subject in detail in their books, *Miracle Mongers and Their Methods* and *Learned Pigs & Fireproof Women* respectively.[1]

Perhaps the most widely celebrated stone eater was an Italian by the name of Francis Battalia, whose strange dietary habit led to him being exhibited all over Europe. Writers described Battalia as the "Italian Lithophagous" ("FAMOUS FOR OSTRICH STOMACHS").[2] A doctor named John Bulwer examined Battalia when he came to London and wrote of his findings in a 1653 essay, "Man transformed, or the Artificial Changling."

In his work, Bulwer describes Battalia as being roughly 30 years old and claims that Battalia had been born with a fixation on eating stones rather than having developed the ability over time. The highly improbable writing alleges that Battalia was "born with two stones in one hand and one in the other; who, as soon as he was born, having the breast offered unto him, refused to suck." As a child he was said to refuse all food and it wasn't until he was offered pebbles that he was content. The dietary preference carried on into adulthood.

Regarding his technique, Bulwer observed:

Engraving of stone-eater Francis Battalia. Hollar, Wenceslaus. Francis Battalia, The Stone Eater. 1641. Medical Historical Library, Harvey Cushing/John Hay Whitney Medical Library, Yale University.

His manner is to put three of four stones into a spoon, and so putting them into his mouth together, swallows them all down one after another; then (first spitting) he drinks a glass of beer after them. He devours about half a peck of these stones every day; and when he chinks upon his stomach, or

---

1. Two very fine works that contain great information that may be of interest to readers of this book.

2. Lithophagous is a somewhat outdated term that means "stone-eating" ("litho-, comb. form." OED Online).

shakes his body, you may hear the stones rattle as if they were in a sack; all
which in twenty-four hours are resolved.

As an adult, it was said that Battalia had attempted to eat conventional food but the food did him no good, so he opted to instead sustain himself solely on stones, beer, and tobacco (Caulfield 92-96).

Another stone-eater who achieved great fame during his time was a man simply known as the Stone Eater. A 1788 playbill notes him as "The Original Stone Eater" and indicates that he was doing performances from noon to 7pm every day except Sunday. For an added fee, he was also available for private performances ("The ORIGINAL STONE EATER").[3]

Irish dramatist J. O'Keefe actually wrote a song called "The Stone-eater's Song" in the late 18th century:

Make room for a jolly Stone-eater,
For stones of all kinds I can crunch,
A nice bit of Marble is sweeter
To me, than a Turtle or Haunch.
A street that's well-paved is my larder-
A Stone you will say is hard meat;
But, neighbours, I think 'tis much harder,
When I can get nothing to eat!

Chorus: - With my crackledy mash, ha! Ha!
And a jolly Stone-eater am I.

London Bridge shall just serve for a luncheon-
Don't fear- I won't make it a job:
The Monument next I will munch on,

---

3. Possibly due to the technology at the time, those behind the Stone Eater's press were unfamiliar with Battalia and the others who came before him. Or perhaps, much like today, sometimes stretching the truth slightly in show business to claim to be the originator of something is simply an effective marketing strategy.

For fear it should fall on my nob;
Ye Strand folks, as I am a sinner,
Two nuisances I will eat up;
Temple Bar will make me a good dinner,
And then on St. Clement's I'll sup.
I think, if my mind does not alter,
The Spaniards some trouble I'll save:
I'll eat up the rock of Gibraltar,
And still if my stomach should crave,
I'll eat up Pitt's diamond at Paris,
I'm told 'tis the rarest of stones-
If Monsieur inclin'd then for war is,
At Cherbough I'll eat up the Cones.
The Ostrich, Sir, I can beat hollow,
Through smartly he gobbles horse shoes!
So, cut out in stone, and I'll swallow
An Ostrich for Michaelmas Goose!
Though with Stones I came here to be treated,
Whilst Liberty Britons enjoy,
The Rock where the Goddess is seated
May no Stone-Eater ever destroy.

With my crackledy mash, ha! Ha!
And a jolly Stone-eater am I (Urban 386).

Around this same time, there was a famous gluttonous German stone eater by the name of Kohlnicker. It seems that his oral fixation ran in his family, and it was rumored that his mother had even eaten some of her children. In addition to large quantities of food, Kohlnicker himself began eating stones and non-food objects as a child to help satisfy his extreme hunger. When he was an imperial soldier, his appetite was said to be equal to that of eight men. One interesting albeit slightly improbable story was that during his time as a soldier, he suffered a gunshot wound to his abdomen after an attack. However, because of all the stones in his mid-section, the bullet simply bounced off, causing only a minor flesh wound. When he died, the contents of his stomach were a pound and a half of stones, metal buttons, and pieces of buckles (Mieg 118).

There are references to several other stone-eating performers throughout the 1700s. The following century, in late 1858, a man named Guiset who was purported to eat nothing but paving stones was exhibited in New York. The playcard on the showroom of his public exhibit read as follows:

The wonder of the nineteenth century! - Mons. Guiset, the great stone eater. This wonderful man eats nothing but paving stone, pebbles, rocks, &c., for his breakfast, dinner and supper. He will swallow a number of large rocks in presence of the audience. He lives and subsists entirely on the above food, drinks nothing but water, and has perfect health. Physicians cannot account for this unparalleled living wonder ("A STONE EATER").

The Great Eater of Kent

There are a number of accounts of early geek-like figures who not only ate disgusting food but also ate obscene quantities of food. An extreme example was Nicholas Wood, the Great Eater of Kent.

Nicholas Wood was a glutton from England who performed eating feats at county fairs and festivals during the early 17th century. He frequently took on various bets related to eating. These included eating a meal intended for eight people at a royal dinner and, in another instance, eating seven dozen rabbits.

Occasionally he was tricked and lost bets, such as one instance where he was bet that a two-shilling meal could fill his appetite. After he took the bet, twelve loaves of bread soaked in a strong ale were given to him. These caused Wood to pass out partway through the meal.

In 1630, Wood's appetite caught the attention of poet John Taylor, who witnessed the eater win a bet by consuming a leg of mutton, 60 eggs, three pies, black pudding, and a large duck (eating everything save for the quills and beak). Taylor was so amazed by what he saw that he created a plan to bring Wood to the stage in London to perform his feats of consumption at the Bankside bear garden. Wood accepted the invitation and made his way to London.

Taylor wrote about his experiences with Wood and his thoughts about him in detail in a pamphlet called "The great eater, of Kent, or Part of the admirable teeth and stomacks exploits of Nicholas Wood, of Harrisom in the county of Kent His excessiue manner of eating without manners, in strange and true manner described."

In this work, Taylor described his vision for Wood's performances in London:

Now my plot was to have him to the Beare-garden, and there before a house full of people, he should have eaten a wheelbarrow full of tripes, and the next day, as many puddings as should reach over the Thames (at a place which I would measure betwixt London and Richmond) the third day, I would have allowed him a fat calf, or sheeps of twenty shillings price, and the fourth day he should haue had thirty sheepes geathers, thus from day to day, he should have had wages & diet with variety.

However, this big break in Wood's performing career was not meant to be. Wood was getting up in age and began to fear that he would not be able to live up to such a prestigious engagement. He had also recently lost all his teeth except one during a bet where he ate a quarter of mutton (including the bones). As a result, Wood broke off the engagement and the London performances never came to fruition. John Taylor concludes his work on The Great Eater of Kent with the following poetic verse:

Like as a River to the Ocean bounds,
Or as a Garden to all Britain's grounds,
Or like a Candle to a flaming Linck,
Or as a single Ace, vnto Sise Cinque:
So short am I of what Nick Wood hath done,
That having ended, I haue scarce begun:
For I haue written but a taste in this,
To shew my Readers where, and what he is (John Taylor 142-148).

Nicholas Wood, The Great Eater of Kent. Unknown Artist. Woodcut from The great eater, of Kent, or Part of the admirable teeth and stomacks exploits of Nicholas Wood, of Harrisom in the county of Kent His excessiue manner of eating without manners, in strange and true manner described, by John Taylor. 1630. https://upload.wikime-dia.org/wikipedia/commons/3/3b/Nicholas_Wood_the_great_eater_of_Kent.jpg

Charles Domery

A glutton who had a tendency to eat unusual and still-living things was the Frenchman named Charles Domery, who was also known as "The Voracious Pole" ("REMARK-ABLE MEN"). The moniker was likely due to the fact that he was a rather tall man, standing at 6'3". Despite his reputation as a glutton, he was of slim build ("Coal Heaver's Capacity").

Charles Domery enlisted in the French service but was captured by the English in 1799 and ended up in a Liverpool prison. Previously, when he was in the army camp, if his bread and meat rations were scarce, he would make up for it by consuming four to five pounds of grass per day. In one year during his army service, he consumed 174 cats, many of which he ate while they were still alive. When his ship was in the process of being surrendered, he was so desperate for food that he began feasting upon a man's leg that had been shot off. That is, until a sailor saw him, ripped the leg from his grasp, and tossed it overboard in disgust ("REMARKABLE MEN").

As a prisoner of war, Domery was once observed eating a cat and about 20 rats. In addition to his prison rations, he enjoyed eating raw beef and candles. He would also drink the medicine that was prescribed for his fellow prisoners.

The doctors at the prison were so surprised by his eating habits that they decided to test him. On September 17, 1799, the doctors witnessed Domery eat the following for his breakfast and lunch:

- 4:00 am - Four pounds of raw cow udder.

- 9:30 am - Five pounds of raw beef, twelve tallow candles, and a bottle of porter.

- 1:00 pm - Five pounds of beef, one pound of candles, three bottles of porter ("Coal Heaver's Capacity").

Tarrare

Perhaps the most extreme and bizarre case of an early geek-like eater was the Frenchman known only as Tarrare, born in 1772 (Oliver).

There are accounts of Tarrare's life and the study of him, including in the *London Medical and Physical Journal* from 1819, which profiles him under the section on "pol yphagism."[4] Much of this history is based on the investigations of physician Baron Percy, which begin to paint a picture of the unusual life Tarrare led.

At the age of 17, Tarrare weighed a mere 100 pounds. Despite his small size, he was born with insatiable hunger. He would often eat quantities of food suitable for a small village all by himself in a single day. Even stranger was that he was fairly indiscriminate with his eating habits, often consuming non-food objects as a means to attempt to satisfy his constant state of hunger.

---

4. "Polyphagism" or "polyphagy" refer to "The habit of feeding on a variety of different foods" ("polyphagy, n." OED Online). In the context of many of these pre-1900 medical journals, it relates to the condition where the individual lacks the ability to feel satiated from a meal, so they continue to feed on whatever is at their disposal.

After leaving home, he wandered the streets as a beggar, though he later ended up putting his skills on display as a street performer. During one documented performance, he dared the audience to satiate him. In this instance, he ended up eating a basket of apples, flints, corks, and other random objects given to him from the audience.

He later joined the army where he was, unsurprisingly, known to eat large quantities of food, to the point where his food rations were quadrupled. In a few instances, he was known to eat all the dinners prepared for 15 German laborers. Disturbingly, this was still not enough and he would often eat anything he could get his hands on, including cats, dogs, live snakes, and, in at least one instance, a large eel. The chief physician of the army once observed him devouring a large living cat by ripping its belly open with his teeth, drinking its blood, then eating it piece by piece until nothing remained but the bones. Tarrare did, however, vomit up the fur later.

Doctors tried everything from opium to tobacco to cure his hunger but to no avail. Soon Tarrare had taken to drinking the blood of blood-letting patients at the hospital and begun attempting to eat the corpses there. The staff finally chased Tarrare away when a 14-month-old child went missing from the hospital and they suspected Tarrare as being responsible.

Tarrare did not re-emerge until four years later, when the doctors that had previously treated him encountered him in a hospital where he was sick and wasting away. He passed away in the hospital at the age of 26 as a result of tuberculosis. Doctors examined his corpse and noted that it putrefied at a shocking rate. His entrails were covered in pus and his excessively large stomach was lined with ulcers. The stench of his body was so extreme that, after a period, the physician doing the examination was unable to continue the investigation to any further extent.

It is unknown what drove Tarrare to such extreme and often filthy eating habits as well as how he was physically capable of achieving such things. Though he was a slender man, he was known to have a very wide mouth and a balloon-like torso, where the skin from his belly could nearly wrap around his body if he had not eaten recently. Perhaps he was the product of an unusual physical abnormality that affected his digestive system. He was known to sweat profusely and had incredibly strong body odor, which was particularly potent after meals, and emanated off his body in the form of a visible vapor. After eating a large meal, it was observed that "the vapour from his body increased, his cheeks and his eyes became of a vivid red; a brutal somnolence, and a sort of hebitude, came over him while he digested." A doctor noted that beyond his insatiable drive to eat, his overall mentality "was almost devoid of force and of ideas" (Baron 203-205).

Regardless of the cause of this strange affliction, Tarrare, it seems, truly did live to eat.

Jacques de Falaise

Not all eaters of inanimate objects and live animals were driven by gluttonous hunger, however. Frenchman Jacques De Falaise, who was born Jacques Simon in 1754, spent most of his years living a fairly normal life, working as a field laborer along the quarries of Montmartre, near Paris. It was not until he was an older man that he discovered his unique ability (*Notice Sur Jacques De Falaise*).[5]

When he was 60, his talent was discovered on a fluke one day while he was attending a colleague's wedding. At the event, people were playing a game where they hid jewelry from one another. Falaise took a chain and locket and hid it in his mouth. When the other players caught on to him staying silent, he ended up swallowing the item without thinking, then showed the other players that his mouth was, in fact, empty. Discovering no ill effects from having swallowed the object, he would later go on to repeat the feat as well as consume other objects, such as keys. Soon he moved on to swallowing other household objects like roses (thorny stems and all), playing cards, and stovepipes. He even started swallowing live animals (*Notice Sur Jacques De Falaise*).

In a different telling, it is alleged that when he was 62, after a long day working at the quarry, one of his fellow workers dared him to eat a nearby caged canary at an inn in which they were drinking and dining. He ended up accepting the challenge and swallowed the live bird whole, surprised at how seemingly easy it was for him ("Case of Polyphagia").

Jacques de Falaise was eventually hired to work as an entertainer, performing his unusual skills for local quarry workers. He would perform eating animals and household items during his performances, surrounded from all sides by a large crowd and often doing multiple shows per day. The shows featured audience participation, as he would happily oblige anyone who challenged him to swallow their pocket watch or coins that they had brought with them to his show. Soon, he caught the attention of a theater manager in Paris and moved on to doing theater stage shows. At one point he even had a five-year theater agreement where, in exchange for his performances, he would be provided with

5. For a full translation of "Notice Sur Jacques De Falaise," see Appendix 1.

food, clothing, 400 francs per year, and the condition that anything he swallowed during performances, including money, would become his property ("Case of Polyphagia").

The animals that he would swallow alive included mice, sparrows, eels, snakes, and crayfish. He could often feel the animals moving around inside his body prior to them succumbing to the digestive process. In cases where the animals were too active and causing him discomfort, he would drink a rum mixture to calm them down (*Notice Sur Jacques De Falaise*).

The crabs and eels were the most challenging for him to control. In fact, he refined his technique after a mishap with a live eel. During one stage performance, after swallowing an eel whole, the creature actually made its way painfully back up his esophagus mid-show. Once it had made its way back up to the inside of his mouth, he bit down and smashed its head, then immediately re-swallowed it. After that experience, he got in the habit of quickly crushing the heads of the animals he was about to swallow with his molars just prior to swallowing them whole ("Case of Polyphagia").

Interestingly, he also used his ability to master the art of sword swallowing and was capable of swallowing a 20" sword to the hilt and then pulling it out without harm (*Notice Sur Jacques De Falaise*).

However, his ways caught up with him over time as he began suffering from gastroenteritis which resulted in several long-term hospital stays. Eventually, at the urging of physicians, he gave up his performing career and ended up working at the hospital. Though his health eventually recovered, his spirits did not, and he hanged himself one night after drinking.

After his death, his body was studied. Overall, his organs seemed relatively normal, though his esophagus was found to be abnormally large, which would explain how he was able to swallow objects and animals whole with relative ease. It was observed that the stomach was distended, and there was evidence of former ulcers in his cecum, a testament to the damaging nature of his act ("Case of Polyphagia").[6]

Ultimately, it wasn't the predisposition of an insatiable hunger that drove Jacques de Falaise but rather the allure of the spotlight.

---

6. The cecum is a pouch or large, tubelike structure in the lower abdominal cavity that receives undigested food material from the small intestine and is considered the first region of the large intestine ("Cecum," Encyclopædia Britannica).

Le Poliphage JACQUES *de Falaise,*
chez M. Comte.

Jacques de Falaise with the various objects he was known to swallow. Un-
known author. 1820. https://upload.wikimedia.org/wikipedia/common
s/2/23/Le_polyphage_Jacques_de_Falaise.jpg

Jacques de Falaise performing. Lanté, Louis-Marie. Hand-colored engraving from the series Le Bon Genre published by Pierre de la Mésangère. 1816. https://upload.wikime dia.org/wikipedia/commons/8/86/Jacques_de_Falaise_le_polyphage.jpg

Portrait woodcut print. Jacques de Falaise swallowing a sword while holding a live snake and rat in his hands, with bird perched on his shoulder. Unknown author. 1816. MS Thr 949 (59), Houghton Library, Harvard University. https://upload.wikimedia.org/wikiped ia/commons/1/11/Jacques_de_Falaise_1816.png

Chapter 4
Eats 'Em Alive!

T hough biting the head off a chicken is a common stereotype of a sideshow geek, the animals most commonly associated with early geek shows were actually snakes. The concept of the snakes themselves being symbolic of something forbidden and myste- rious goes all the way back to biblical times with the story of Adam and Eve, for it was the serpent that tempted Eve to taste the forbidden fruit. In Greek mythology, there is also the tale of Medusa, who had live snakes for hair and whose appearance was so shocking that those who laid eyes upon her turned to stone. Ancient esoteric symbolism also utilizes serpent imagery, such as with the ouroboros, depicted as a snake eating its own tail.

Snakes have been used in performances for generations, long before geek shows became an established form of entertainment. Pre-20th century snake shows consisted of displaying exotic snakes in boxes, snake charming, and handling venomous snakes. Some of these exhibits continue to this day in various forms.

Snake Charming and Handling

Snake charming is an ancient art form that involves the performer "hypnotizing" a snake. Scholars indicate that it arose originally in India and was common at Indian markets and festivals, though it has since fallen out of popularity. Typically, it involves a person playing a wind instrument traditionally known as a *been* (Singh) over a basket which contains a snake. The snake slowly rises up from the basket and moves back and forth, seemingly hypnotized by the charmer's song. In reality, the snake doesn't actually hear the music and is instead focusing on following the tip of the instrument as it slowly moves back and forth, which causes the snake to appear entranced (Flintoff). Regardless the cause, it creates a striking visual. In carnival sideshows, many belly dancers working with live snakes are also billed as snake charmers, using their gyrating movements to seemingly charm the snake.

The earliest references to snake charming date back to the Bible:

Psalm 58:3–5:
The wicked backslide from the womb;
liars go astray from birth.
Their venom is like a snake's venom—
like a deaf cobra's—one that shuts its ears
so it can't hear the snake charmer's voice
or the spells of a skillful enchanter.

Ecclesiastes 10:11:
If a snake bites before it's charmed,
then there's no profit
for the snake charmer.

There is also Mark 16:17-18:

These signs will be associated with those who believe: they will throw out demons in my name. They will speak in new languages. They will pick up snakes with their hands. If they drink anything poisonous, it will not hurt them. They will place their hands on the sick, and they will get well.

This verse in particular spawned an offshoot of some churches known as "Snake Handling" churches, who take this wording literally. At these churches, followers handle live poisonous snakes during services of worship. There have been numerous fatalities as a result. Snake handling churches started around 1910 in Chattanooga, Tennessee, and the practice continues to this day, primarily in the Appalachia region of the United States (Scott).

A snake charmer in India. From the author's private collection.

Vintage photograph, female snake charmer Messaouda.
From the author's private collection.

1882 newspaper depiction of a female snake charming act.

From the author's private collection.

The Rise of Bosco

When it comes to geeks, they were not known to achieve widespread popularity as performers or have long careers in the profession. However, there was one major exception: the geek known as Bosco.

Bosco was a glomming geek who ate snakes and was very popular in the early 1900s. His performances of eating live snakes at carnivals, street shows, and circuses saw him travel extensively. He also regularly received media coverage over the course of his career, which spanned several decades.

Once he was established, the term "Bosco Eats 'Em Alive" became the trademark phrase used to describe his performances. As his fame grew, "eats 'em alive" became a tagline used for numerous geek shows, then grew further into a sort of recognized popular culture phrase around the turn of the 20th century (Mannix, *Freaks* 90). The catchphrase even made its way into social commentary and political humor. For example, in 1900, the *Times* of Richmond, Virginia, wrote of two political opponents, saying that "in their claims against each other remind us of Bosco. They eat 'em alive" ("Last Joke of The Campaign").

Though not something that would appeal to today's mainstream entertainment standards, Bosco's bizarre performances saw him making appearances all over the world, and he was frequently in the press. He thrilled audiences at Coney Island and was even said to have performed for royalty during his time in Europe around the turn of the 20th century ("Bosco Will Be Here").

To fully examine the origin of Bosco the geek and discover how he became so incredibly prolific, we must first take a look at a bit of magic history.

There once lived an Italian conjurer by the name of Bartolomeo Bosco (born 1793) who rose to prominence with his performances in the mid-19th century. He was an extremely talented performer and was very well known for his highly skilled cups and balls magic routine (Neutert 320). He also did a number of acts involving live birds. One of Bartolomeo Bosco's signature performance pieces with birds was an illusion that involved him decapitating birds of different colors and swapping their heads. He would do this trick with pigeons, one black and one white, so when he finished the effect, the black head would end up on the white body and the white head on the black body. However, even though the trick itself was an illusion involving an alternate set of concealed birds, the technique he utilized to make the trick as convincing as possible involved actually slicing the heads off of the first set of birds, killing them, and allowing the blood to flow freely in view of the audience before swapping them out (Schiffman 258). Despite the macabre nature of his performances, Bartolomeo Bosco was so influential that after his passing in 1863, other emerging magicians started using the Bosco name as a means to elevate their own careers (Houdini, "Reading and Rubbish" 49).

Bartolomeo Bosco. Image courtesy of the American Museum of Magic.

Poster for Bartolomeo Bosco's show, 1827.
Image courtesy of the American Museum of Magic.

With high official approval

Bartholomeo Bosco
will perform

a
great evening of entertainment
in two parts
on Wednesday, August 8th, 1827
in the Grand Ballroom,
Bischofsstrasse, Hotel de Pologne.

The undersigned will have the honor of performing five more shows: today on the 8th, Friday the 10th, Sunday the 12th, Monday the 13th and Wednesday the 15th. Further detail is provided so that the esteemed audience may be informed on the content. Since such detail might convey very little, the undersigned will eagerly do his utmost to exceed expectations.

Details of the first part:

1) The popular cups and balls routine.
2) An isolated painting with transformations.
3) Liquids which separate themselves.
4) Living cards.
5) The isolated clock.
6) The comedic flower-metamorphosis.
7) The magic jug.
8) For the first time, a highly incomprehensible vanishing of a shawl, an extremely striking piece worthy of your attention.

Details of the second part:

1) The truth-telling Mercury.
2) The numerous family of cups.
3) The invisible wandering delivery boy.
4) His return trip.
5) The burnt yet intact map.
6) The money that multiplies in a stranger's hand.
7) The funny disappearing plume.

At the end of the show:

The famous magic frying pan of the well-known knight Von Pinetti, in which up to 15 live birds, beaten to death and plucked, will be fried; and after the honorable audience has convinced itself of this truth, the same fried birds, to everyone's surprise, will fly away alive and well.

Ticket prices:
Numbered seats: 15 Sgr.   Parterre and first gallery: 10 Sgr.   Second gallery: 5 Sgr.

Tickets for numbered seats are available daily in the Hotel de Pologne.
The box office opens at 6:30 p.m.
Show starts at 7:30 p.m. and ends at 9:30 p.m.

English poster translation. Note the macabre end of show act description involving birds. English translation by Gary Varney and Petra Schweigert Otto. Image re-design by Nathan Wakefield.

Another famed magician from that time period was the Frenchman Jean-Eugène Robert-Houdin (1805-1871). He spent much of his early life as a clockmaker, patenting many innovative designs. Later, he reinvented himself as a stage magician and was able to use his creative, mechanically inclined mind to develop unique illusions, which brought him great fame. Robert-Houdin also authored numerous books on magic theory as well as a book of memoirs (Karr 46-50).

In his memoirs, Robert-Houdin writes extensively about Bartolomeo Bosco after having witnessed one of his performances, though his tone is rather rivalrous toward his fellow conjurer. Robert-Houdin discredits Bosco's skill level as a performer and draws attention to the element of authentic animal cruelty involved in Bosco's methods in working with birds. In addition to his head-swapping trick, Robert-Houdin describes an additional effect that involved Bosco stuffing a bird into the barrel of a gun, then having a spectator fire the gun and Bosco stabbing the bird out of midair onto the blade of a sword (Robert-Houdin 184-191).

Illustration from 1860 of Bartolomeo Bosco with his cup and balls. Eerily and somewhat prophetically, he is pictured here with a live snake. As pictured in "Satana: Raccolta Universale, Biografica, Aneddotica delle Avventure di Bosco." From the author's private collection.

Robert-Houdin's accusations that these illusions involved actual animal fatalities resonated so much at the time that soon Bartolomeo Bosco's very name became associated with violence toward animals. Years later, when a man decided to forge a path in show business as a full-time snake-eater and was in need of a performance name, one that had already become linked with animal cruelty in the realm of live performance seemed like a logical choice, so he assumed that very handle. As a result, Bosco, a name once associated with a skilled magician, became instead widely known as the moniker of a depraved snake-eating fiend ("The Original Bosco---The Famous Italian Magician").

There was another magic performer named Ehrich Weiss (1874-1926) who came along after both Bartolomeo Bosco and Robert-Houdin. The mainstream popularity of Weiss would eventually become so great that it would dwarf that of both Bosco and Robert-Houdin. In fact, Robert-Houdin inspired Weiss so much that he used a derivative of his name that he would go by for the rest of his life: Harry Houdini (Rydell and Gilbert 96).[1]

Though Harry Houdini was inspired by Robert-Houdin and looked up to the deceased magician early in his career, that all changed during a strange publicity incident gone awry. While visiting France, Houdini decided to visit the grave of Robert-Houdin to place a wreath upon it. Houdini had heard that Robert-Houdin's daughter-in-law, Madame Emile Houdin, was still alive, so he wrote her a letter requesting permission to place the wreath upon Robert-Houdin's grave and suggested that they meet up while he was in the area. Much to his surprise, Madame Emile did not respond to his request for permission and refused to meet with him. Houdini ended up placing the wreath and taking photos anyway but was extremely embittered by the experience (Houdini, Unknown Facts Concerning, 6-9). In his journal, *Conjurers' Monthly Magazine*, Houdini wrote of the experience:

An iconic photo of Harry Houdini from 1899. McManus-Young Collection, Library of Congress, 1899. https://upload.wikimedia.org/wikipedia/commons/3/37/HarryHoudini1899.jpg

I was most discourteously treated by Madame W. Emile...Personally, I think she should have shown a little common courtesy to the memory of

1. Interestingly, Jean Eugène Robert-Houdin was born simply as Jean Eugène Robert and only added "Houdin" to his name after marrying his first wife, Josèphe Cecile Houdin (Karr 47). Had it not been for Josèphe, both Jean Eugène Robert-Houdin and Harry Houdini would have had very different stage names, and the historical connotation of the very name Houdini that is prevalent to this day would not exist.

Robert Houdin, especially as she is now living in her old age on the proceeds of his endeavors.

As Harry Houdini's own fame grew, he continued to research his boyhood idol and talk to other magicians about him. Over time, Houdini came to the belief that Robert-Houdin was a largely unoriginal and overrated magician. Perhaps it was this feeling of disillusionment, the rebuff by Robert-Houdin's daughter-in-law, or a combination of the two that led Houdini to release his infamous book *The Unmasking of Robert Houdin*. Originally intended to be a work on the history of magic, by the time the book was released, it had adopted a focus of discrediting the accomplishments of Jean Eugène Robert-Houdin.

In this book, Houdini strongly criticizes Robert-Houdin in a number of ways, including his negative assessment of Bartolomeo Bosco. Houdini praises Bosco as having been a brilliant magician and blames Robert-Houdin for being the one who perverted Bosco's good name as being synonymous with cruelty:

Robert-Houdin devotes the greater part of chapter X., American edition of his autobiography, to belittling Bosco, a conjurer whose popularity all over Europe was long-lived. First, he pictures Bosco as a most cruel creature who literally tortured to death the birds used in his performances. Here, as in his attack on Pinetti, Robert-Houdin throws the responsibility for criticism on the shoulders of another. His old friend Antonio accompanies him to watch Bosco's performance, and it is Antonio throughout the narrative who inveighs against Bosco's cruelty and Antonio who insists upon leaving before the performance closes, because the cruelty of the conjurer nauseates him.

At that time no society for the protection of animals existed, and, even if it had, I doubt whether Bosco's performance would have come under the ban. Certain magicians of to-day employ many of Bosco's tricks in which birds and even small animals are used, but the conjuring is so deftly done that the public of 1907, like that of 1838, thinks it is all sleight-of-hand work and that the birds are neither hurt nor killed. Even in Bosco's time the bird trick was not in his répertoire exclusively. All English magicians employed it. Apparently the head of the fowl was amputated, but often in reality it was tucked under the wing, and the head and neck of another fowl was shown by sleight-of-hand. Quite probably the Parisian public did not consider Bosco cruel. Robert-Houdin and his friend Antonio, being versed in sleight-of-hand and conjuring methods, read cruelty between the deft movements. Certain it is that the name of Bosco has not been handed down to posterity by other writers as a synonym of cruelty.

The Unmasking of Robert-Houdin was published in 1908, at which point in time geek shows were becoming increasingly popular, and Bosco the Snake Eater was already appearing in fairs and sideshows throughout England and America. In the book, Houdini expresses extreme contempt for snake-eating Bosco the geek and notes how unfortunate it is that his act is dragging down the good name of such a legendary magician as Bartolomeo Bosco:

A man of noble birth and brilliant attainments was the original Bosco, and his name became a by-word all over the Continent as the synonym, not of cruelty, but of clever deception, yet never has posterity put the name of a great performer to such ignoble uses. For who has not heard the cry of the modern Bosco, "Eat-'em-alive"?

To-day I can close my eyes and summon two visions. First I see myself stand-ing bareheaded before a neglected grave in the quiet cemetery on Friedrich-strasse, Dresden, the sunlight pouring down upon the tombstone which bears not only the cup-and-balls and wand, insignia of Bosco's most famous trick, but this inscription: "Ici repose le célèbre Bartolomeo Bosco.—Né à Turin le 11 Janvier, 1793; décédé à Dresden le 2 Mars, 1863." The history of this clever conjurer, with all its lights and shadows, sweeps before me like a mental panorama.

The second vision carries me into the country, to the fairs of England and the side-shows of America:

"Bosco! Bosco! Eat-'em-alive Bosco. You can't afford to miss this marvel. Bosco! Bosco!"

Follow me into the enclosure and gaze down into a den. There lies a half-naked human being. His hair is long and matted, a loin cloth does wretched duty as clothing. Torn sandals are on his feet. The eulogistic lecturer dilates upon the powers of this 20th century Bosco, but you do not listen. Your fascinated gaze is fixed on various hideous, wriggling, writhing forms on the floor of the den. Snakes—scores of them! Now the creature, half-animal, half-human, glances up to make sure that attention is riveted upon him, then grasps one of the serpents in his hideous hands and in a flash bites off its head. The writhing body falls back to the ground.

You grip the railing in a sudden faintness. Has your brain deceived your eyes, or your eyes your brain? If you are a conjurer you try to convince yourself that it is all a clever sleight-of-hand exhibition, but in your heart you know it is not true. This creature, so near a beast, has debauched his manhood for a few paltry dollars, and in dragging himself down has dragged down the name of a worthy, a brilliant, a world-famous performer (Houdini, The Unmasking, 307-308).

Houdini references Bosco the Snake Eater again in his 1920 work *Miracle Mongers and Their Methods* and recalls a time that he saw Bosco perform live in America earlier in his career:

I also witnessed the disgusting pit act of that degenerate, Bosco, who ate living snakes, and whose act gave rise to the well-known barkers' cry HE EATS 'EM ALIVE! If the reader wishes further description of this creature's work, he must find it in my book, The Unmasking of Robert Houdin, *for I cannot bring myself to repeat the nauseating details here* (Houdini, Miracle Mongers 164).

Though he had great admiration for the magician Bartolomeo Bosco, clearly Bosco the Snake Eater was not appealing to Harry Houdini's refined tastes.

But an important question remains: How did Bosco, a geek, manage to achieve so much fame throughout his career, unlike his successors? The answer is rather simple, actually: Bosco the geek wasn't a single performer – rather, Bosco was a character portrayed by many.

During the start of Bosco the Snake Eater's career, the word *geek* had not yet become widespread in sideshow, and the attraction was only beginning to become commonplace on fairgrounds. As such, the acts were simply known as "Snake Eaters." As snake-eating "wild man" displays rose in prominence, the word Bosco cropped up as a term to describe geek shows before the word *geek* had caught on. As attention for the attraction grew, many traveling carnivals and circuses hired their own snake-eating "Boscos."

Houdini references this phenomenon in *The Unmasking of Robert-Houdin*:

> *Of the 20th century Boscos there are, alas, many. You will find them all over the world, in street carnivals, side-shows, fair-booths, and museums, and why the public supports such debasing exhibitions I have never yet been able to understand. I have seen half-starved Russians pick food from refuse-barrels. I have seen besotted Americans creep out from low dives to draw the dregs of beer-barrels into tomato cans. I have seen absinthe fiends in Paris trade body and soul to obtain their beloved stimulant. I have heard morphine fiends in Russia promise to exhibit the effect of the needle in return for the price of an injection. But never has my soul so risen in revolt as at sight of this bestial exhibition with which the name of Bosco, a nobleman and a conjurer of merit, has been linked* (Houdini, The Unmasking, 308).

Bosco as a farmer. The *"Topeka State Journal"* - February 26, 1902.

Charles Kinnebrew of the Kinnebrew Brothers' Sideshows was very open about his use of multiple Boscos to accommodate the demands of his business. When interviewed for *The Topeka State Journal* in 1902, he explained that he had several different Boscos with his touring show and one of them worked as a farmer during the off season. Kinnebrew also received some Bosco-related publicity when one of his boxcars was burglarized and the perpetrator opened up Bosco's box of snakes, not realizing what it was, and inadvertently released 65 of the serpents ("He Found Snakes").

It is even said that accomplished filmmaker Tod Browning worked as a Bosco back in his early days as a sideshow performer prior to his career in film (Mank 165). Browning would later go on to direct several films that had carnival themes, including the sideshow classic *Freaks*.

In a testament to how dangerous it can be working with venomous snakes, in 1899 a man named Richard Bailey died as a result of a Bosco performance. During his act, while Bailey was attempting to put a rattlesnake into his mouth, the snake bit him on the hand, and he later passed away as a result of the venom ("'Bosco' Dead").

Illustration of the Bosco burglary incident. The "Topeka State Journal" - February 26, 1902.

Two career showmen known as Beneker and Blubber used a local tramp (to whom they supplied whisky during each performance) to portray an Australian snake-eating Bosco at their show. The ballyhoo they used went like this:[2]

> *Step right in! Costs you but a dime! He eats 'em alive! Bosco, the wonderful snake eater from Australia! He eats 'em alive! Cr-r-r-ushes their heads! He br-r-r-reaks their bones! Eats 'em alive! Eats 'em alive!* ("The Snake-Eating Game").

Another Bosco ballyhoo from the early 1900s, this time coming from a talker who went by the name Professor Layton, went like this:

> *La-deees and Gentle-men: Permit me to call your attention to the world renowned, justly celebrated only and original Bosco, the Snake Eater! He eats them alive! He bites their heads off! He gro-vels in a den of loath-some reptiles! An ex-hit-it for the ed-U-ca-ted! And a show for the sen-si-tive and re-fined!* (McCardell 13).

---

2. "Ballyhoo" or "bally" is a hype speech done by the outside talker in carnivals to promote an attraction (Keyser).

There is evidence that Bosco even made his way into the large-scale traveling circus scene. In 1927, a former Bosco named Will "Steamboat" Davis passed away while incarcerated in Fort Madison, Iowa. In his death announcement, the press stated that Davis had traveled with the Barnum and Bailey and Ringling Brothers circuses, where he played the role of Bosco the Snake Eater before he was imprisoned for murder ("Relatives of 'Bosco' Circus Freak, Are Sought").

Bosco was also portrayed as being a woman in some shows, occasionally billed as an "Abyssinian woman" ("Prefers a Diet of Snakes"). However, in one instance, "Bosco the Abyssinian Female Snake Eater," while performing in Pittsburgh, was exposed in the press as actually being an Irishman named O'Leary playing the part. O'Leary had suffered from sunstroke some time earlier and, as a result, was no longer able to work at his previous job as a brickyard laborer, so he fell into the role of a snake-eating carnival performer instead ("'Bosco' Left Town").

With all these Boscos running around eating snakes, one may wonder who the first Bosco the Snake Eater was. At one point, someone had to originate the idea of eating snakes alive in a performance setting and adopt the last name of illusionist Bartolomeo Bosco. There are several clues in old press articles that shed some light on the identity of the first snake-eating Bosco.

In 1929, there was a series of news stories about a decrepit old man, age 75, who had checked himself into a hospital. The press noted that this man was actually Bosco, who had resurfaced from obscurity after having retired from the snake-eating business many years before. The mysterious man, whom the press implied was the original Bosco, went by the assumed name of Michael Griffin (real name said to be Moran) and had worked more recently as a night watchman ("Aged 'Bosco' In Hospital").

Befitting what's expected of a sideshow geek, what ultimately landed him in the hospital was alcoholism ("Volstead Rum Ruins Bosco"). Unsurprisingly, the press had a field day with sensationalized articles about how a man who had once made a career of using his digestive system to withstand eating live snakes, glass, and nails had later in life found that liquor was too much for his stomach to take. An article from later that year notes his full name as Frank Moran and indicates that he began his career as Bosco in 1901 ("After Eating Snakes").

While there are numerous media accounts discussing Moran resurfacing and noting his career as Bosco starting in 1901, there are other references to Bosco the Snake Eater that predate them. One in particular stands out as the probable source of Bosco's true origin.

A 1911 article in the *Pittsburg Headlight* titled "Bosco Original 'Eat-Em-Alive'" profiles a man by the name of John West who claimed to be the original Bosco and to have originated the snake-eating act. West only had one arm, as he had to have the other amputated after he was bitten by a rattlesnake in his act. He also claimed to have invented the idea of a snake-eating character performing in a carnival and implemented it himself ("Bosco Original 'Eat-Em-Alive'").

An announcement from 10 years earlier, in 1901 from Wellington, Kansas, seems to support the claim of Mr. West being the innovator of the Bosco character. The local paper stated that a major contract with "the world famous 'Bosco,' the snake eater" had been secured for their jubilee celebration and describes him further by stating "This is the original snake eater--all others are imitations." The manager who booked Bosco admits to having booked an imitator for a previous year but notes that that year's jubilee would feature the real Bosco. This announcement article goes on to describe the real Bosco that they had booked as being a one-armed man who lost his arm from a venomous snake bite during a performance in Baxter Springs, Kansas, the year before ("Bosco Will Be Here").

Sure enough, there was news on September 3, 1900, that reported that the "famous" Bosco had been bitten in the arm during a performance in Baxter Springs, Kansas, where he was "drawing immense crowds" to his shows. Though he lived, this initial report seemed grim and indicated that he was not expected to survive the bite ("'Bosco' Is Dying from a Snake Bite").

Several days later on September 8, 1900, the *Pittsburg Daily Headlight* reported that Bosco's condition was improving and he was expected to survive though his left arm had to be amputated. the *Headlight* mentions John H. West by name as being "Bosco, the Australian Snake Eater." West is described as a 35-year-old man who was born in New York City and later relocated to San Francisco before becoming involved in the snake business. Prior to his hospitalization, he was said to have performed for more than 16,000 people during a stint in Oklahoma City ("Bosco Is Better").

Though there are smatterings of historical mentions of snake eaters that date back hundreds of years, snake-eating did not really exist as a widespread form of entertainment at organized events before Bosco came along. If John West was the first Bosco, that would mean that he is not only responsible for the creation of the widely popular "Bosco the Snake Eater" character, but he could also be seen as the father of the glomming geek act.

SOME OF THE ATTRACTIONS:

The Famous Patterson Ferris wheel from the World's Fair; the renowned
streets of Cairo with trained Egyptian camels and donkeys; the original Bosco.
the snake wonder. who lost his arm from the bite of a diamond rattler at the last
reunion; Patterson's magnificent $7,000 carousal. Colorado Charley's Wild West
Show. one of the largest vaudeville and variety shows on the road. Tschudi's
Moving Pictures of the war and vivid army and naval battle scenes, a solid half
mile of Midway shows. theatrical amusements. games and curiosities. making a
glittering galaxy of star performers never before exhibited in Southern Kansas.

*Event from 1901 that references the original Bosco having lost his arm. "Galena Weekly
Republican" - July 18, 1901*

Interestingly, John West's personality and characteristics seem quite different from
what one might expect of an early sideshow geek. West spoke to the press directly several
times regarding his Bosco creation, coming across as very humble and articulate. In fact,
after he ended up surviving his snake bite and amputation, he wrote a two-part op-ed
piece which was featured in the September 22 and September 29, 1900, *Baxter Springs
News*. In the piece, he describes his near-death experience and recovery as a professional
snake eater after being bitten by a black diamond rattler. He also offers the reader advice
on what to do in the event that they are bitten by a snake themselves. Reading West's
account in his own words gives great insight into his thought process behind the creation
of Bosco.

John West began his career in 1896 when he started working with a showman named
Arizona Bill, who exhibited reptiles. West saw the opportunity for money and, unlike
some workers, did not fear handling snakes, so he began working in that field.[3] Regarding
the selection of the name Bosco, West notes, "Of course the reader will understand that a
showman always adopts some name suitable" (West, 4). John West, it seems, had a good
PR sense and leveraged the reputation of animal violence tied to Bartolomeo Bosco's
name to carve out his own unique niche in show business.

Given the countless imitators of John West's Bosco that would soon emerge and the
historical impact his act had, it is fascinating that in the last paragraph of his article, West
states:

---

3. Though there are several newspaper references to the Bosco character throughout
   the late 1890s, no references could be located mentioning Bosco the Snake Eater that
   predate West's claim of starting the act in 1896.

In concluding this article I would further warn the reader, while hunting or otherwise engaged in the country, that they cannot be too careful when they come across a poisonous reptile, and do not try to copy my exhibitions that many of you saw me give here, that of handling a poisonous snake, for they surely will get you sooner or later, and when that saying that has been the by word in your town and cities and has followed me wherever we have shown, "Have you seen Bosco? You'll have to Hurry" has entirely been forgotten, you may still remember the few words of advice that I gave to you while at Baxter Springs.

I am, Yours Truly, "BOSCO" (West - Continued, 4).

The aforementioned *Pittsburg Headlight* article that was printed in 1911 features several direct quotes from John West regarding his Bosco character. By that time, he had long given up snake-eating though was still very much involved in show business, working as a carnival talker. He also offered several intriguing insights on his life and act.
On the snake bite that cost him his arm:

The accident was all my own fault for it was always up to me to "fix" the snakes and I was careless, that's all, and here is the result.

On how he feels now about starting the snake-eating act:

I was the first man to start it but I did not stop until I was forced to by the big rattler. I look back upon those days and wonder why I ever thought of such an uncivilized proposition. It made me money while I was at it, though and when I first started out the tent where the den was located could not hold the people that looked on with a morbid curiosity at the wild man who lived on snakes alone. They reasoned that nothing but a wild man, a savage, would eat snakes alive. No civilized person would attempt it, they believed.

On how he came up with the act:

The stunt came to me all at once one cold winter day while I was in St. Louis. I reasoned it out that a man could start a stunt like that and carry it out would be the attraction in any carnival company. I figured that to "fix" the snakes, was the only thing necessary and then I could do anything with them. I got everything ready in my mind how to handle the business and engaged with a carnival company that was to make the fairs and reunions.

On his imitators:

Others got into the game, however, and made snake eaters got very common. They did not draw like I did for I was the first one ever to think of such an inhuman show. That was the best money making stunt ever originated by me and it was the last ("Bosco Original 'Eat-Em-Alive'").

It is worth noting that while the Bosco character's cultural popularity in shows is primarily due to the name being synonymous with many performers doing a similar act in the following decades, West himself was widely sought after and his act highly popular on an individual level. Not only is this indicated with the frequency of his newspaper mentions but also in written praise through other sources, such as the *Billboard* archives.

The October 6, 1900, edition of the *Billboard* features an article about a showman who had been trying to book the "widely heralded" original Bosco for his carnival, but it was during Bosco's recovery from his snakebite accident, so he was unable to secure him. Feeling that the show simply wouldn't be complete without a snake eater, in a panic the showman secured a local alcoholic to eat snakes and billed him as "Beno the Snake Eater." Perhaps it was Bosco's high demand coupled with his unavailability during his injury that increased the wave of his imitators ("Beno, The Snake Eater").[4]

The following week, the *Billboard* featured a letter to the editor from a man discussing a recent street fair, which featured a snake eater as one of the attractions. The author of

---

4. There is also a popular American Midwestern food called "Bosco Sticks" which are long breadsticks filled with mozzarella cheese. Despite the name and snake-like appearance, no reference could be located showing any relationship between Bosco Sticks and Bosco the Snake Eater.

the letter noted that the performer was "not as good as 'Bosco,' who recently lost his arm, and is now recovering in Baxter Springs" ("Emporia, Kan., Events").

There are several descriptions of West's act that give insight as to what may have set his Bosco performances apart from his imitators and explain the acclaim he received over other snake eaters. While many snake-eating geeks were alcoholics who sat in a pit chewing on snakes and biting pieces from them, West's act incorporated more creative techniques. Information on his specific performances can be found in several news articles. the *Leavenworth Weekly Times* noted on September 6, 1900, that his performances before his near-fatal injury involved the following:

> *Bosco stands at the head of his profession as a snake eater. He not only eats live snakes, but goes barelegged into a den of fifty rattlesnakes, permits them to bite him anywhere on his body and hangs them by their fangs out his arms* ("'Bosco' Is Dying from a Snake Bite").

On August 22, 1901, an article in the *People's Voice* newspaper out of Wellington, Kansas, hyped up a comeback appearance after his injury:

> *He not only eats 'em alive, but eats 'em whole. To prove this, he bares his belly to the admiring multitude so that the critical eye may see the snakes wriggling and writhing in his stomach* ("Bosco Will Be Here").

With showmanship like that, it is no wonder that John West's Bosco performances stood out among countless other snake eaters.

Regarding the historical correlation of Bosco the magician and Bosco the geek, there is a certain degree of irony to be found when comparing the two. One Bosco is a well-dressed and highly skilled magician accused of engaging in casual animal cruelty in order to achieve illusions. The other is a seemingly unskilled performer dressed in rags whose sole purpose is to engage in blatant animal cruelty for the sake of entertainment.

Both Bartolomeo Bosco and John West also had numerous imitators using the Bosco namesake to try to propel their own careers in stage magic and early geek performance respectively. History does indeed repeat itself, sometimes in the most curious of manners.

Chapter 5
The Snake-Eating Craze

A fter Bosco the Snake Eater's initial rise to fame, there was a sudden burst of popularity when it came to snake eaters performing at events. Not only were there countless imitators carrying the Bosco name, but there were also many other snake eaters who did the same style of performance but used different monikers. Though many snake eaters eventually adopted exaggerated wild man garb for performances, as evidenced by old cabinet cards, there were some snake eaters around the turn of the 20th century who dressed more akin to South Asian aesthetics, possibly influenced by Indian fakirs and snake charmers.

Cabinet card featuring "Rattlesnake Tan The Serpent King". Image courtesy of Nat Sharpe.

For snake eater monikers, the common trend was to take a primitive-sounding name of three to five letters in length and follow it with "The Snake Eater." By mid-1900, no street fair or carnival was complete without a snake eater as one of the featured attractions.

The *Billboard* took notice of this unprecedented explosion of snake-eating performers in December 1900, stating that "If there was a street fair held during the past six months at which there was no snake eater, that fair should go down in history as a wonder." To further illustrate how widespread the practice had become, the issue went on to describe how the Keokuk Street Fair received 21 letters from snake eaters attempting to get booked for that year's event, noting that of the snake-eating applicants, there were eight Boscos, five Esaus, four Unos, two Sunos, one Isaw, and one Rasco ("Many Snake Eaters").

It is important to note that in this particular instance, the name "Esau" came in as the second most popular snake eater name after Bosco. This is not a coincidence, as of the many Bosco imitators, Esau stands out from them as having also achieved some degree of widespread notoriety. Like Bosco, Esau was treated often in the press as a singular being but was actually a character portrayed by many different performers.

The Emergence of Esau

The usage of the name Esau emerged in the realm of sideshow-style entertainment with showman P.T. Barnum. During his career, Barnum promoted bearded woman Annie Jones (1865-1902) at various points in her life. Early exhibitions billed Jones as "The Infant Esau" during her show days as a small child. This was a reference to Esau, the famously hairy brother of Jacob, in the Old Testament of the Bible (Dimuro).

The first mentions of Esau as a snake eater in the press begin around 1899, just a few years after the original Bosco began performing but before Bosco Fever had infected midways in earnest.

A couple of the ballys that were used to promote Esau are as follows:

> *Come and see Esau*
> *Sittin' on a see-saw*
> *Eatin' 'em raw!"* (Maurer 331).

Also:

> *Esaw [sic] eats them alive. He picks out the one he likes best and eats them*
> *like a boy does hot cakes. He would rather eat snakes than candy* ("ESAU
> LIKES SNAKES").

Like Bosco, Esau was often regarded in the press as both an originator and superior performer compared to other snake eaters on the circuit. the *Davenport Morning Star* ran a story on June 28, 1902, about an amateur snake eater named "Osco the Snake Eater" who had his show shut down. The paper made a point to state that Osco's show "lacked the cleverness of the performance put up by Esau, the originator of snake-eating attractions" ("Osco The Snake Eater Is Out of the Business").

GRAND OPENING MONDAY NIGHT!

GRAND and LACLEDE **ELKS'** June 2d to 15th.

40 Shows CHARITY CARNIVAL 10 Bands

Something Doing from Noon to Midnight.

Attractions by BOSTOCK-FERARI CO.

Trained Animal Arena.	Chiqueta.
Crystal Maze.	Beautiful Orient.
Egyptian Theater.	Moorish Palace.
Fair Japan.	Wild Minnie.
Dog and Monkey Circus.	Edison's Phantoscope.
Ferris Wheel.	Barnyard Circus.
Venetian Glass Blowers.	Esau, Snake Eater.
Spirit of Niagara.	Famous Watson Sisters.
Golden Chariots.	Miss Murphy, Balloonist.

Great Grant—Electric High Wire. German Village.
Deborah Bros.—Triple Horizontal Bar.
Barlow's Herd of Performing Elephants.
Speedy, Champion High Diver of the World.

ADMISSION, 10 CENTS.

Carnival advertisement listing Esau as one of the featured attractions. "St Louis Post-Dispatch" - June 1, 1902.

At one point, Bosco and Esau were portrayed to be rival snake eaters. In October 1900, Bosco filed a lawsuit against the Wells Fargo Express company for failure to deliver a shipment of snakes to him. Though the snakes had made it through transit safely, several had died while the package sat in a storage room awaiting Bosco's pickup. Concerned that the package may never be claimed, the local agent sold what was left of the snakes to Esau. When Bosco arrived to pick up the snakes and found out the particulars, it was reported that he was not pleased and filed suit as a result ("Bosco Wants Snake Money").[1]

Bosco and Esau were even mistaken for each other in the press. Shortly after the original Bosco was hospitalized from his snakebite and news circulated that he was not expected to live, the *Coffeyville Weekly Journal* ran a story on September 7, 1900, stating that Esau the Snake Eater had died in Baxter Springs from a snakebite. This news release is

---

1. Though this story was picked up and circulated by a variety of credible news outlets, the absurdity of it lends to the possibility that it may have simply been a publicity stunt. Regardless, it's interesting to note the way the press treated Bosco and Esau as two competitors in the snake-eating industry.

fairly romanticized and includes a vague account of how Esau, the blood-sucking snake eater, had allegedly curled up in his pit and died after being bitten by a snake. The paper does address its questionable speculative journalism by stating on Esau's death "how much truth there is in this The Journal does not know." Though the *Journal* ultimately concluded that "If Esau is dead he is probably better off than he was when alive" ("'Esau' Is Dead").

The following week, this same publication posted a correction piece called "It Was Bosco, Not Esau" and noted its poor reporting by stating that the previous article contained "information [that] was slightly inaccurate although well meaning."

With the sudden explosion of snake eaters, it became increasingly evident just how dangerous and occasionally fatal the act was. Accidents working with the snakes were common and became even more so once eating them became popular. Just looking at the number of snake eaters that received serious injuries performing as Esau is astounding.

Ad that mentions Esau the snake eater as well as a wild man and wild girl show. "Chillicothe Gazette" - May 11, 1901.

Perhaps the earliest record of such injuries comes from December 1899, when a man named G. F. Parker, who was the manager of an Esau, confirmed that his snake eater had passed away recently after being bitten under the eye by a rattlesnake during a performance. Parker used the opportunity to let the press know that the incident was evidence that his performer was the real deal and was not faking his act in any way ("About Esau").

In the summer of 1901, a man named Charles Lapearl was bitten by a rattlesnake while performing as Esau. While he was in recovery, his partner Mooney took his place and was also bitten. Both men spent time in the hospital, narrowly surviving their injuries. When Lapearl was released, he went back to his snake-eating ways as Esau and was promptly bitten again, resulting in another hospital stay ("Snake Eater Bitten Again").

A man named John Rufe was wounded in a very obvious, gruesome manner during an Esau performance in Louisiana during October 1903. When he had placed the head of a live rust-head moccasin snake into his mouth, the snake managed to sink its fangs into his tongue prior to being decapitated. Rufe's tongue became so swollen that he began to choke on it as venom spread through his system. He was given little chance of recovery ("Snake Eater Bitten by Moccasin").

Like John West's Bosco, who lost his arm in September 1900, an Esau performer named Thomas McAlister lost his arm the following month after being bitten while performing in Texas ("Snake Nearly Ate Snake Eater").

In one interesting case, a fugitive assumed the role of Esau the Snake Eater as a means to elude authorities. In the fall of 1900, a man who was wanted for a murder committed in Kansas was apprehended after a three-year manhunt. The man had been traveling around as Esau, and a detective who had been searching for him heard that he was traveling with a show in Texas. Cleverly, the snake-eating man wore a mask and wig during his performances which further concealed his identity under the guise of theatrics. The detective tracked him to Nocona, Texas, and hung around the snake-eating tent, watching performances for three days before finally making his move. The detective confronted Esau, had him remove his wig and mask, confirmed his identity, and then arrested him ("THE END OF ESAU").

Snake eaters, particularly Bosco and Esau, made their way into other facets of popular culture as well. For instance, the 1902 book of oddball short fiction stories *Welsh Rarebit Tales* features a story called "The Strangest Freak," about an alcoholic snake eater at a sideshow. The character's name in the story is Esau Bosko.

On the subject of fiction, the highly influential work *Dracula* by Bram Stoker was published in 1897. The novel is notable not only for the oral-centric concept of the vampire that feeds on the living's blood to survive but also for the character Renfield, an insane minion who eats live bugs, rats, and birds as a means to absorb life force.

The Procurement and Commerce of the Snake Business

Snakes themselves have a long history in live shows. In many cases, they were captured and exhibited by those knowledgeable in the field of collecting them in the wild.

One such collector and exhibitor was Sam Helms. Helms was an eccentric man who began capturing rattlesnakes at an early age, even going so far as to carry them with him in social situations. As an adult, he made a great deal of money traveling the country exhibiting his collection of snakes in the mid-1860s. He even invented a special apparatus to display his snakes, which would exaggerate their appearances to make them more shocking to audiences. The effect was done by putting a giant magnifying glass on the front of the viewing area on the snake box so that when the audience peered into it, the snakes at the other end of the box were magnified, looking much larger and frightening than they actually were.

Helms was also involved in an unfortunate and unusual incident involving a live bear. After he had returned home from a snake venture, a man from New York offered Helms $40 if he could capture a live bear and bring it to him. Though he was accustomed to capturing snakes and not large game, Helms accepted the offer. He was successful at trapping a bear and, after putting restraints on it, he boarded a train with the bear to transport it from Pennsylvania to New York, sticking the animal in the baggage car. Unfortunately for Helms and the rest of the passengers, the bear got loose and began running amok in the baggage car. Helms sprang into action and began wrestling the bear. The battle eventually spilled out of the train and ended up on a riverbank, where Helms was able to successfully tie down the bear and attempted to continue transport via a raft. However, the bear once again got loose and made it ashore. Helms pursued the bear through the woods, but the animal was eventually shot and killed by a local farmer, ending the chase and destroying Helms's chance at $40 (SAM HELMS' $40 BEAR).

Another collector was Elijah Pelton from Hawley, Pennsylvania, who in 1886 was known to have nearly 200 rattlesnakes in his private collection, which he caught himself and kept in a giant caged den, all of them with the fangs intact. Pelton refused offers to sell his collection but did intend to exhibit it at Coney Island and other summer resorts at one point ("Two Hundred Live Rattlesnakes").

With all the various types of snake shows being put on in different venues, there was a strong demand from showmen for reliable sourcing of snakes for their shows. Naturally, the show business industry was also big business for those with expertise in snake collecting.

An early snake supplier was Charles Bishoff, aka Montana Charley and Rattlesnake King of the Rockies. He was a successful snake dealer who regularly supplied snakes for established circuses and traveling menageries throughout the 1890s. He had a boat loosely modeled after Noah's Ark, which included small living quarters for him and his family and a large space used for his snake cargo ("CARGO OF SNAKES").

The most notable snake supplier was William Abraham King, aka Snake King (1877-1952), who not only had a long career selling snakes to those in the outdoor entertainment industry but was also a go-to for many geek show operators in the early 20th century.

Snake King got his start in show business when he worked as a carnival snake show operator in his teens. He observed that snakes had a much higher mortality rate when they were being handled all day for entertainment, and as a result there was a constant need for workers to acquire more snakes for their shows. Making note of this growing need for snakes in outdoor shows, he decided to establish a snake farm and set up shop in Brownsville, Texas. Not content to be an ordinary snake supplier, he built a very successful operation while cultivating a larger-than-life image for himself. He called his establishment Snakesville and had the full trade name "W.A. Snake King" registered. King also created elaborate, snake-themed illustrations for his checks and signed his correspondence "Rattling Yours...Snake King" (King Jr. VII - X).

Snake King sold various serpents, including fanged venomous snakes (known as "hot" snakes) and those that he had defanged himself (known as "fixed" snakes), which were safer for end users to work with during geek shows. In one very unfortunate circumstance, a geek customer of Snake King's lost his life due to miscommunication of a single letter of the alphabet. One day King received a rush order by telegraph that read "Rush fifty dollar not fixed rattlers." Noting that the customer did not want fixed snakes and was in a hurry to get them, King quickly sent out the $50 order of hot snakes to the customer. During the geek show, the man acting as a "Wild Man from Borneo" was bitten by one of the venomous snakes during his act and continued to perform, disregarding the wound, only to die a short time later. While his widow was preparing to file a lawsuit against King, he decided to look into the order further. It turned out there had been a transcription error from the original telegraph to the order King received, which made all the difference in the world. The original telegraph had indeed requested fixed snakes, as it actually read "Rush fifty dollar lot fixed rattlers" (King Jr. 74-75).

Though he was widely known as a snake supplier for geek show operators, King later branched out to supply other exotic animals to traveling circuses and carnivals. Various anecdotes about his life are recounted in the appropriately titled book *Rattling Yours...Snake King*, written by his son, W. A. King, Jr.

As snakes often either met a bloody end in geek shows or expired prematurely due to poor conditions, there was a need for a streamlined supply chain in the industry for fresh snakes as showmen traveled from stop to stop during carnival season. A common technique was for geek-show operators to make a note of their routes for the season, with each engagement lasting about a week. While running shows at each stop, the show operators would mail in orders to snake suppliers for fresh snake batches to be delivered to the location where the carnival would be set up for the following week's engagement. If they were in a time crunch, they would instead send in the order via telegraph. Typically, a deposit would be required for each order, then the snakes would be sent to the upcoming location and shipped C.O.D. for the balance, arriving just in time for the show operator to set up and use at the new location (King Jr. 45).

By 1908, snake-eating performances had made such a widespread impact that they were actually starting to cause ecological and economic concerns. The *Washington Post* took note of this and discussed how with all the numerous Bosco and Esau performers consuming such a high volume of snakes during their performance runs, supplies of snakes were running scarce. As a result, the costs for snakes, particularly rattlesnakes, had skyrocketed. Some showmen were even forced to discontinue their snake shows due to an inability to obtain snakes. There was also speculation that certain types of reptiles were on the verge of extinction as a result of so many being eaten by performers ("Boscos' Hard on Rattlers").

Snake-eating also had an effect on local environments. After a snake eater had performed at a street show in June 1901 in Port Huron, Michigan, what was left of his snakes were thrown into the river. The following day, bunches of snakes washed ashore. Many were dead, decapitated and mangled, but some lived and slithered off into the local woods. Not only did the locals then have to deal with disposing of snake corpses, but the snakes that had survived, including rattlesnakes, proceeded to terrorize the local neighborhood, even attacking a local boy. The resultant spike in snake sightings led many of the snakes to be killed in the wild ("Rattle Snakes Ran Rampant After Esau Left Town"). This incident could also serve to answer the question as to what exactly happens to all the snake remnants after a snake eater show.

In July 1904, the *Atlanta Constitution* profiled a professional snake eater named Charlie Pierce, who had run into some legal trouble. Pierce had come into town to perform, but his snake supply was low. He took on a silent partner, who he convinced to give him $5 so that he could procure snakes for the show. However, Pierce ended up spending the money on drugs and alcohol instead and soon found himself in front of a judge. Though the judge initially doubted Pierce's claim of what his profession actually was, he was convinced when Pierce produced numerous letters about his snake-eating ways, including correspondence from a Texas firm where he'd previously purchased snakes. While he was before the judge, Charlie Pierce provided some interesting insight about what it was like to be a professional snake eater during the peak of the act's popularity.

On how the act had impacted the market of snake sales:

Frog snakes and grass snakes are the cheapest, although they are considerably higher than they used to be. Hop snakes and moccasins are away yonder, and rattlers are worth twice what they were two years ago.

On if he ever gets bitten by the snakes while working:

Oh, yes; but you will see by the letter head of this firm that they guarantee all of their snakes. They take the poison out of the glands, you know, and then I always take a lot of morphine, and then I don't care whether they bite me or not. That's the way I got to taking the white stuff. When I first entered the profession, the snakes weren't always fixed, and they used to bite me often. Then it was that I used to drink lots of whisky and take morphine, and I reckon I've got the habit pretty well fixed now.

On his career ambitions and the spike of newcomers to the profession:

I've always wanted to buy a gila monster, but I have never been able to get just the kind I wanted. It's worth good money to eat these things, but they will always draw a crowd. The snake-eating profession is getting to be overrun with a lot of amateurs who don't know the first thing about it and what with their cutting the prices and the price of snakes going up every six months, it's getting pretty hard for an honest snake eater to make a living ("ARRESTED SNAKE EATER TELLS OF HIS PROFESSION").

The Many Faces of Serpentina

Though snake eating attractions were common during this time period, utilizing snakes and snake-like imagery at shows was not restricted to live snake exhibitions and snake eaters. As with Bosco and Esau, sometimes sideshow performers adopted the same common name to portray a character and perform a standardized type of act. Another common sideshow name but one that deviates from this mold somewhat is Serpentina. Though the name has been used by many performers in sideshow, it has been used to describe completely different types of acts, ranging from natural born oddities to snake dancers to illusion shows. The only overlapping commonalities are that Serpentina is female and what she is known for relates to snakes in some way.

The original Serpentina was a freak show performer who was born without the ability to move her body below her arms. This left the rest of her anatomy limp and trailing behind her. Serpentina's pitch book made the claim that she was born without a skeletal structure below her shoulders, which led to her state of being. When she started being exhibited, her appearance resulted in her being marketed as a human snake, and she was called Serpentina the Serpent Lady ("Curiosity Of Nature Will Be Displayed").

Her real name was Mary Krasinski ("'HEADLESS WOMAN' ILLUSION EXPOSED; POLICE CLOSE SHOW"; Uno 75) and she was born in Douglas, Ontario, Canada, in 1900.[2] For her career in show business, her small body was placed on a velvet cushion and she was exhibited at various sideshows. Despite her being branded as a human-serpent hybrid, she had kind eyes and an angelic face (Seay). In some instances, photos of her had her lower body made to look like she was covered in scales, and she was promoted as a real living mermaid ("Serpentina, A Real Living Mermaid?"). She achieved immense popularity in show businesses throughout the 1920s, '30s, and '40s, even being exhibited at large-scale events including the 1933 Chicago World's Fair, where more than eight million people paid to see her ("Serpentina Displayed").

According to her biographical pitch book, her condition was a result of being born with arrested ossification, and as a result she was largely restricted to assuming only three different positions: on her stomach with her head up in her ordinary position, on her stomach with her head down to sleep, and in a twisted position for exercise and to

---

2. Some sources indicate that she may have been born in 1898 or 1908 in Oakland, California. However, given the numerous unrelated period newspapers that list the information stated above, the author is inclined to believe that the information stated is correct.

help prevent organ congestion (BIOGRAPHICAL SKETCH OF SERPENTINA THE SERPENT LADY).[3]

Despite her circumstances, she was known to be an incredibly positive and friendly person who loved her life in show business. In 1922, she told the *St. Louis Star*:

> *Everybody's mighty good to me. I guess I'm the pet of the show. And I have everything on earth that my heart desires. I like the business. I read and crochet and sew - I've taken prizes with my needles - work - and I attend to all my correspondence. And I'm in perfect health-eat three good square meals a day and enjoy them, too. People out front feel sorry for me. But they don't have to, I'm better off than a lot of other folks I know.* ("Serpentina of the Sideshow, Pet of Circus Freaks, Finds It's a Good World After All").

SERPENTINA
HALF SERPENT, HALF WOMAN

Freak show performer Serpentina. From the author's private collection.

There have been numerous performers with live snakes who use the Serpentina moniker. In the mid-to-late 20th century, there are countless instances of Serpentina the Snake Girl, Serpentina the Snake Charmer, and Serpentina the Snake Dancer. In many cases, the entertainer would dance with a large snake, often a boa constrictor, with the act being promoted as an erotic attraction and often performed at nightclubs.

---

3. For her full biographical pitch book, see Appendix 2.

A notable and more recent long-term Serpentina performer is Coney Island's Stephanie Torres, who worked as a snake charmer, dancing with a large snake. As Serpentina, she has made numerous media appearances and first joined the Coney Island Sideshows by the Seashore cast in 1998 (Hartzman, "A Touch of Knowledge...").

There is also a classic sideshow illusion that creates the appearance of a human female's head on the body of a snake. It is in the same vein of the more popular Spidora illusions, which have the same effect but with a human female head on the body of a large spider. The snake girl version is sometimes billed by promoters as Serpentina. The upside to this version of Serpentina is that the head can be played by virtually any female in the show, and there are no actual snakes involved. As such, it's an incredibly versatile and low-maintenance, albeit cheesy, sideshow attraction.

Giving It a Name

It is somewhat challenging to pinpoint exactly when snake-eating attractions became widely known specifically as geek shows.

William Lindsay Gresham's 1946 carnival noir novel *Nightmare Alley* and its film adaptation the following year contributed to the widespread use of the term but were not its origin. However, the works did mark the first mainstream, fictionalized piece of widely distributed entertainment that used the word *geek* in such a context.

Gresham himself first became aware of what a sideshow geek was during the winter of 1938. He details the experience early on in his nonfiction book about variety entertainment, *Monster Midway*. While he was serving as a volunteer medic during the Spanish Civil War, his superior was a man named Clem Faraday, who was an old-time carnival worker.[4] Gresham was fascinated by the sideshow and would frequently ask Faraday for old stories about working there. When Faraday noted that he had a geek show as the "blow-off", Gresham asked him what that was exactly.[5] Faraday said, "That's a fellow

---

4. There is seemingly little to no historical information regarding Clem Faraday. Some publications, such as the "Skeptical Inquirer," state that Gresham's superior was actually carnival worker Joseph Daniel "Doc" Halliday (Polidoro 14). In that case, it is likely that Gresham was using a fictionalized name for Halliday when he decided to publish "Monster Midway."

5. A blow-off is an added attraction for an extra fee at the end of a show (Keyser).

that bites the heads off chickens and snakes." Then he went on to describe to Gresham an African-American geek who would swallow snakes as well as another geek who would bite the heads off baby alligators.

Gresham was taken aback and asked how to find someone that would perform in this kind of show. Faraday told Gresham that geeks are not found, they are made. He then detailed the approach: Find an alcoholic or a drug addict and offer them a temporary job pretending to be a geek in exchange for their fix of alcohol or morphine. Simply have them sit in the pit and give them a razorblade to discreetly cut the chickens and pretend to bite them. When he becomes comfortable after a few days and his addiction has been fed, tell him that faking the act isn't drawing a crowd, and after the following night's show, he is done so that he can be replaced with a real geek. Then give him a bottle of booze, telling him it's the last one he'll get before he has to leave. After that, according to Gresham's conversation with Faraday, "The next night when you throw in the chicken - he'll geek."

After hearing this, Gresham notes that he was "paralyzed by his account of the geek-manufacturing process" and likened it to an account he'd heard of young girls being groomed for prostitution. The tales sparked the idea for *Nightmare Alley*, which Gresham described based on the geek revelation as "a man learns, from working in a carnival sideshow, that a geek is made by exploiting another person's desperate need. Taking this as his guiding principle in life, he rises higher and higher, finally meets someone who works the same process on him, and tumbles back literally into the pit – biting the heads off chickens himself for a bottle a day" (Gresham 13-16).

A similar instance of Gresham's conversation with Faraday is described in Gordon Thomas's biographical book on sideshow performer the Amazing Blondini, titled *Bed of Nails*. In the book, while the subject is learning the art of fire eating from one of the veterans in the show, the instructor mentions that he once knew a man who was training to be a "civilized cannibal." This man did an act where he would dress as a "wild man" and sit in a pit, biting the heads off snakes and birds. However, the veteran notes that the cannibal was a lazy worker and would cheat the act by palming a razorblade and discreetly cut the throats of hens in his pit instead of actually biting them. Once the public caught on that he wasn't actually biting the heads off, attendance suffered. In a last-ditch attempt to save the show, he started biting the heads off for real, but by then those in attendance had already written him off and were still convinced that he was faking it through some other means. So the cannibal gave up the act and went back to selling popcorn. When recalling the instance, the fire-eating veteran concluded with the advice that: "It goes to show that you've got to be prepared to learn the job properly from the start" (Thomas 109).

Though Gresham no doubt helped popularize the term *geek* with *Nightmare Alley*, there are numerous instances of it appearing in the same context that predate that work.

According to David W. Maurer's *Glossary of Carnival and Circus Slang*, published in June 1931, the word *geek* as it relates to the performance type actually originated with an Esau snake-eating performer. This work alleges that *geek* was first used to describe a man named Wagner who achieved fame working as an Esau (Maurer 331).

There are, however, various other early print references connecting the word *geek* to the sideshow act.

For example, in its December 16, 1925, edition, the *Rapid City Journal* featured an article about human freaks migrating toward outdoor entertainment outlets, particularly carnivals. It notes that "Each carnival has its 'wild man,' who is carefully guarded in a pit filled with snakes, the only living creatures with which he will associate." The

> ### Come on, You Geex
>
> Want ad in yesterday's Register:
> "GEEK WANTED TO WORK
> SNAKE SHOW PIT. Write L-668,
> Register and Tribune."

Early example of a classified ad for a geek show that mentions the word geek specifically. "Des Moines Tribune" - July 19, 1922

article later states that the wild man is also known as a "geek" in carnival parlance. This write-up describes the wild man's actions by stating, "He rolls his eyes, grimaces, and seizes large snakes which are all about him." Of the snake pit, it notes that "The 'poisonous reptiles' are large, but harmless snakes, which are anxious to get away from the 'geek,' and wriggle rapidly around the pit, hoping to find some exit" ("Facts About Freaks and Fakes").

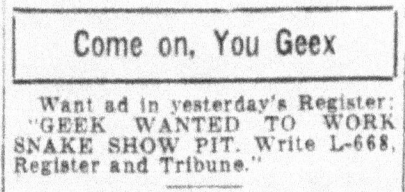

The *Oxford English Dictionary* indicates that the first recorded usage of the *geek* definition was actually in 1919, when it was used in a classified ad in the October 25 edition of the the *Billboard* ("geek, n." OED Online). The classified advertisement referenced is from a man named Carl Elder in Paducah, Kentucky, and reads: "Snake charmer or geek man; 25; would like to join show going South; have own makeup." Appropriately, just a few lines below that is another ad that reads "JOE SAVO, the Great and Only Savo; eats them alive; glass eater, fire eater; swallows watches, rings, money" ("Circus and Carnival Advertisements Section").

Other sources, such as the *Online Etymology Dictionary*, claim this definition of *geek* as coming into language in 1916 ("Geek" Online Etymology Dictionary), and *Merri-*

am-Webster states that the first known use of this definition of *geek* dates back to 1912 ("geek." Merriam-Webster).

Once the geek act had a name of its own, it began to branch off into new territories. Soon performers moved on from snakes and began feasting upon other animals, most commonly chickens, rats, and sometimes pigs. Though snakes were what caused the original boom, chickens eventually became the animal most commonly associated with geek shows in the public eye. The obvious reason for this is that chickens are far cheaper and easier to obtain, particularly in rural areas. Some geek show operators would also move the dead chickens to the cookhouse after the show and the chickens would then be cooked and served for dinner. Soon, the all-purpose term "geek show" became an industry standard to describe this specific type of attraction.

Over the next few decades, more and more want ads for geeks began appearing in the *Billboard*. By the time the 1940s hit, nearly every issue had at least one classified advertisement that referenced a geek show in some way.

At that point, the sideshow geek had come into its own and was at the peak of its popularity as a standalone and established sideshow act.

CHIEF WON A PONY \ DECEASED \ TAKEN IN 40's \ EMPLOYED BY W.T."SLIM" KELLY

"Chief Won A Pony" with a snake. He was managed and exhibited by W.T. "Slim" Kelly
circa 1940's. Image courtesy of Rhett Bryson.

"Chief Sundown" performing with snakes in 1960. From the author's private collection.

Chapter 6
Historical Geek Profiles

Individual geek performers were not typically known to achieve great personal fame and were often seen as expendable by those who hired them. Some had poor physical and mental conditions and were taken advantage of to lure them into performing, and others simply led unreliable lives. Not all geeks had a down-and-out lifestyle, but for promoters, sourcing from vulnerable populations was a common way to obtain geek performers, given the turnover rate. That coupled with the gross nature of geek show acts resulted in geeks not being held in high regard as performers and generally being seen as the lowest act of sideshow entertainment.

The information in this chapter focuses on individual performers. It is not intended to be all-encompassing or to provide thorough biographies but rather to focus on slice-of-life stories about those who worked as geeks at some point.[1]

Snake-Oid

Working firsthand with snakes, one might expect some of the more astute geeks to have a strong expertise with the animals. That was indeed the case with accomplished showman Cary "Snake-Oid" Jones, who went on to become both an expert on snakes and have a successful career after dabbling as a performer in geek shows.

Cary Jones started out in sideshow in 1890, where he began exhibiting snakes. He then became a geek, and later an established authority on snakes. He had his own snake farm and did consulting work on the subject of snakes. Throughout most of his career, he did not like his name in print and went simply by "Snake-Oid" (sometimes "Snakeoid" or "Snake Oid"). He was a wealthy family man and travelled extensively. The *Tampa Tribune* wrote of him in 1921 that he was "a man of considerable means, remarkably intelligent and far above the average usually found in a sideshow as a snake charmer, or a so-called 'snake eater'" ("'SNAKEOID' IS READY TO QUIT").[2]

Indeed, Jones's quick wit and analytical perspective was not like that of the traditional wild man that some were used to seeing in geek shows. During one performance where he was swallowing snakes, the question arose from the crowd about how to determine a snake's gender. Snake-Oid paused mid-performance and cracked, "Just put his head down on your arm and if HE bites you

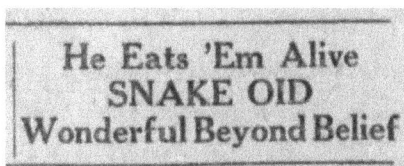

He Eats 'Em Alive
SNAKE OID
Wonderful Beyond Belief

Snake Oid promotional clipping using the popular "Eats 'Em Alive" tagline first used by Bosco the Snake Eater. "Tampa Bay Times" - March 9, 1919.

---

1. For some, I have included additional biographical information where applicable.

2. It is possible that there were other snake eaters using the "Snake-Oid" moniker as well. However, the sources used in this section match with this Snake-Oid being from Jones's city of Muncie, Indiana. He was also widely known by the name, and later articles that use his real name as a snake authority also reference his early days as a snake swallower.

it's a Him, and if SHE bites you it's a HER." A moment later, as he was getting ready to swallow another snake, he noticed that his sock was coming down and remarked on his observation out loud during the performance ("Eats Garter Snake When He Finds His Socks Coming Down"). Clearly, one must ensure that their attire is in proper order when working as a geek.

Though he was occasionally called the "Original Snake-eater," Jones's geek technique was much more strategic and humane than that of his counterparts. Rather than biting the heads off snakes, he would instead swallow small garter snakes whole, then regurgitate them. Jones described his technique and geek philosophy:

> *I do not eat snakes, as is generally supposed. It is true I swallow them and by muscular control am able to throw them out again in a living condition. It took a great effort and much practise [sic] to be able to do this. I feel safe in saying I have the only legitimate snake show in the world today. Back in the old days when I started out, many tried to imitate me. Some of them would bite the head of a snake off for the benefit of the gathered crowd. It did not appeal to the public, and I kept right on to success with my show* ("'SNAKEOID' IS READY TO QUIT").

Content not just to exhibit snakes, Jones believed in educating the public as an advocate and lecturer on snakes. Despite his geek ways, he was against killing non-poisonous snakes and said that they should be protected by law, claiming that killing non-poisonous snakes cost the country $220,000,000 per year, since they ate rodents and pests that destroyed farmers' crops ("SAYS IGNORANCE ABOUT SNAKES COSTS COUNTRY $220,000,000 ANNUALLY").

Unlike other snake eaters of the time, Jones did not swallow venomous or even fixed snakes. Rather, he would use non-venomous garter snakes. However, he exhibited other snakes and worked with venomous snakes in other capacities. He had actually developed a general immunity to snake venom through ingesting anti-venom serum and allowing poisonous snakes to bite his arms in controlled circumstances throughout his career. Jones passed away from natural causes in 1939 at the age of 60 ("MUNCIE MAN, BITTEN").

Kafoozelum and Michizupo

In the early 1900s, the student body from the University of Michigan held yearly carnivals billed as county fairs in Ann Arbor, Michigan. They featured various vaudeville-style performances, a parade, and a midway that contained numerous sideshows put on by the college's fraternities and sororities.

There were several mystery attractions as well. The students even had specialty badges made and handed them out to those that attended these mysterious attractions, some of which were early geek and wild man shows.

In 1902, the carnival featured a strange sideshow attraction called Kafoozelum. Those who had the bravery to observe it were rewarded with badges that read "I have seen Kafoozelum eat snakes in the Persian Garden."

A few years later, in 1905, a similarly named attraction called "Michizupo" was featured at the carnival. It was promoted as a mystery attraction with a sign outside on the first night, which simply stated that there was "something inside" as a means to lure those passing by (Event and Comment 402).[3] Much like Kafoozelum, Michizupo also had badges made as souvenirs for attendees. These read "I have seen the Michizupo."

The attractions are not described in any preserved University literature. However, an article from the April 19, 1908, *Detroit Free Press* about the University of Michigan's upcoming county fair provides interesting details on both of the attractions.

On Michizupo:

> *Then the cage enclosing the wild ferocious Michizupo came into view, and the crowd roared again as the features of a diminutive pickaninny protruded through a black, curly dog skin.*

On Kafoozelum:

> *In the Persian garden was located the famous Kasloozelum, who ate snakes. Kasloozelum spent the evening in chewing up a boa constrictor, but the body of the snake was "almost" like a striped barber pole, and the head was found*

---

3. Note the first two syllables of the attraction and the name of the university.

later to be made of cloth. Because of Kasloozelum's ferocity and the size of the
snake, a large crowd was constantly before his cage and his keepers earned
considerable money for the union.

It is unclear if the newspaper accidentally misspelled the name of Kafoozelum or if the attraction's name evolved in subsequent years. The article does strongly imply that, with the case of the Kafoozelum attraction, any glomming was likely a gaff involving a fake snake.[4]

The article also recounts a humorous anecdote from a previous year when one of the fraternities had ordered and promoted a "wild man" for the carnival event. A rival fraternity, not wanting to be outdone, claimed to have gone and ordered their own "wild man" from a zoo. When the carnival happened, the fraternities buried the hatchet when they realized that their respective "wild men" both ended up being two of the University varsity football players in costume (Kahn 6).

Original tickets and badges from the Michigan Union
Country Fair including those referencing Kafoozelum
Michizupo. From the author's private collection.

---

4. Gaff is a general term for fakery used in an attraction. It can refer to a secret mechanism used to control the outcome of a carnival game, the secret apparatus used to achieve a magic trick, or the props utilized in a fake freak exhibit (Keyser).

Neola

Fred Bloodgood was a pitchman who was active in show business beginning in the 1920s. He began with Vanderburg Brothers Greater Combined Shows circus shortly after he graduated from high school, then later started running his own carnival shows. Bloodgood was well known for his medicine shows.[5] In these performances, he would wear a surgeon's outfit, complete with stethoscope, and enthusiastically sell bottles of a natural remedy that he called "Doc Foster's Hospital Tonic." Despite his image, he never claimed to be an actual licensed doctor, as it was all for the show. Bloodgood was also his birth name, not a stage name, hence he often went by "Doc Foster" during his medicine shows because it sounded less contrived. He was quite successful selling his miracle tonic during the winter seasons throughout the 1920s and '30s. During the summers, Bloodgood ran geek shows.

His first attempt at a geek show was short-lived, as the geek, who went by the name Neva, proved to be unreliable. He eventually found success with a new geek in the form of a man called Shorty whom he hired from another showman. Shorty, so called due to his short attention span, proved to be an enthusiastic worker (Isay and Wang 192-193). After fitting Shorty in a wig and marketing him as a female to increase appeal, Bloodgood's new geek Neola was born. Some said that Shorty was previously a piano player in a brothel in Northern Georgia prior to joining the carnival. Being a geek assured him of a nutritious repast several times a day—no guarantees as a piano player (Bloodgood). Because the attractions did not have a loudspeaker system, Bloodgood favored choosing geek names that had long vowel sounds since they carried better acoustically, hence names like Neva and Neola.

Neola's setup was that of a traditional canvas pit, held up by two-by-fours. The attraction went through live snakes so quickly that Bloodgood had to have a standing order in place with a large snake vendor in Texas. During the show, Neola would cradle the snakes in her (his) arms like a child, then periodically throw inner tubes, made to resemble snakes, into the crowd. In other instances, Neola would simply let out a loud scream and leap

---

5. Medicine shows were an entertainment attraction where the performer would pitch a cure-all miracle medicine to the audience, often making absurdist claims and incorporating comedy for the sake of entertainment value.

towards someone in the audience for the roust, always making a point to target those in attendance appearing the most terrified, which would occasionally result in them fainting.

Bloodgood also worked with chickens in his Neola show. For these performances, Neola would crawl around on her hands and feet and Bloodgood would toss a chicken into the pit, causing Neola to let out a scream before grabbing the chicken and biting its head off. Bloodgood noted that though he worked many shows of this nature with Shorty, he never saw him get sick from doing this (Isay and Wang 193).

The doctor image that Bloodgood utilized for his medicine shows also lent well to his geek shows, as he promoted the attraction as being so shocking that there needed to be a medical man in attendance at all times.

Bloodgood and his crew also engaged in several clever guerilla marketing and theatrical displays to help promote their geek show. Occasionally, while tickets were being sold, Bloodgood and his inside man would run inside the tent, feigning a panic as though Neola was out of control. They would then crack bullwhips and shoot pistols (with blank cartridges) inside. The sounds alone were enough to gain the attention of those nearby, who simply had to buy a ticket to see what the commotion was all about. Sometimes Neola would become so "unmanageable" that she would knock two of the tent poles out of position. To defend themselves, Bloodgood and his inside man would grab the other two

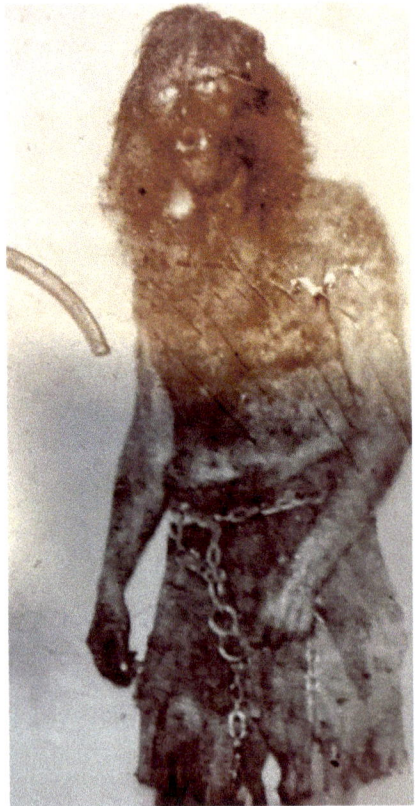

The Strangest of all Strange Creatures, Neola. Image courtesy of David Bloodgood.

poles to keep Neola at bay, thus removing the remaining tent supports and literally bringing down the house on their audience (McNamara 39-56).

Another promotional tactic they would employ whenever Neola caused a girl to faint in the audience, the inside man would pick her up off the ground and carry her around the carnival frantically yelling "Is there a doctor in the crowd? Is there a doctor in the crowd?"

while those nearby became intrigued about just would could have possibly happened to cause such a reaction (Isay and Wang 193). Some onlookers may have noticed that, curiously, it was often the same girl fainting in every show (Bloodgood).

Another activity involved Bloodgood and his partner walking to the other end of the midway, then loudly getting into an argument where Bloodgood would accuse his partner of "seeing" Bloodgood's wife, until Bloodgood would finally pull out a gun and threaten to kill him. His partner would then run away, with Bloodgood chasing after him, firing blank rounds from his pistol, until they ultimately both ran into the door of their Neola attraction. By the time the crowd had caught up to them to see what was going on, Bloodgood had already jumped into the ticket box to sell tickets to the show (Bloodgood).

The relationship between Bloodgood and Shorty proved successful in the long term, as they ran for several seasons their geek show called "That Strangest of All Strange Creatures, the Girl Whom We Call Neola" (McNamara 39-56).

Fred Bloodgood eventually left the world of outdoor show business after being drafted in 1940. He later married and had a son, David. When putting David to bed as a child, Fred Bloodgood would tell him larger than life bedtime stories about his carnival years. In addition to his time working medicine shows and geek shows, he also told tall tales of exhibiting the preserved body of John Wilkes Booth, scuba diving all over the world, and having dinner with the likes of historical notables such as Harry Houdini and John Phillip Sousa.

David Bloodgood eventually grew up to use a professional title similar to that of his father's "Doc Foster" sideshow persona. Only instead of pursuing show business and playing the part of a doctor-themed character, David obtained an actual doctoral degree and spent his career working primarily as a relationship therapist. Dr. David Bloodgood, PhD, has fond memories of his father and the stories he told him as a child. On his father's approach to storytelling, David notes:

I think he treated the truth much the way an oyster treats a grain of sand. It takes something insignificant, maybe even ugly and it begins to coat it and begins to work with it and continually dress it up until it finally ends up this beautiful pearl. I think that's probably the approach my father took to most things.

David theatrically describing the climax of his father's Neola show using some of Fred
Bloodgood's original verbiage:

*Once and once on every midway, my father would throw a live long horn
chicken down into the bottom of that pit and you'd see a strange change
come over Neola. Her eyes would begin to glow like two red hot coals of fire.
She would emit one soul-searing scream, leap halfway across the arena and
grasp that foul in her teeth. Now, you may have noticed that she had a
double row of teeth on the upper jaw, single row of them on the lower jaw,
and her head tapered at the top like that of a coconut. She had long long
arms that hung way down to here. But she would then proceed to rip the
head from that quivering foul, and then suck, drain, and draw the blood
from that bird just like you would drink water from a glass.*

On the controversies of his father's show relating to the animal fatalities:

*He said things have changed dramatically. I doubt that there was anybody
in the audience that hadn't either killed a chicken or seen a chicken killed,
because it was standard. It happened every Saturday night across the South.
Somebody took a chicken out, butchered it, then they had it for lunch the
next day. They weren't buying it in cellophane wrapped Styrofoam, they just
went out and got one. And he said "I don't think that troubled people, I think
the idea of this strange creature screaming and yelling and jumping around
and then ripping the head off of it, drinking the blood..." He said that wasn't
standard fair in the barnyard...I don't think that he saw what was being
done to the chickens at all as being any way cruel. I mean, it's what everybody
was doing. It wasn't suffering either. He didn't torture them. They just did
the same thing that you would do in the chicken yard. He swung it around
by it's neck, and killed it, and then ripped the head off and that was the end
of it.*

On the human ethics of his father's geek show:

I've refused to watch, Nightmare Alley...*I guess I don't want to think of my father as having the capacity to treat somebody the way he was treated. There was never, as far as I know, there was never any kind of mistreatment. But that would trouble me. He always spoke very fondly of those years.*

Much later in Fred Bloodgood's life, during his golden years, there was a renewed interest in his past as a carnival showman, since that form of entertainment was largely extinct by that time. He would later go on to relive his carnival years by doing re-enactments of his medicine shows for organizations and telling tales of his years in the sideshow to the media. At this stage in his life, Fred Bloodgood became a bit of a local celebrity and was featured in numerous books and documentaries.[6] He continued to entertain audiences with his tales of the midway until passing away in his mid-80s.

Regarding his father's John Wilkes Booth exhibit:

My father said that one of his most successful shows was the John Wilkes Booth exhibit. He said, "Everything I ever said was the truth, but I believe the Booth show may have been even truer than the others." The stiff had a broken tibia, a mangled thumb, six toes on one foot, and a mysterious signet ring top lodged in his bronchial passage that had the letter B embossed on it. In a nod to the movie Big Fish *I will say that* Life *magazine did an article showing a stiff with all those manifestations.*

David Bloodgood describes these later years of his father:

It was an absolute dream for him, because those were among the happiest days of his life and then to be able to relive them at age 70 and early 80s. He said in the broadway thing [documentary featuring Fred Bloodgood], they sold medicine at the end of the show for a dollar a bottle. It was a souvenir bottle for the show. He said the first night, speaking as a showman, it was exactly what heaven must be like to see every single arm go up and each

---

6. Notably, the 1984 medicine show documentary "Free Show Tonite" prominently features Fred Bloodgood.

hand held a dollar. That was something he had dreamed about all his life
(Bloodgood).

Fred Bloodgood selling tickets to his Neola sideshow attraction. Image
courtesy of David Bloodgood.

The Donaldsonville, Louisiana, State Fair Geek of 1938

There exists a phenomenal series of photographs that were taken during a live geek act
at the Louisiana State Fair in 1938. Several of the images can be found online through

various photo archives. These images are notable not only in their high quality but also in that they are among the few historic photographs that capture a truly authentic glomming geek performance in the context of a traditional fairground carnival during the act's relative heyday.

The photos in this series were captured by professional photographer Russell Lee (1903-1986) during his time working for the Farm Security Administration (FSA) project ("Farm Security Administration/Office of War Information Black-and-White Negatives"). These photos are incredibly captivating in that Lee's expert eye and timing led to beautifully captured images that contrast starkly with the grim and vile nature of their subject. Though this particular geek's origin is unknown, there are a number of interesting things that can be learned through visual analysis of these photographs.

The first common photo in this series (photo: "Closeup Bally - A") shows the geek standing outside the tent, appearing mid-bally. This was not common placement for geeks, who were usually restricted to the inside of the tent and in the pit. As the geek stands, a large snake is placed between his teeth, though this is done in a somewhat playful and non-destructive manner, as if to tease and entice the people passing by with what he will actually do inside during his act. His clothes are fairly normal for the time period and his appearance well-kempt, implying that he was doing a straight geek performance without the guise of a wild man gimmick. This is possibly the reason why he is outside doing a pre-show before the performance rather than being hidden away as a captive wild man who customers had to pay first to see.

The geek is a person of color, as was common for the act. There is a second photo that is nearly identical to this first image, undoubtedly taken just a few seconds later, that tells a greater visual story. In this image (photo: "Closeup Bally - B"), the positioning of the geek and photographer is virtually the same, but the snake is held slightly differently and more of the geek's lower half is visible. In this photo, it is revealed that this geek is handicapped, having only one leg. His right pant leg is folded up, and he holds a crutch under his arm behind the snake.

The next common photos take place inside the tent during the geek show. The geek performs while the audience looks on. Between the geek and the crowd is a barrier, as the setup appears to be that of a common pit show. One common photo (photo: "Placement") shows the geek positioning the snake between his teeth. Gone is the playful interaction of the snake in the mouth from the first photo from outside the tent, instead replaced by calculated placement of the snake's head into the side of the geek's mouth, careful positioning with the fingers in preparation to deliver the death bite. The next common photo (photo: "Bite") is impeccably taken just after the bite has taken place. The geek's neck muscles are tense and his teeth grit tightly with the snake's severed head between them while he pulls the snake's body away with his arms. There is even a slight motion blur from the action taking place, and a piece of the snake's flesh remains upright in the side of the geek's mouth from the fresh removal.

Though these photos are easily found circulating online, tagged collectively in image archives, there are a couple other images Russell Lee took of the geek that were not widely circulated. One appears to have been taken before the first in the commonly circulated photo series, and one after the last. The first uncommon photo is an exterior wide shot (photo: "Wide Bally") that shows the geek show attraction outside from afar. The attraction has giant lettering that reads "onGo," which likely has an additional consonant cropped off from how the photo was taken, indicating the name of the geek show.[7] A man stands with a snake around his neck while the geek hunches over and stares at the snake. Though difficult to correlate the attraction to the other images and identify the geek specifically, he is recognizable by his clothing, the presence of a snake, and by the fact that he is standing to the right of a giant "n" on the bally stage. In photo "Closeup Bally," he is also seen standing to the right of the giant "n" on the bally stage.

The other uncommon photograph of the geek looks to have been taken after the photo "Bite." This photo (photo: "Aftermath") shows the geek looking around his pit with his mouth open and holding what appears to be the dead snake while a stunned audience looks on. These additional two images are likely not associated with the three common photos due to the geek not having been identified in the "Wide Bally" photo previously and the "Aftermath" photo having some damage to the negative. All six images are included here in proper sequential order.

---

7. In a 1980 interview, showman Clarence Samuels references a notable one-legged snake-eating geek named Pongo. Based on the description and name, there is a strong possibility that the geek pictured in these images is Pongo, in which case the out-of-frame consonant would be the letter "P" (Samuels).

The Louisiana State Fair Geek of 1938, "Wide Bally" photo. Lee, Russell. 1938. Farm Security Administration. Library of Congress, Prints & Photographs Division, FSA/OWI Collection, LC-USF33-011768-M3.

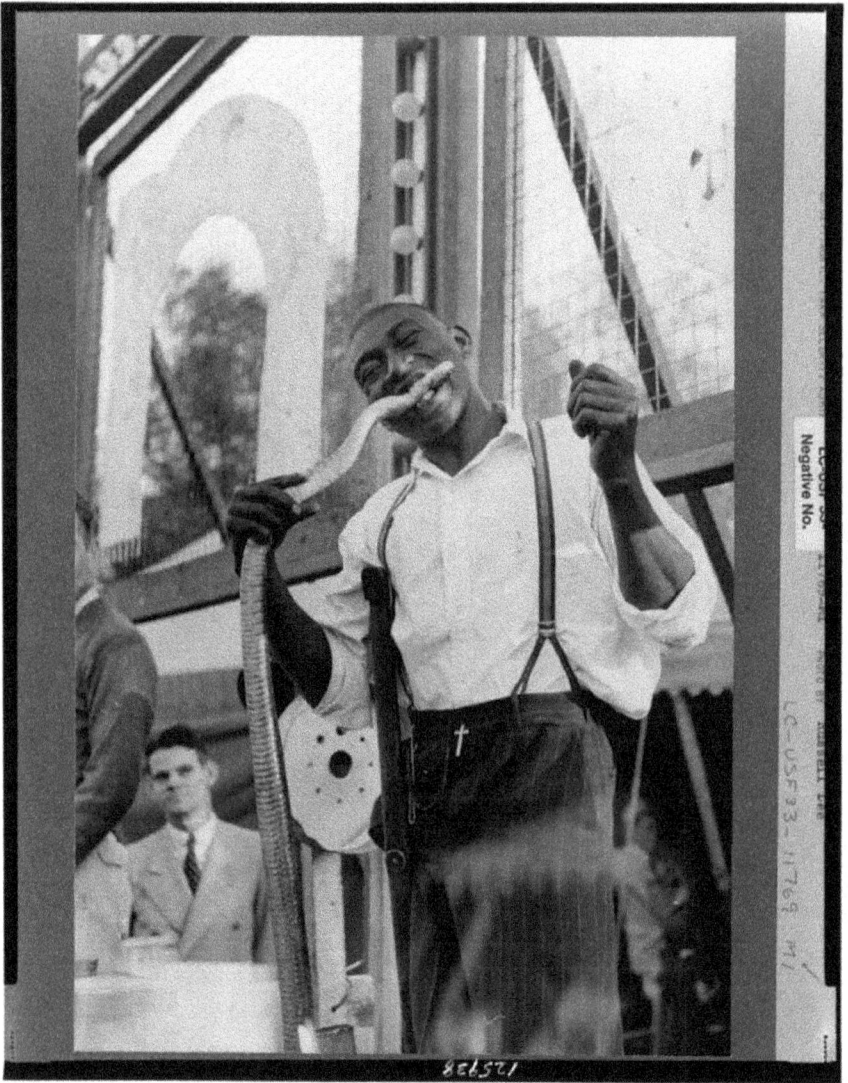

The Louisiana State Fair Geek of 1938, "Closeup Bally - A" photo. Lee, Russell. 1938. Farm Security Administration. Library of Congress, Prints & Photographs Division, FSA/OWI Collection, LC-USF33-011769-M1.

The Louisiana State Fair Geek of 1938, "Closeup Bally - B" photo. Lee, Russell. 1938. Farm Security Administration. Library of Congress, Prints & Photographs Division, FSA/OWI Collection, LC-USF33-011769-M2.

The Louisiana State Fair Geek of 1938, "Placement" photo. Lee, Russell. 1938. Farm Security Administration. Library of Congress, Prints & Photographs Division, FSA/OWI Collection, LC-USF33-011767-M1.

The Louisiana State Fair Geek of 1938, "Bite" photo.

Lee, Russell. 1938. Farm Security Administration. Library of Congress, Prints & Photographs Division, FSA/OWI Collection, LC-USF33-011767-M2.

The Louisiana State Fair Geek of 1938, "Aftermath" photo. Lee, Russell. 1938. Farm Security Administration. Library of Congress, Prints & Photographs Division, FSA/OWI Collection, LC-USF33-011767-M3.

Big Doc

Magician Henry Valleau once recalled working with a glomming geek early in his career. At the Marine Firestone's sideshow in the summer of 1939, a man named Doc Klingman, who was a tall, half-Cherokee man with long black hair, was the geek show operator and performer. People in the sideshow simply called him "Big Doc."

For his act, Big Doc would sit in a small canvas pit wearing gunnysacks, with his face made up to look like a wild man. In his pit were snakes, chickens, mice, and rats. He would bite the heads off these animals throughout the show and spit them out. Valleau remembers that "he was blood and dirt all over." Snakes in particular were Big Doc's specialty. He developed a knack for throwing snakes into the audience just right, so that they would wrap around a woman's neck. When he did this, people would scream and clear out of the tent, which would result in even more people stepping up to buy a ticket, overtaken by curiosity. He also had a special move where he would bite a snake's head off, spit it out, then rip the snake's body open with his teeth from the bloody stump down to the tail.

Valleau also remembers helping Big Doc defang a shipment of hot rattlesnakes by removing their fangs with a scalpel and pliers. Though there were no incidents during this ordeal, Big Doc was later bitten on the hand by a snake during one of the shows, and Valleau came to his aid and poured iodine onto the wound. Sticking to the mentality of "the show must go on," Big Doc opted to finish out the show performing as the geek and didn't have the wound properly cleaned and sutured until after his audience had left.

Shortly after that, Big Doc's show was shut down by an animal rights organization, and thus the glomming geek left the carnival (Valleau and Hudson 32-33).

The Augusta Maine Geek of 1940

Oddity collector and Tote Em In Zoo animal park founder George Tregembo once recalled the details of seeing a rather extreme glomming geek show in Augusta, Maine around 1940.

Just before the show, the geek, an African American male with one leg, stepped out onto the bally platform. He then proceeded to walk back and forth on a home-made

crutch while presenting his own bally to the audience.[8] Tregembo remembered the geek's
bally:

I will eat live snake and chicken as sure as there's a lord above - Regular
price to the show 50 cents, 1st show special 35 cents.

Many people purchased tickets for the show and the inside of the tent was packed.
Once inside, the geek situated himself in the bottom of his pit and picked up a blue racer
snake. He then bit the snake's head off, peeled back the skin, then stuck about four inches
of the snake's bleeding neck into his mouth and chewed on it.

At this point, many in attendance walked out in disgust and several others vomited,
though the geek's performance was far from over. Once done with the snake, the geek
reached into a crate and pulled out a live chicken as well as a sharp knife. The geek then
proceeded to cut the chickens head off, then stuck the chicken's squirting neck stump
into his mouth so that the blood shot into his mouth.

Though the crowd was rather thin by this point, the performance continued. The
geek next took a large bite out of the decapitated chicken's midsection and sucked out
a mouthful of guts while remarking to the few left in attendance that it was "just like
spaghetti." This was enough to successfully gross-out what little audience remained, as
even Tregembo admitted that after that, he had "a woozy feeling about the belt line"
(Tregembo).

Bozo, The Rat-Eating Geek

Showman and sideshow book author Joe McKennon shared his geek experience during
his time in the carnival. Furman University Professor Rhett Bryson notes from his com-
munication with McKennon in 1982 describe the geek that he worked with:

---

8. The time period, description of the geek's appearance, and behavior of him also
working the bally stage before the show lends to the likelihood that this very well may
be the same geek pictured in Russell Lee's photos at the Donaldsonville, Louisiana,
State Fair in 1938. It's also possible that this geek's name was Pongo (Samuels).

Joe once had a geek on a sideshow that he managed and did the front talking for. Joe called him the rat-eating geek. He would eat live rats. He would snap the heads off with his mouth and then suck the blood. The managers of the shows would have to take the bodies from him or he would eat them too. If he was allowed to do that, he would get full and would not want to do as many shows as was necessary for the day. A sort of wire screen had to be put up in front of the bally platform to keep the rats from getting into the crowd and frightening them. This same geek would often reach down and unscrew one of the light blubs on the front of the bally and eat the hot bulb. This geek was described as a "feeble-minded jig". He would also cut himself on the stomach with a knife (Bryson, Notes from Joe McKennon interview).

McKennon further described this geek, named Bozo, several years later in a 1987 letter:

In 1936 I did know one. An East Dallas mental defective jig (black) called Bozo. We used him as a wild man Ballyho attraction on front of our big freak show (United Shows of America).

Bozo was a compulsive "glomer" Ate glass, razor blades, etc., in addition to live things. Had to screen the bally footlights that season as he would screw out the hot bulbs and eat them during his cavorting. Bozo had been used as a geek by other shows. His show was "slaughtered" in Fort Worth in the early thirties and everyone connected with it "made the can" as vags (vagrants). Bozo was "gloming' live rats that season. Yep, he ate them, squealing and screaming. His manager only let him eat two whole ones a day, if he got full, he would go to sleep and not work. So, they let him bite off the heads, suck the blood from the quivering body but snatched that body away. He was allowed to eat the head. Quite a sight with brains and blood running out of his mouth.

Quite a sight, wasn't it? Yet the suckers lined up in droves and paid 25 cents (a lot of money in those days) to see this (McKennon, Letter to Rhett Bryson).

Bola-Bola the Wild Man from Africa

Alonzo "Bola-Bola" Gill was involved in show business for around a decade and spent
much of that time with Bee's Old Reliable Shows carnival, where he worked as a ride
operator during the 1943 season ("Bee Combo's Ky. Trek a Winner; Spending Is Up").
While he was with Bee's carnival, however, Gill was most well known as "Bola-Bola, the
Wild Man from Africa."

Sitting in a traditional geek pit setup with live chickens, Bola-Bola was clad in a grass
skirt and had metal rings in his ears and nose. He would lunge at the audience throughout
the act and was a full glommer, biting pieces from the live chickens in his pit while the
audience looked on. Decades later, in April 1979, when he was asked in a profile piece by
the *Courier-Journal* if he actually ate the live chickens during his geek days, he responded,
"Well, I took enough off of 'em to say I was eatin' 'em."

He was also known to eat glass throughout his carnival career, frequently breaking glass
that people had brought to the show and shoving it into his mouth. Gill admitted to being
a heavy drinker at that time in his life, as intoxication was necessary for him to commit
such acts while he played the Bola-Bola persona.

Throughout his career as Bola-Bola, he claimed to have only broken character once.
During one performance, after snatching the purse of a female onlooker, her husband
promptly drew a pistol on Bola-Bola, at which point Gill had to defuse the situation by
reasoning with the onlooker, stating that he wasn't actually a wild man from Africa and
it was only part of the act.

When commenting to the *Courier-Journal* on whether he had eaten any glass since his
Bola-Bola days, Gill said, "Oh maybe a few times around town here, just to show people
I could do it...I miss it, but I can't do it now....I've lost all my teeth" (Crawford B1).

After his carnival days were behind him, Gill retired comfortably to Lawrence-
burg, Kentucky, and passed away in November 1979 at the age of 77 ("Alonzo Gill
[1902-1979]").

Perooney

Born into the home of a fundamentalist minister, Bobby "Perooney" Sanders always had
a very independent mentality. Unable to live up to his father's moral code, he ended up
leaving home before he had even reached his teens. With only a third-grade education and

no work skills, Sanders had very few job prospects until he found himself getting involved with the carnival.

Unsurprisingly, his first gig with the carnival was that of a geek. Sanders would disembowel and eat live chickens while onlookers watched. "I played like I was crazy and ate chickens and all that. I was smarter than the people who paid money to see me," he told the *Cincinnati Enquirer* in 1987 when reflecting on his time as a geek in his youth.

He also utilized the popular geek trade move of throwing a fake snake (strip of rubber) into the audience to get a rise out of the crowd. At one point in his career, one woman was so upset by the trick that she struck him with a plaster carnival prize, which left a scar on his face.

Through his time traveling with the carnival, Sanders also worked as the person who would stand against the target while the knife thrower would throw knives around his body. He was known to do glass and fire eating, too. Like many geeks, he was a heavy drinker and was occasionally so intoxicated during the knife act that the thrower had to take him by the shoulders and line him up against the backboard beforehand.

Eventually, Sanders got in with the Ringling Bros. and Barnum & Bailey Circus, where he worked as a roustabout, setting up seats and taking care of the elephants. He later spent time as a groom at the racetracks, working and traveling with horses. When his circus and animal days were behind him, he became a hermit and lived in Hesler, Kentucky, during the 1980s. Though he had no electricity or running water, he seemed by all accounts content with the memories of his traveling experiences and the solitude that he had (Hicks A9).

Byebye Breakfast

The *Indiana Gazette* featured an article on May 22, 1996 by writer Dave Putnam, who reminisced about seeing carnival shows from his youth. On the subject of watching geek shows, Putnam wrote, "A good geek would open his act by biting the head off a live chicken and then move on to the more obnoxious stuff involving snakes, pigs, etc."

He went on to describe one "great geek act" in particular that he remembered seeing a few times back in the 1950s. The appropriately named geek attraction was called "Byebye Breakfast," and the geek was promoted as being native to Borneo. Utilizing a clever marketing strategy to arouse customer curiosity, the outside of the geek's tent not only featured warning signs indicating that the attraction was not for the squeamish but also included signage noting that due to the attraction's extreme nature, there was a nurse on duty inside the tent. Naturally, people took the bait and "lined up for blocks" (according to Putnam) just to see just "ByeBye Breakfast" in action (Putnam 9).

Rose, Wild Cannibal Girl from Bohemia

In his autobiography about carnival life, showman William T. "Fats" Usher wrote about his experiences on the midway, which included working geek shows. One of the shows that illustrated the seedier side of carnival life was the attraction known as "Rose, Wild Cannibal Girl from Bohemia."

The banners outside depicted a wild jungle woman eating snakes and biting the head off a chicken. Inside, a male geek playing the role of Rose sat inside a pit filled with a variety of snakes. Rose would put the snakes' heads in her mouth and lunge at the crowd. There was also another worker present inside playing the role of a geek tamer, who would whip at the geek and shoot a gun full of blank rounds now and then.

Those working the attraction had rolled out a system to maximize their profits. Inside, there were pickpockets who were involved with the show. The ticket taker, who saw which audience members (the "marks") had the most money in their wallets when they paid for tickets, would discreetly point them out to the pickpockets as they entered the tent. When the show was underway, the pickpockets would position themselves next to the marks. Then, when the tamer noted they were in position, he would crack his whip and fire at the geek with his gun. This would cause the geek to lunge at the audience, and the crowd ran backwards, madly bumping into one another in an effort to flee the proximity of the geek. The pickpockets would make their move during the commotion, snatching the wallets of the marks. They would then take the cash out and discard the wallets underneath the sidewall of the attraction. At the end of the night, the pickpockets would divvy up the money and share a percentage of it with the show operator (Usher 26-27).

Blah Blah

In the middle of the 20th century, a showman who went by the name "Side Road Shorty" worked at a geek show down in Georgia. The geek's name at this show was Blah Blah, and he worked with chickens.[9]

For his act, Blah Blah would bite the head off a chicken and yell "blah blah blah blah" while waving the chicken around, spraying blood everywhere in the process. As in many geek shows, the action would cause members of the audience to flee in terror, running out of the attraction, which would intrigue those outside the tent to purchase a ticket to see what was causing all the fuss inside. Shorty admitted that while the blood and decapitation was real, the geek did not actually eat the chicken's head – rather, he inconspicuously spit it out while the audience ran off in a panic.

Shorty noted that other show people typically avoided Blah Blah when it came to mealtime in the cook shack. Regarding his manners and charisma behind the scenes, Shorty said of Blah Blah: "My geek was a pretty good fella, except when he was bein' a geek, of course, but I never ate with him, anyway. He ruined my appetite. Sometimes he'd come in from a show with dried blood all over his face. I finally had to tell him to wash his face before he went out to eat. He didn't have a whole lot of social grace, but he wasn't a bad guy, for a geek" (Ives C11).

Veronica Shant

One extremely atypical story of a glomming geek is that of Veronica Shant. In many ways, Shant was a true inverse of the archetypal geek. She was an attractive young female of sound mind and strong religious convictions who regularly attended church.

Writer Arthur H. Lewis traveled around the carnival circuit for six months, interviewing attraction owners and performers alike. Lewis released a written account in 1970 in the form of a book called *Carnival*. The chapters of his book mostly relate to different facets and acts within carnivals, particularly in the realm of sideshow. Naturally, there is

---

9. In the book "Endangered Species," William T. Usher writes about working a show with a geek named Bla Bla during some Midwestern and Southern dates during the same relative time frame. It is possible that this was the same geek, or perhaps just a name that caught on and was used for multiple geek shows in that area.

a chapter relating to geeks. In this chapter, showman Lou Pease discussed working with geeks and mentioned that the greatest geek he had ever seen was a woman named Veronica Shant, whom he worked with for five years until her departure in 1950.

Pease described Shant as a short, buxom brunette who would very enthusiastically perform as a glomming geek. Pease notes that her work ethic was that of a true artist and, in the course of a single evening, she would "bite off and swallow a half-dozen heads from live chickens and three or four field mice whole and maybe a garter snake or two." Her performances were so extreme that they would often cause half the people in the audience to vomit.

After leaving the sideshow, Shant married a fellow carnival worker by the name of Darby in 1958 and had a child shortly thereafter. Darby spoke to Lewis about Shant and described her as an attractive but strange woman who rarely spoke about her past other than to say she was an only child whose parents had separated. Darby said that what set her on the path of being a geek was coming home at the age of 14 and finding her mother in bed with the delivery boy.

Shant left her husband one day and put their child up in foster care, leaving both show and family behind. She was last seen in Elmira, New York. Despite numerous attempts made by Lou Pease, Shant was never heard from again (Lewis 297-300).[10]

Georgette Dante

Dale Collins, better known by her stage name Georgette Dante, has enjoyed a lengthy and illustrious career as a variety performer. A star of stage and screen all her life, when asked to describe herself professionally, she simply remarks with enthusiasm "Showbiz all the way!" Her beginnings in entertainment are both humble and highly unconventional by modern standards.

---

10. This story of Veronica Shant is quite an incredible account, though other than a few small mentions in other publications likely also using Lewis's "Carnival" as source material, the author of this book was unable to find any additional references to Veronica Shant performing or even existing, which seems unusual given her esteem on the midway. However, the fact that Lewis purportedly received primary source accounts directly from both Lou Pease and Darby during separate interviews about Shant lends to the credibility that she likely was, in fact, a real person and performer.

Her parents, Bob and Delilah Collins, worked in the carnival sideshow business when Georgette was just a little girl and it was very much a family endeavor. Beginning in the 1950s, Georgette started performing in the carnival, working as a "pretend midget" for an exhibit starting when she was only three years of age. She starting dancing in the sideshow when she was five.

Growing up on the carnival lot, the young Georgette also learned how to pickpocket, using a razor blade to cut the pockets of carnival-goers and take their wallets. She would then give the money to her father, who would gamble it away at the G-top.[11] During this time, her family also had a geek in their show, an alcoholic from Detroit named Shadow.

Georgette remembers Shadow working in her parent's show:

Shadow was our geek and all he'd do is sit in that damn pit and bite chickens' heads off. Not all the time, just when we had a good crowd, as long as he got his wine. He'd shit and piss and everything else in that damn pit and he didn't care. "Just give me my wine" [he'd say]. At the end of the night, we'd take all of the chickens, all the carnival people would get in the back and make a big bonfire. We'd go out and get tomatoes and lettuce – the farmers around us would bring corn and come out to make goulash and chicken stew almost every night.

On how her family brought in Shadow each year:

At the end of the year, every year at wintertime, we'd take him back to Detroit and drop him off. He'd run through the alleys, he was a bum, that's all he cared to do. So come summertime every summer, my dad would go out in his truck and drive up and down the alleys going "Shadow! Shadow! Anyone know where Shadow is at?" and we'd find Shadow. He'd go back in the truck and go back to the carnival.

---

11. A G-Top is an "after-hours club" open only to carnies. The "G" is for "gambling" (Keyser).

After working as their geek for a few years, Shadow passed away. In need of a new geek in order to keep the show going, Georgette's parents formulated a plan. Her mom took a potato sack, cut some holes in it for appendages, fitted it over her daughter and tied it around her with some rope. Georgette, who was only around six years old at the time, then had her skin smeared with burnt cork to appear dirty and was placed inside a snake pit. Once inside, she would crawl around and was billed as "The Wild Girl from Africa" (sometimes "The Wild Girl from Borneo") by her father. Her father's bally for her went as follows:

> She crawls around on her belly like a reptile. Playing with snakes like you and I would play with a puppy dog or a kitten... The Wild Girl from Africa!

Now in the role of a sideshow geek, Georgette thought back on the skills she learned with a razor blade as a pickpocket several years prior and adapted it to her new act:

> A few years later, maybe two or three years later, I'm a geek now. So I remembered that razor blade. So I'm supposed to be biting that damn chicken's head off, so I take the razor blade and of course I would start biting "Arrrararar!" you know, I'd slit the damn throat. Boop. I would throw the head or the body to the screen and people scream or throw up and get all excited.

Georgette would then pull out a snake and the operator would turn the lights out in the tent. She would run through the crowd terrorizing the audience. This new geek show proved to be a lucrative attraction. She remained a geek for about three years, retiring from the act well before she was even a teenager.

On the importance of showmanship in sideshow, she recalls an attraction that her father once exhibited:

> He took a plate and put a horsefly in the middle of the plate and a red light inside the pit. On the microphone he would say "We don't know what it is. It's hairy, it's on a plate, it has little red beady eyes, this strange looking hairy thing. You have to see it! Ten cents!" So people would go in there and

laugh at it, and come out and say "Hey, you gotta go, you gotta go, you gotta go!" It's a horsefly, on a plate, with a blinking light and talking the right way. So when it comes to geeks, honey, it's just showmanship. You know how many people look at horror movies and monster movies and all that. People go nuts over it. That's their excitement. Something different.

After her carnival days were behind her, Georgette Dante continued in show business and went on to have an extremely extensive career as a performer, doing everything from fire eating to magic to burlesque. She has also appeared in numerous films and done additional work throughout her career as a writer and producer.

Though geeks may have a reputation for not going far in the entertainment industry, Georgette exemplifies that that is not always the case as she reflects upon her achievements:

I'm in fourteen books, one museum, nine movies, I was magician of the year...I'm involved in so many good things, so let people know that a geek can go far (Dante).

Georgette Dante with a snake. During one promotional stunt in her career, she was buried with 102 live rattle snakes (Dante). Image courtesy of Georgette Dante.

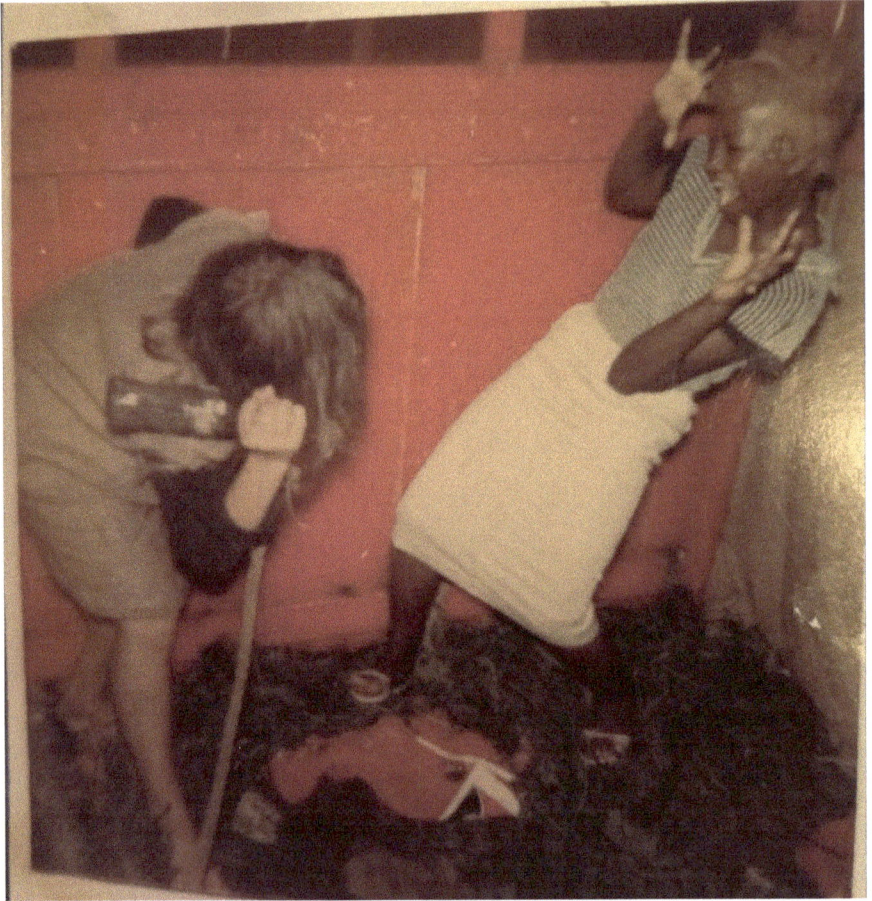

Georgette Dante working as a geek during her childhood. Image courtesy of Georgette Dante.

Georgette Dante working as a geek during her childhood. Image courtesy of Georgette Dante.

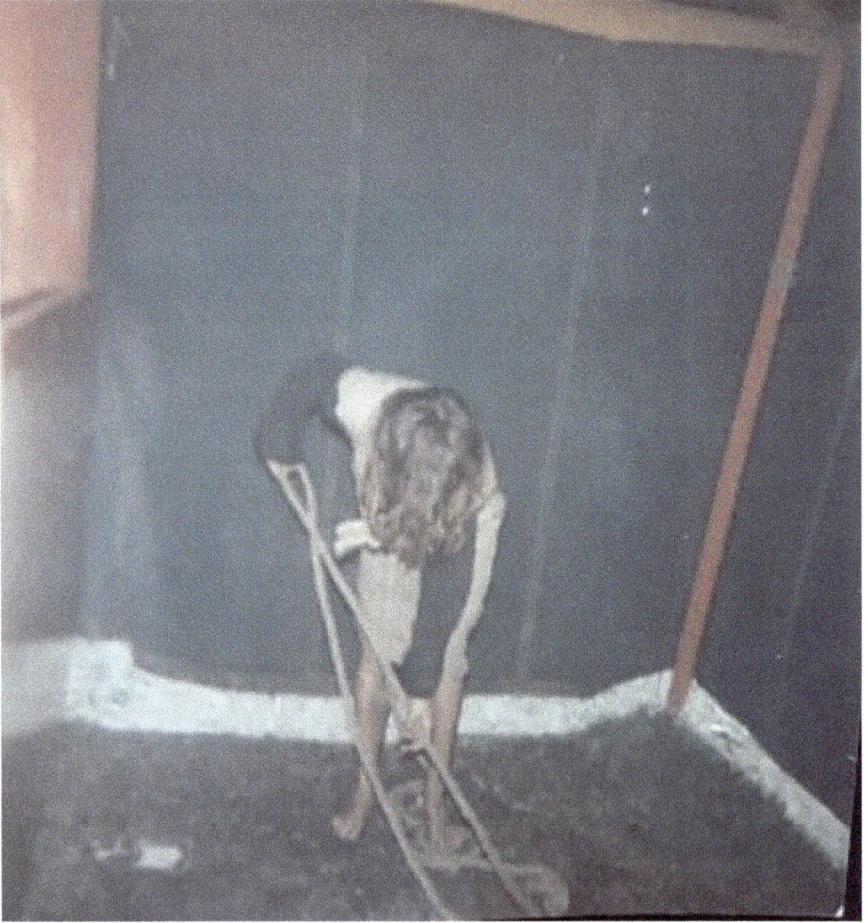

Georgette Dante working as a geek during her childhood. Image courtesy of Georgette Dante.

Ali Boo

Showman Clarence Samuels worked with a geek named Ali Boo back in the 1960s and early 1970s. According to Samuels, Ali Boo was unlike many other geeks in that he greatly enjoyed his work and was very hands on, often acting as both a performer and producer in the shows he was a part of.

When working with Samuels, Ali Boo's performed both geek and wild man versions of his show. This depended on the territory since some places he could not perform the geek act, so he would do the wild man act instead.

In his role as a wild man, Ali Boo would apply fake hair, put in fangs for teeth and dress in overalls while in a cage, which he would walk around in while people would pay to watch him. He would glare at the audience one by one as they came in and when a large crowd had accumulated he would break out of the cage and chase them out.

For his geek act, he wore a slightly more simplified costume, with no hair other than a small peak on the top of his head and just pants for clothing. As the geek, he would be in a canvas pit rather than a cage. The animals he performed with included snakes, pigs, chickens, frogs, and insects. When performing, he kept his animals in boxes in the pit with him. With the frogs, he would swallow one, open his mouth to show it was gone, close his mouth, then a moment later spit the frog right out. With the pigs, he wouldn't necessarily kill them, rather he would simply pull out small pigs and bite them until they squealed enough to add to the show. During this act he would be chained to a post and would shake the chain, though much like his wild man show, at the end of his geek act, he would eventually burst out of the pit and chase the audience away.

Ali Boo was a fully independent entertainer who booked himself and worked year round. When the carnival season ended on the East Coast, he would make his way to the fairs in California. He passed away in the late 1970s at the age of 74. In 1980, Clarence Samuels reflected on his time working with Ali Boo and noted that when it came to geeks, "He was about the best." (Samuels).[12]

---

12. To read the complete transcript of this interview, see Appendix 3.

Spiderman the Geek

Though it is not uncommon to see modern sideshow performers doing geek-style acts with large insects, it is typically done as just one part of that performer's repertoire. It is also more commonly done in a nightclub or indoor event rather than at a standalone grind show.[13] Geek shows in the traditional sense nearly always utilized common vertebrates characteristic of the act, such as snakes, chickens, and rats. The setting and presentations of these two interpretations are quite different. For geek showman Malcolm Garey, however, some outside-the-box thinking lead to an early hybrid approach.

Garey ran a number of geek shows throughout his career, and in the 1970s, he decided that he wanted to do a geek show that he had never seen another showman do. So he abandoned the traditional animals, brought in spiders, and "Spiderman the Geek" was born.

For the show, Garey took his geek and painted a spider web on his face. The geek then sat inside a pit filled with spiders and behaved like a geek. At one point, he even began holding a tarantula in his mouth and showed it off by sticking it out on his tongue, much to Garey's delight.

One night after a show, an old lady in a pickup truck pulled up to the midway. Spiderman the Geek hopped in and was never seen again (Stencell 239).

Prince Keeyama

For some, the topic of New Orleans voodoo conjures up visions of macabre imagery and animal sacrifice. Stories about life in the swamps often feature such elements – they're exciting, but not always based in fact. However, it is true that some voodoo rituals have involved activities with snakes, such as dancing with live serpents. In traditional Haitian voodoo mythology, the god Damballah is portrayed as a giant white snake (Filan 132-13 3).[14] Historically speaking, animal sacrifice has been an element of voodoo, particularly in Haiti, as a means to provide an offering to the spirits. The animals may include goats, pigs,

---

13. A grind show is a show or attraction the customer can walk through and see at any time without being guided through (Keyser). They operate with the talker of the attraction speaking a continuous and repetitive pitch, hence they "grind" away.

14. More appropriately known and spelled as "Haitian Vodou."

chickens, and other barnyard animals. Though not widespread or universally embraced by all followers, the practice does continue in some communities (Rosenberg). In New Orleans voodoo history, there are also larger-than-life figures that have become iconic historical figures of voodoo, one of which was the real-life voodoo priest geek, Prince Keeyama.

Despite his unusual moniker and "voodoo priest" image, Prince Keeyama's real name was actually Fred Staten and his parents were from Cleveland. He claimed to have learned voodoo from his Haitian-born grandparents when he was a child. As an adult, he adopted an over-the-top persona focused on Haitian voodoo and settled into a life in New Orleans, Louisiana, where he became a local figure of note during last quarter of the 20th century. Staten had dreadlocks, wore a top hat, and carried a long staff in public, frequently boasting about his supernatural voodoo powers and offering to sell potions to those he encountered. Naturally, he was widely popular with New Orleans tourists. Staten was also known for his kindness, often mentoring black teenagers in the underprivileged neighborhoods that spanned the city.

In addition to being a local character and seller of voodoo paraphernalia, he was a nightclub performer. During his cabaret shows, Staten would perform geek feats with his voodoo persona in full effect. He would handle snakes, chew glass, and stick pins into his throat. For his finale, he would bite the head from a live chicken on stage and drink the blood. These performances resulted in a new moniker for Staten – "Chicken Man" (Filan 103-104).

The antics of his stage show eventually caught up to him, however. In 1973, he was charged in criminal district court on the grounds that he "did criminally, negligently mistreat a chicken in such a manner as to cause unjustifiable physical pain, suffering and death of said chicken." This was after two witnesses testified that they saw him bite a chicken's head off and drink its blood during a live performance. While the case was pending, Staten agreed to forgo using chickens in his act until the case was resolved ("Chickens Now Safe From Prince").

By 1988, Fred Staten had settled down from his wild stage performances and was quietly running a voodoo store on Bourbon Street. He noted that as an older man (he was then in his 50s), he no longer used his voodoo powers to harm anyone or anything. Around that time, his shop was frequented by Republicans who turned to him for political gain. Seeing financial opportunity, Staten was more than happy to sell them gris-gris bags[15] for luck to help aid in the election of George H. W. Bush as US President.[16]

Staten also wore dentures by that time. When reflecting on his previous chicken-biting ways, Staten told the press, "I used to bite off the heads of lot [sic] of chickens. It was part of the voodoo ritual. They gave me raw energy. Sometimes they still call me the Chicken Man. But either the chickens got tougher or I got older" ("Chicken Man Makes Magic for the GOP").

There were other instances when people tried to enlist Fred Staten to use his powers to help them, too. In 1984, a struggling New Orleans bar owner named Earl Barnhardt was on the verge of losing his business due to low patronage. As a last resort, he hired Staten to bless his bar. That seemed to do the trick, as Barnhardt's establishment became an overnight success, and he went on to open up numerous other businesses. Barnhardt even went so far as to fly Staten out to Houston so that he could bless his bar there as well.

Fred Staten passed away from natural causes in 1999 at the age of 61. Though he was a local celebrity, he died penniless, and his body was held at the local coroner's office for more than a month because there was no money to bury him. The famed Chicken Man, it seemed, was destined for a quiet and uncelebrated farewell.

However, when the then-wealthy businessman Earl Barnhardt caught wind of Staten's passing, he decided to personally see to a more appropriate farewell. Barnhardt still attributed the success of his bar business to Staten's powers and wanted to repay the recently deceased. Upon hearing about Staten's passing and the lack of funding for a memorial, Barnhardt took it upon himself to not only pay for the general funeral expenses but also hire a horse-drawn carriage for the procession and fund a full-scale "jazz funeral," the traditional New Orleans farewell for prominent community figures.

During Fred Staten's New Orleans memorial, jazz music filled the air, voodoo priest-esses blew cigar smoke into Staten's casket, and onlookers sang and danced in the streets.

---

15. A gris-gris bag is a common voodoo charm that is concealed in one's pocket. These herb-filled bags originated in western and central Africa. Some gris-gris bags contain animal remains and even human bones. The bags are used to grant protection or achieve other goals of the owner (Filan 213).

16. Bush won the 1988 presidential race with 426 electoral votes and 53.37% of the popular vote.

It was an over-the-top spectacle of a service befitting of an over-the-top local character, Prince Keeyama the Chicken Man (Bragg).

Red Stuart

John Lawrence "Red" Stuart (born 1951) is a career sideshow entertainer and a true renaissance man of the midway. Though widely known as a sword swallower, since getting into the business he has done everything from fire eating to human pincushion to reptile work to acting as an outside talker. The sideshows he has worked run the gamut from torture shows to illusions shows, girl shows, and many others. In his early days working the carnival lot, he worked as a human ostrich where he ate lightbulbs, chains, nails, and razorblades (Burdette 1). During that time, he also worked as a glomming geek.

In 1969, Red met a man named Ollie who was a glomming geek. Ollie was an African American carnival worker who was college educated, spoke four languages, and had his front teeth removed so that he could better swallow live animals. He had previously played the role of a glommer, though after being run out of towns, Ollie developed a more humane regurgitation act. Instead of ripping animals apart with his teeth, he would swallow them and bring them back up again alive. He was especially known to do this with live frogs.

Ollie passed on his knowledge of animals to Red. "All the glomming stuff I learned from Ollie and how to work with snakes," said Red. "My fundamentals with working with reptiles and all the glomming."

In the early 1970s, throughout the midwestern United States, Red made several appearances as a glomming geek, performing the act four or five times. When he started in the business, many of the shows that he was with were racket shows, owned by those with a hand in organized crime. The shows were often able to operate by using a patch.[17] Given that true geek shows had largely fallen out of favor by that point, the shows used the patch to get away with having a glomming geek show without any repercussions. To further avoid any trouble, the shows in which Red did the geek act were always on the last

---

17. A patch is a carnival employee who handles payoffs to local police and settles customer complaints arising from rigged games (Keyser). This is done as a means to allow rigged games and more controversial attractions that would not be permitted to run otherwise.

day of the carnival, only running for a performance or two. Oftentimes, the rides were already in the process of being torn down and all that was left standing from the sideshow was a tent, pit, and a ticket box.

The reasoning for doing the impromptu act was to make fast cash just before the sideshow left town. Though audiences widely viewed the show as disgusting, their morbid curiosity and willingness to pay to be grossed out created an easy means of maximizing profits on the last day of the carnival.

Red expanded upon the reasoning for setting up a geek show on the last day:

If we could get away with something to give us a little extra push, we didn't make enough money to pay the sheriff off or run to the flat stores[18] or the alibi stores[19] or whatever, or if we were rained out, we would ask if we could work some extra money to have the glommer and we would give them a little extra cash for us to do it. And we'd do it. The amount of money would cover for damn near everybody to get off the lot and into the next spot. And that's how it worked. Otherwise we rarely did it because it was more of the so-called ace in the hole on a racket show. The ace in the hole.

For his role of the geek, Red would dress up as a wild man and rub his body with a soap that turned his skin a red/brown color. He would then enter the pit with snakes and a chicken in it and behave like a wild man, placing snakes in his mouth, speaking gibberish, and throwing rope (that the audiences assumed was snakes) at the people. When it came time to do the actions of the glommer, Red described his performance and method:

---

18. A flat store is a game at which the agent has total control over winning or losing. Usually a game at which money is the prize rather than goods. So called because the "wheel of fortune" or whatever other rig is played there, once set vertically for all to see, is now set flat horizontally so that only the player and the agent can see it (Keyser).

19. An alibi store is a game in which the agent gives you an explanation of why you didn't win. Maybe "you threw the ball too fast," or somehow you violated the rules (leaned over the foul line, etc.) He often offers you a "better" chance to win (for another fee, of course) but you'll never win a thing, there's always some reason that disqualifies you (Keyser).

I would spread the legs of a chicken open, take a nice sized chunk out of it, pull half its guts out, and let the chicken run around with his guts hanging behind him. It isn't me eating the chicken or biting the chicken's head off, it's how long that chicken is going to be squawking like hell, running around the pit with his guts and blood dragging behind before it keels over. That's the show.

To end the geek act, Red would do the following:

For the so called blow off, where you blow the people off to get ready for another show, as soon as the animal keels over, you pick up the animal, guts and all and start spinning it around and smearing it all over your body and stuff. That's when people puke, or most of the time they just split. And that would be the show and then we would do it again. We'd do it for 80 to 100 people per show for two shows, at five bucks a pop, that's good money to what we call "blow off on," you just blow the town and that would be extra money.

On his technique:

The best method to do it was to spread the legs of the chicken and pull the guts out and let it drag or do the same thing with a pig, a piglet. But the piglet is a little nosier, a little messier, takes a little longer for the animal, the animal can attack you, and things of that nature. But with the chicken, it's best to pull its guts out of its belly, same thing with the pig. You don't want to bite the head of the chicken off, because then you don't hear it squawk, making noise. You want it flapping its wings and running around.

On the pros and cons with working with chickens vs. pigs during a glomming geek act:

I wasn't particularly all that fond of the chicken, because there was a lot of dirt, taste of the dirt, and the nastiness of the ooze and oils that's on the feathers, on the chicken's feathers. The pig was okay because you could always

clean it before you throw it into the pit, but the skin was a little tougher to
tear into.

In order to better penetrate the stronger skin of the pig, Red would use a small razor knife that he discreetly held in his hand to make an incision along the underbelly of the pig during the act prior to biting it open.

I would do a slight tear with my hand to get the skin started, so I could hook my incisors in it and just tear into it while the thing is kicking at my head and everything else. That was a little more of a gory part of the show for people to enjoy, or walk out, or scream, or holler. Everyone has their own opinions. In my business you would do it for the money. You would do anything.

On the difficulty of tearing into pig skin as opposed to a chicken:

The skin of a pig is just like a human. You can't just turn around and like bite into a human with your teeth and tear the flesh. The skin is a lot more elastic and thicker. Whereas a chicken, I mean, you can take a raw chicken and put your teeth into its breast, its skin on the breast and just tear into the skin.

Though his time as a glomming geek was brief, it was certainly a memorable albeit controversial point in his early career. On his future as a sideshow entertainer, Red has no intention of stopping. "I learned these sideshow acts," he reflected. "I can do them until I drop dead and I plan on keeping on doing them forever" (Stuart).

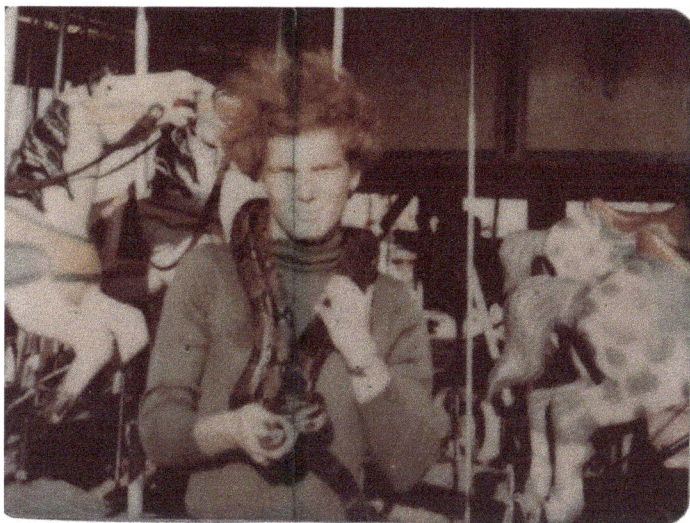

John "Red" Stuart with a snake in 1971. Photo courtesy of John Stuart.

Author Nathan Wakefield and Red Stuart in 2017. From the author's private collection.

Joe Coleman

Joe Coleman (born 1955) is an American artist based out of New York City. He is primarily known for his work as an accomplished painter. His creative output has also extended into the realm of film and underground performance art.

Coleman has long been a fan of the unusual, particularly carnival sideshows. As a child, he frequented sideshow attractions in Connecticut at the local fairground. "I saw for the first time real sideshow freaks and it really captured my imagination," Coleman recalled. "I was more fascinated by the sideshow than I was just about anything else that was going on at that time." Coleman even traveled briefly with the Coleman Brothers Shows (no relation), drawing images based on what he saw during his time with them. The only geek performer that Coleman met in person was Hezekiah Trambles, who was performing as "Congo the Witch Doctor" when Coleman saw him perform at the American Theatre of Magic.

When he was most active as a performance artist in the 1970s and 1980s, Coleman had created a stage character that he would portray called Professor Mombooze-o, the name being a combination of what he called his mother and father ("Mom" and "Booze-o"). While in the persona, Coleman would perform extreme acts, such as detonating fireworks strapped to his body and behaving as a glomming geek. Coleman described the character as "a fire and brimstone preacher that also bit the heads off live animals and blew himself up with explosives. It was also a kind of merging of both the barker and the geek into one being."

Coleman cited the 1947 film adaptation of William Lindsay Gresham's *Nightmare Alley* as the source of much of his inspiration with the geek act, particularly the main character Stanton "Stan" Carlisle's descent into becoming a geek.

Coleman described his philosophy on what the geek represents:

> *The geek is more than just a sideshow figure to me. The geek to me is kind of a religious figure. He crosses a boundary, he crosses over beyond reason and beyond morality and ethics to a kind of primitive, either sub-human or certainly pre-industrial but even pre-civilized state. In some ways it is a debasement of the human, but it's almost a way of freeing humanity too, from the constrictions that were forced upon it by becoming civilized.*

The animals that Coleman would bite the heads off of were mice and rats which were purchased as snake food, and chickens procured from a slaughterhouse. To help achieve the decapitations, he sharpened his teeth by filing them down. Though Coleman was able to successfully bite the heads off all the animals, he noted that the chicken was his least favorite animal to geek with. "It just goes crazy," Coleman recalled of the chicken. "It's a real battle."

He performed the geek act in clubs about six times over the course of around ten years, starting in 1979, always in the Professor Mombooze-o character. People found the act horrifying, and there were instances where he was arrested for animal cruelty. On the performances, Coleman said, "I was experiencing some kind of internal chaos that had no verbal language, but there was a symbolic language that I found in the geek."

Coleman made the news for his shocking underground performances, and footage of him performing in his geek role exists. Video of him geeking can be seen in the films *Mondo New York* (1988) and *Rest in Pieces: A Portrait of Joe Coleman* (1997).

He made his final geek performance in 1989, just after his mother had passed away. His father had died a year and a half prior, and with his mother gone, Joe Coleman decided to put Professor Mombooze-o to rest after one final performance.

He saw this final show as a funeral ritual, which took place at The Boston Film & Video Foundation. His performance began with a blank screen that had pornographic clips from the 1950s projected on it. Coleman then burst through the screen, hanging upside down by a harness, and ignited explosives that were attached to his body. After blowing himself up, he was cut down, and he produced two live mice, noting that they were named "Mommy" and "Daddy." He bit Daddy's head off and spit it into the audience, then bit off Mommy's head and swallowed it (Frank).

Joe Coleman described what it was like to physically commit the geek act:

It's horrific. It's really painful, and they would bite me. I was getting tetanus shots and I was getting arrested for these performances too. I have the arrest warrants framed. They were truly on the brink when I was doing those performances. They took me to a really really dark place. If you're talking about the sensations, you can feel bone crunching, you can feel the cartilage rip in your mouth, and blood shoots to the back of your throat and you're bit up. It's pretty disturbing.

On his reasoning for doing geek performances:

It was something for my psyche that I needed to do. There were some demons inside of me that I needed to face. I certainly didn't do it for money; it cost me money to have done that and it cost me a certain amount of sanity, but that's what I needed at that time.

On the geek as a primitive state of being:

I had lost all faith in humanity and felt, at the time, that spiritual re- demption could be found only in extreme transgression/regression. There's a kind of hideous grace in going beyond, because you've transgressed so far. You're beyond humanity. You're not even a human anymore; you're less than human. But in a way you're free of humanity (Coleman).

Coleman also has a large collection of oddities and sideshow artifacts in his home, including items from William Lindsay Gresham himself. He draws artistic inspiration not only from the sideshow, but also diverse and fringe figures from history, literature and the arts. He also documents his own struggles in self-portraits and devotional paintings of loved ones. Joe Coleman continues as an in-demand artist with his main artistic passion of painting.

Koyuki Tayu, the Snake Lady

When one considers the live entertainment cultural history of Japan and compares it to the heyday of the carnival sideshow on fairground lots in rural America, the two forms of entertainment may seem to have little to no crossover. However, there are some parallels.

While Japan might be known to some Westerners for its refined and theatrical en- tertainment, Japan itself had its own form of sideshow entertainment, known as *mis- emono*, which loosely translates to "things for showing." It was a crude form of cheap entertainment that was frequently held outdoors inside tents around temple grounds and was especially popular during the Edo period (1603-1868). The acts included common variety working acts like magic, acrobatics, and feats of strength. Additionally, misemono included freak show acts, showcasing individuals born with unusual physical deformities (Shores 184-189). In short, Japanese misemono very much resembled traditional Western sideshow entertainment, and there are still shades of misemono-style entertainment that pop up occasionally in Japan at festivals and street shows.[20]

One of the more recent misemono performers in Japan was a female glomming geek known as Koyuki Tayu, the Snake Lady.

Rather than adopt the crude wardrobe of a wild jungle person, Koyuki had a much different approach: one of beauty. She performed her act in elegant, geisha-like makeup and wore a flowing red robe.

小雪太夫

Koyuki Tayu's name written in Japanese.

She traveled around Japan, and her performances were frequently seen in tents as part of more recent *misemono* throughout the early 2000s. Koyuki would take the stage dressed with her trademark white face and red robe, occasionally taking time to put an apron on over her outfit to reduce the impending mess. She would then produce a bag and remove a snake, toying with it for a moment to elicit movement, likely as a means to demonstrate to the audience that it was indeed a live snake. Her specific geeking technique was to then hold an end of the snake in each hand, extend her tongue, then in a continuous motion, lick the entire length of the snake from tail to head. Once she got up to the top of the snake, she would either place the head of the snake into her mouth or place a segment of the snake between her teeth. After placing the snake, she would bite down hard and pull the body away from her face with her hands, resulting in the head being removed. Sometimes she would then chew the head and eat it. In other performances, she would spit out the severed segment and raise the snake's body to her mouth, tilt her head back, and drink the blood from the neck of the snake. The snake's blood would then drip out of her mouth onto her white face, creating a strong

---

20. There are also Japanese publications that feature documentation of actual misemono performances featuring geek acts. For example, the 1999 book "Misemono-goya no bunkashi" features an image of a row of women placing snakes in their mouths during a performance and a series of photographs of another performer chewing a live chicken apart.

visual contrast. Sometimes she would also throw a fake snake into the audience afterward
to give them a fright, much like in a traditional American geek show.[21]

Unlike most geeks, Koyuki seemed to achieve a notable degree of popularity and had
her own following in Japan. There are numerous works of art and even images floating
around on the Internet of tattoos depicting her eating snakes.

Though best known for her glomming geek act, Koyuki also performed other traditional sideshow feats, such as mental floss and fire breathing.[22]

Koyuki Tayu made her final stage appearance as The Snake Lady on November 19,
2010 at the Tori no Ichi festival at the Hanazono Shrine in Tokyo's Shinjuku Ward
("Carnival 'Snake Lady' at Hanazono Shrine in Shinjuku").

---

21. There are numerous photos and videos of her performing the geek act on the
    Internet, most easily found by searching the Japanese characters of her name.

22. Mental floss is a common sideshow feat where a flexible object such as a chain or
    string goes into the nose and is pulled out the mouth.

Chapter 7

Wild Men and Women

W ild men were commonly associated with the geek act. Some wild men were actual Indigenous people who were pushed into show business by promoters for financial gain, but most were simply local citizens who were playing the part of a wild person from a foreign land. The costumes of wild men tended to be exaggerated jungle attire, often displaying racist overtones. This particular wardrobe frequently included things such as animal fur and face paint, sometimes incorporating wigs and tusks. Other wild men interpretations appeared more monstrous in nature and were marketed as being part man and part beast. Others still just simply maintained an overall unkempt appearance. However, not all wild men engaged in geek behaviors and not all geeks dressed as wild men, so the two acts, while closely related, are not completely synonymous. Perhaps a strong differentiating factor is that while wild man geeks worked with live animals, non-geek wild man acts tended to emphasize more over-the-top character theatrics and performed without animals, though sometimes incorporating raw meat. Wild man shows were quite popular both before and during the same period of geek acts, though unlike geeks, there is more information recorded about some of the wild man shows and notable performers. There are far too many to cover, though some of the more interesting wild men deserve noting.

Naturally, due to the bleed-over between wild men and geeks, lumping some of the individual performers into one category over the other can prove challenging. A few of these performers may have geeked, though they are more known for wild man acts not involving animals.

Wild man in outfit.
From the author's private collection.

A wild man on stage at a traditional 10-in-1 sideshow in 1938.

From the author's private collection.

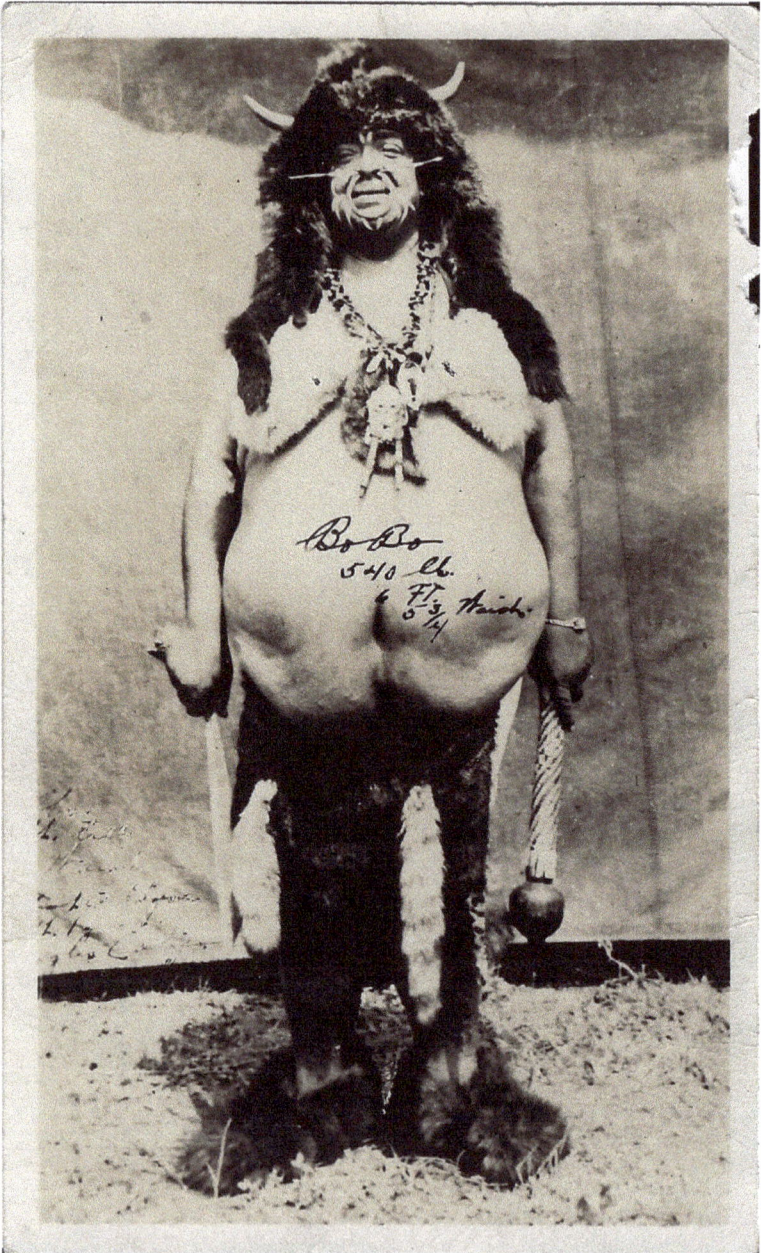

Wildman Bo Bo. From the author's private collection.

Moko the "Missing Link." Image courtesy of Joe Petro III.

1890s Wildman George Stall, who was known for his long fingernails. From the author's private collection.

Waino and Plutanor, the Wild Men of Borneo

When one considers the notion of a wild man exhibit, a common phrase that comes to mind is the "Wild Man of Borneo." Though there were numerous performers in the 19th and early 20th century who were billed with this title and origin, the original wild men from Borneo weren't even from Borneo. Rather, they were two brothers who lived in America.

The brothers were Hiram and Barney Davis, born 1825 in England and 1827 in New York, respectively. They were little people, standing only three and a half feet tall, and were severely mentally disabled. Adding to their unusual appearances, both brothers had long hair and facial hair.[1]

Newspaper drawing featuring Plutanor. The "Star Press" (Muncie, IN) - December 10, 1905

While living with their widowed mother near Gambier, Ohio, they caught the eye of showman Lyman Warner, who offered to purchase them and serve as their guardian. Their mother accepted the offer, and Warner began exhibiting the brothers in dime museums and sideshows beginning in 1852. As a means to create marketable intrigue and take advantage of their unusual appearances, Warner gave them the stage names Waino and Plutanor and created an elaborate background story about how they were savages from Borneo.[2] He even detailed their fictional capture in a promotional booklet titled *What We Know About Waino and Plutano, Wild Men of Borneo* ("Hiram and Barney - WILD MEN OF BORNEO").[3]

---

1. Some sources indicate them being closer to four and a half feet tall, but the prevailing thought is that three and a half is likely their accurate heights.

2. Sometimes also called "Plutaino" or "Plutano".

3. To read this booklet in its entirety, see Appendix 4.

During performances, they would act strangely and speak gibberish, though occasionally they would recite poetry in English. Despite their small stature, they were extremely strong and would often display their strength by lifting up members of the audience.

After Lyman Warner passed away in 1871, guardianship of the two brothers was transferred to his son, Hanford Warner, who continued to display them. They were also involved with P.T. Barnum, who exhibited and billed them as twins from Borneo, building upon their wild man mystique and growing their popularity even further (Heinke 2).

The brothers retired from show business in 1903. Hiram (Waino) passed away in 1905 at the age of 80, and Barney (Plutanor) passed in 1912, at the age of 85.

Waino and Plutanor, the Wild Men of Borneo. From the author's private collection.

A promotional piece regarding The Wild Men of Borneo. MS Thr 1835 (Folder 10), Houghton Library, Harvard University.

SEE THE WONDERS OF NATURE!
NOW ON EXHIBITION!

WORDS

DEDICATED TO

"WANO" AND "PLUTANO,"

THE

WILD MEN OF BORNEO.

Air— Carry me back.

Ye gentlemen and ladies fair,
　That dwell both far and near,
In palace great or cottage small,
　For a moment please give ear.
The truth to you I will declare,
　In language simple, plain,
If strict attention you will give
　You may some knowledge gain.

Then I'll carry you back to Borneo,
　Where the Wild Men used to roam,
Until a number of years ago,
　With us they found a home.

This island lies far to the East,
　Of note and high degree,
Beyond the Cape of old Good Hope—
　Across the Indian Sea,
A hunter with his dog and gun,
　Whilst rambling did espy,
Two things like beasts in human form
　On a tree suspended high.
　　Then I'll carry, &c.

They dangling, hung upon a limb,
　Suspended by one arm,
This hunter, with his dog and gun,
　Gave these Wild Men great alarm,
They quick descended to the ground,
　And ran with all their might,
Upon all fours, or straight erect,
　To escape this hunter's sight.
　　Then I'll carry you back, &c.

They scrambled o'er the rocks and hills,
　At length a cavern sought,
And in this dark and drear abode,
　By stratagem were caught;
Though somewhat like the Ourang Outang,
　They are more wondrous far,
For a hundred would a thousand thrash,
　Of Ourangs when at war.
　　Then I'll carry you back, &c.

The power of speech they do possess,
　Which Ourangs do not have ;
They can be trained to well behave,
　Likewise to understand;
In stature small, though giants in strength,
　They delight and much astound,
Men of all rank, and talents rare,
　And science deep, profound.
　　Then I'll carry you back, &c.

Hutchinson, Printer, 128 Washington St., Boston.

Wild Men of Borneo broadside. From the author's private collection.

THE WILD MAN OF BORNEO.

Illustration of a Wild Man of Borneo from the 1896 book "Among the Freaks." Alden, W. L. 1896. Among the Freaks. London: Longman's. Available through: Adam Matthew, Marlborough, Victorian Popular Culture, http://www.victorianpopularculture.amdig ital.co.uk.libproxy.wustl.edu/Documents/D etails/NFA_ALDE_1108

The Wild Men of Borneo and the ensuing popularity of other Borneo-based wild men became a popular cultural motif, even to the point that soon a folk song emerged based on the Wild Man of Borneo concept. This song was commonly sung in the late 1800s through the early 1900s and was occasionally referenced in the press. As with many folk songs, there are numerous lyrical variations, though the original was called "The Wild Man of Borneo Has Just Come to Town" and was written by George Le Brunn. It follows a cumulative song format, where each verse builds upon the previous. It begins with the lyric "The Wild Man of Borneo has just come to town," and this first verse repeats four times. Each new verse builds upon the previous verse by indicating that another associate of the Wild Man of Borneo has also come to town. As the song progresses, more associates are added and the verse lengths increase to the point of absurdity. The ninth and final verse of Brunn's original reads in full as:

The wind that blew through the whiskers on the flea in the hair on the tail of the dog of the daughter of the wife of the Wild Man of Borneo has just come to town (Brunn).

The Wild Man of Borneo motif also crept into other realms of popular culture such as motion pictures. In 1920, a silent short film called *Circus Days* was released. The motion picture tells the story of a young boy who is unable to go to the circus when it is in town, so he puts together his own circus, complete with his own version of the Wild Man of Borneo act. In that case, the wild man is another little boy dressed up and painted for the attraction.

Another Wild Man of Borneo reference can be found in a 1933 comedy short film, *The Kid from Borneo,* which was released as part of the *Our Gang* (Little Rascals) series.[4] In the short, the kids visit a local sideshow where they mistake the wild man from Borneo at the attraction for their uncle George. The wild man, who has an appetite for candy, soon escapes and runs amok, chasing the children around and repeatedly saying his catchphrase, "Yumm, yumm, Eat-em-up! Eat-em-up!" while eating everything in sight.[5] There was also a 1941 comedy film, *The Wild Man of Borneo,* which starred Frank Morgan of *Wizard of Oz* fame.

Poster for the 1920 short film "Circus Days." Reelcraft. 1920. https://upload.wikimedia.org/wikipedia/commons/5/58/Circus_Days_1920_poster.jpg

Zip the Pinhead

Perhaps the most popular and prolific wild man was William Henry Johnson – or Zip, as he was better known throughout his career.

Johnson was an African American man from New Jersey who was born in 1857. His head was unusually small and slightly elongated. As he grew into adulthood and his body filled out, the disproportion became even more noticeable.

Word of Johnson's strange appearance got to the Van Emburgh's Circus, which added him to their sideshow. Once his popularity spread, Zip was eventually picked up by

---

4. At the time of this writing, both the "Circus Days" and "The Kid from Borneo" short films are available to view in their entirety on the Internet via streaming sites.

5. Likely an intentional albeit more family-friendly version of Bosco's popular "Eats 'em alive!" catchphrase.

P.T. Barnum, who branded his attraction the "What Is It?" as a means to arouse public curiosity.[6]

To accentuate Zip's "pinhead" appearance, Barnum shaved off all of Zip's hair, save for a small tuft on the very top of the point on his head. Zip wore a fuzzy costume and Barnum promoted him as a wild man, a link somewhere between monkey and man.

Under Barnum, Zip's career reached great heights, as he was exhibited frequently and given a good salary. He later went on the tour extensively with the Ringling Bros. and Barnum & Bailey Circus as one of their star sideshow attractions. During his later career, Zip developed a more sophisticated persona, often dancing and playing a fiddle, occasionally even dressing in a tuxedo ("Zip The 'What Is It?'").

There is some debate regarding the true nature of Johnson's physical appearance and his mental capacities. Though his general appearance was akin to that of a microcephalic and he was largely silent or seen speaking gibberish in public, there is some evidence to suggest that he may not have been mentally impaired. Johnson's sister once noted that he would "converse like the average person, and with fair reasoning power."[7] In one incident, while he was performing at the Coney Island, Zip heard the cries

> ## Greatest Vaudeville Show on Earth
>
> A Laughable Travesty on the Old Time Circus Side Show with a Congress of Genuine Living Freaks including:
>
> # ZIP
>
> "What Is It?"
>
> Barnum's Original Wild Man, The Pioneer of all Freaks.
>
> **ZIP** *IS 86 YEARS young and wilder than ever — Don't fail to see him!*

Newspaper advertisement for Zip. The "Bridgeport Telegram" (Bridgeport, Connecticut) - February 5, 1923

---

6. Though Zip most popularly carried this title, he was not the first "What Is It?" Barnum had previously used the title to describe a deformed English actor named Harvey Leech, after hearing Charles Dickens remark "What is it?" during a meeting. Barnum felt that the phrase had a marketable ring to it ("Zip The 'What Is It?'").

7. A microcephalic is someone born with an abnormally small head ("Facts about Microcephaly"). Due to their unusual appearance, microcephalics were popular sideshow attractions, particularly around the early 1900s. As a result of the condition, those with it also tend to have severe intellectual disabilities.

of a seven-year-old girl drowning in the surf. He promptly jumped into the ocean and saved the young girl's life. Previously, Zip had allegedly also worked as a farmer ("Famous Freak, Zip, 83, Dying"). It is possible that he was simply born with an odd cranial structure and facial features that made the structure appear even more pronounced.

Zip continued to perform until just three weeks before his death, when he was taken ill and hospitalized. He passed away on April 9, 1926 ("Zip The 'What Is It?'").[8]

The legacy of Zip is very strong. During his lifetime, it is estimated that more than 100 million people viewed him. The press gave him titles such as "Dean of the Freaks" and "The Pioneer of All Freaks." He was also one of the inspirations for the popular comic strip *Zippy the Pinhead*. Not bad for a sideshow wild man.

William Henry Johnson, AKA Zip the Pin-
head. https://upload.wikimedia.org/wikipe
dia/commons/d/da/Brady_Johnson.jpg

8. Curiously, while numerous newspapers as well as Johnson's death certificate note him as being 83 at the time of his passing, his tombstone reads "William H. Johnson 1857-1926," which would have made him 68 or 69 years of age at the time of his death.

"What is it?" exhibition poster from Barnum's museum. Currier and Ives, Public domain, via Wikimedia Commons. https://upload.wikimedia.org/wikipedia/commons/6/68/Wh at_is_it_poster.jpg

Oofty Goofty

One notable performer who worked during the Borneo wild man craze was Oofty Goofty.
Oofty Goofty was born in Berlin as Leonard Borchardt in 1862. He first came to
America at the age of 14 as a stowaway on a ship. He was eventually caught and forced
to work out his passage on the ship back to Germany before he was successfully able to
immigrate to the United States. He landed in New York and traveled from state to state,
doing whatever he could to earn a living before eventually winding up in Detroit, where
he enlisted in the United States Cavalry. While there, he was stationed at the Jefferson
Barracks Military Post in St. Louis. Soon, orders came in for the recruits to be sent to the
Washington territory out West. Borchardt ended up deserting, later recalling that "the
soldiers told me that if the Indians caught me they would scalp me, so I deserted, sold
my horse and gun to a farmer, and footed it to Sacramento." Little did Borchardt know
that he was about to find unexpected fame and adopt a new name ("Oofty Goofty in
Helena").

Borchardt eventually made his way to San Francisco where he was approached by a man
who gave him an interesting proposal. The man suggested covering Borchardt in tar and
hair and exhibiting him to the San Francisco public at the local Market Street sideshow
as a wild man. Eager to earn money, Borchardt agreed.

After being covered in tar and hair, Borchardt was displayed in a cage and billed as a
wild man captured in the jungles of Borneo. In character, he was fed raw meat and stalked
around his cage, rattling the bars while wildly muttering the gibberish phrase "Oofty
goofty! Oofty goofty!"

The attraction was a success, and he was a sensation for about a week. However, when it
came time to step out of character, Borchardt found that he had great difficulty removing
the tar and hair from his body. He was unable to perspire due to the coating and was
hospitalized as a result. The medical staff was also unable to easily remove the tar and
hair, so they doused him in a tar solvent and set him out in the sun for several days. The
experience nearly killed him, but the tar eventually melted away and he returned to health.
Though he did not make further attempts at being a wild man, his run as The Wild Man
of Borneo on Market Street was so memorable that he soon became a local celebrity and
became known simply as Oofty Goofty.

Oofty Goofty was ultimately arrested for desertion. While on trial in 1885, he attempted to plead insanity but was deemed sane enough to stand trial. The *San Francisco Examiner* noted that "Although his actions in the past have been somewhat eccentric, the Commisioners [sic] decided that he was perfectly sane" ("Exit of Oofty Goofty").

While imprisoned, he attempted to be granted release by faking epileptic fits, though the prison staff was not convinced by his performances. He was later released from prison after, in an act of desperation, he jumped off a cliff and injured himself ("Odd Characters in Houston [No. 4.]").

Goofty later attempted to reinvent himself as a singer and dancer in variety shows. After one poorly received performance, he was thrown out onto the street. During the experience, he noted that he felt no pain and proceeded to further reinvent himself as a pain-proof man.

Oofty would travel around and allow people to strike him for money. For 10 cents, he would allow a participant to kick him. For a quarter, they could hit him with a walking stick, and for 50 cents, they could hit him with a baseball bat. Naturally, Oofty carried the baseball bat with him to make sales easier. The strange endeavor was remarkably successful for Oofty for a number of years until one day when professional boxer John L. Sullivan decided to take him up on his offer. When Sullivan struck the willing Oofty with a billiard cue, the blow was so fierce that it severely injured Oofty's back, and he was never quite the same afterward ("The Bella Union").

Though he was primarily known as Oofty Goofty throughout his life, Leonard Borchardt had several other nicknames at various stages of his performing career. When he first came to San Francisco and was doing various odd activities to earn money prior to his wild man fame, he was briefly called "Wild and Woolly and Full of Fleas." During his pain-proof man days, he was often referred to simply as "Professor," and in reference to his wild man days, he was sometimes called "The Hairy Man." His physical appearance was once described by the *Seattle Post-Intelligencer* as "a small German Jew, weighing but 130 pounds and standing five feet five inches. He dresses in a natty manner, and in his shirt front wears an immense imitation diamond" ("Wild Man of Borneo").

Goofty's entertainment career did not end with his time spent as a wild man and pain-proof man, however. Ever the career showman and lifelong eccentric, Goofty also attempted assorted feats and unusual pursuits during his life:

- **Entering Competitive Walking Matches** - Oofty Goofty entered several competitive footraces in his life, often performing poorly against the other competitors. In one 1889 instance, there was an organized world record attempt to see who could achieve the most distance by foot in a 27-hour period. It was held in a pavilion, with 17 laps equaling one mile. At one point during the race, an aching Oofty Goofty asked one of the trainers to rub him down. But when the trainer attempted to accommodate his request, Goofty began screaming in pain so loudly that it was heard all over the pavilion ("Albert Still Leading"). During a six-day footrace a couple months later, the *San Francisco Chronicle* covered the start of the race: "The pedestrians as they stood straining every nerve for the start looked a remarkable sturdy and well-trained lot of men, as with the notable exception of 'Oofty Goofty' they all showed their bronzed features and prominent muscles, the effect of earnest preparation for the match" ("Opening of the Six-Day Walking Match").

• **Eating 30 Quails in 30 Days** - After moving to Texas, Oofty Goofty engaged in a series of quail-eating contests, where he would wager money that he could eat 30 quails in 30 days. Goofty once remarked that the feat was "one of the hardest experiences of my life, but I consider myself the champion quail eater of the United States and bar nobody from a quail-eating contest" ("Odd Characters in Houston [No. 4.]"). The *Waxahachie Daily Light*, when covering one of his quail-eating contest wins, noted "Oofty's feat has often been accomplished" ("Looking Backward").

• **Mailing Himself from San Francisco to Sacramento** - Intended as a holiday joke, a man paid Oofty $20 to mail himself to a friend in Sacramento. Unfortunately for Oofty, no one wrote "This Side Up" on the box, and he ended up spending the night in a warehouse completely inverted, though he eventually made it to his destination ("Wild Man of Borneo").

• **Consume a Glass of Beer with a Teaspoon and Smoke a Cigar in One Minute** - Goofty displayed this strange talent in public places in exchange for a small purse. It was also one of his acts during his time as a vaudeville entertainer ("Odd Characters in Houston [No. 4.]").

• **Drink Six Glasses of Beer in 10 Minutes Using a Teaspoon** - Goofty performed this act during a stint at a variety theater between singing songs and relaying his life story in 1892 ("Wild Man of Borneo").

- **Pushing a Wheelbarrow from San Francisco to New York** - As part of a wager, Goofty attempted to push a wheelbarrow from San Francisco to New York. After 40 miles, he stumbled upon a group of farmers while he was traveling at night. They were startled, so they knocked him and his wheelbarrow from a bridge. After that, Goofty sold the wheelbarrow and walked to Sacramento, where the governor paid him $10 to leave town, calling him a nuisance ("Oofty Goofty in Helena").

- **Playing Romeo in an Unusual Production of *Romeo and Juliet*** - Oofty Goofty's co-star was a severely overweight conwoman turned singer/dancer known as Big Bertha, who played Juliet. During the balcony scene, the slight-in-size Romeo was up in the balcony, while the 280-pound Juliet re-mained stationary on the stage. The intentional pairing proved oddly successful, though the production lasted less than a week, as Bertha complained that Goofty was too physically rough when they were acting together ("The Bella Union").

- **Playing the Mascot of the San Francisco Baseball Team** - While playing the mascot, Oofty made an agreement with the team: If they won, they would pay him $20; if they lost, they got to kick him. The team ended up losing both of their scheduled games, and after kicking Goofty, they made him walk back to Fresno ("Oofty Goofty in Helena").

- **Trying to Sell Obscene Content to Law Enforcement** - Goofty was once tried in court on a misdemeanor charge after he entered a police station and attempted to sell the police sergeant a "surprise box" that was labeled as "domi-noes." When someone touched a spring on the box, an indecent picture popped into view. The sergeant was not amused and ordered Goofty locked up. In court, Goofty claimed that he had purchased the box from a friend and was unaware of the true contents ("Oofty Goofty - He Goes to the Wrong Place to Sell His

---

9. Several newspapers covering this particular incident noted Goofty's real name as being Louis Switzer. However, given the date, location, and the papers' additional references to his past experience with sending himself through the mail, it was most likely Borchardt simply using a different name.

Wares").[9]

- **Playing a Human Baseball Target** - After his failed stint as a baseball mascot, Goofy was hired to stand in front of a canvas where people paid to throw baseballs at him. If they succeeded in hitting him, they won a cigar (or two, if they hit his head). Oofty quit after suffering a broken nose when a baseball struck him in the face ("Oofty Goofy in Helena").

- **Performing a Water Jump** - During an exhibition when swimmer and water stunt performer Paul Boyton was in town, Goofy was offered $50 if he could replicate one of Boyton's jumps. Though Goofy did not know how to swim, he succeeded in making the jump ("Oofty Goofy in Helena").

- **Competing in Roller Skating Races** - In addition to his footraces, Oofty did roller skating races. In one instance, Goofy took to the starting line of a roller skating race covered in heavy diamonds and medals. He fell down twice before passing the starters' stand and then sprawled to the floor 13 times before finishing the first lap ("Rolling Off the Miles").

- **Competing in a Broadsword and Wrestling Contest** - Once again pairing with Big Bertha, Goofy was promoted for an event by this name, which took place at the Cremorne Theatre on Market Street in San Francisco ("Local Brevities").

- **Performing Sketches with a Little Person** - In 1889, vaudeville press coverage noted that Goofy was "playing sketches with a midget at a San Francisco music hall" ("Minstrels and Vaudevillers").

- **Fighting in Boxing Matches** - There are several accounts of Goofy competing in boxing matches. In one 1887 match, he fought against a local San Francisco fighter known as Jimmy. Goofy billed himself as "Professor Hardness" and won the bout after Jimmy verbally conceded defeat ("Pugilistic").

Oofty Goofty.

An illustration depicting Goofty during one of his footraces. The "San Francisco Examiner" - May 12, 1889.

NAME.	Present Race. Miles.	Laps.	Last Race. Miles.	Laps.
Albert................	238	5		
Guerrero.............	214	0	92	3
Hart.................	194	2	221	0
Klatt................	188	0		
Howarth.............	186	5	219	0
Peterson.............	183	6		
Vint.................	181	5	185	0
Crozier.............	180	0		
Old Sport...........	180	0	185	6
Taylor..............	154	5		
Morgan.............	118	3		
Broeder	112	4		
Skinner.............	106	0		
Oofty Goofty.	104	2	111	5

Competitor rankings of a race that Goofty participated in. The "San Francisco Examiner" - May 12, 1889.

Oofty Goofty during one of his drinking-beer-with-a-spoon challenges. The "New York Press" - August 22, 1897.

John L. Sullivan striking Oofty Goofty. The "New York Press" - August 22, 1897.

Oofty Goofty was interviewed by the press numerous times throughout his life. On his experience as a wild man and receiving his trademark moniker:

I was walking along Market Street one day when a man tapped me on the shoulder, said he had met me in New York, and told me if we could get $50 together we could make a fortune. I only had $25, which he took and opened a dime museum with. He stripped me, tarred me, from head to foot with glue, put on hair, and laid me for five hours on the roof to dry. Then he put me in a cage, with handcuff on my wrists, fed me on raw meat, and made me go 'oof oof.[10] *There was a big picture on the roof showing how they captured me on one of the South Sea islands, while a man on the sidewalk kept calling out: 'Walk in and see the wild man of Borneo. He speaks 21 languages and understands none. Only when you say beef he says oof.' The women fed me on peanuts. The manager made a barrel of money out of me and skipped town, and I lay six weeks in Hamam baths to get the glue and hair off. It cost the city of San Francisco $300 to get me clean. It came near killing me. The glue had stopped up the pores of the skin and I had to be fed through tubes. All the doctors and medical students came to see me. When I got well I was known as Oofty Goofty all over California* ("Oofty Goofty in Helena").

On his secret to absorbing physical blows:

My stock in trade was a leather pad I wore in the seat of my trousers and my customers were young men, who would pay from ten cents to $2, according to the thickness of the cane with which I would allow them to strike me one blow as I bent forward over the back of a chair ("A Peculiar Professor on Trial").

---

10. In other interviews, Borchardt mentions that he yelled 'oofty goofty' specifically during his time as a wild man. Perhaps he used both of these variants or was abridging the sound for this particular interview.

On misadventures during his pain-proof days:

They [boys who paid to strike him] could not hurt me much with my pad,
but one night they caught me without it and I was held over a chair by
some while others nearly cut me in two with their sticks. I remember another
time when Whister, the wrestler, offered me a dollar for a blow with an
ordinary-sized stick, and while I was not looking used a five-pound Indian
club. It nearly broke my back and sent me sprawling into another room ("A
Peculiar Professor on Trial").

Later in life, Oofty Goofty moved to Houston, Texas, where he made his living selling
imitation diamonds ("Odd Characters in Houston [No. 4]"). Whether he is remembered
as a failed renaissance man, an unlikely entertainer, or simply a man willing to do anything
for a buck, one thing that can be said about Oofty Goofty is that he certainly did not live
a dull life.

"OOFTY GOOFTY."
Oofty Goofty. The "Houston Daily Post" -
August 10, 1900.

Projea, the Wild Man of Mexico

Though Harry Houdini voiced extreme contempt for Bosco the snake-eating wild man in his written works, it is interesting to note that very early on in his career, Houdini actually worked as a wild man in a circus himself.

In the spring of 1895, when he was just 21 years old, Harry Houdini joined the Welsh Brothers' Circus as part of the touring cast. As wild man acts were in high demand during that time period and the circus was in need of one, the young newcomer Houdini was plugged into the role and became "Projea, the Wild Man of Mexico."[11] Houdini rumpled up his bushy hair, painted his facial features, and wore old sacks as clothing. During the act, he was placed in a cage where he would growl and tear at raw meat (Kellock 72-77).

Houdini reminisced about the experience years later when he was covering some freak shows in Europe. He reported to the *New York Dramatic Mirror* in 1902:

> *It reminded me of the time when I was traveling with the Welsh Brothers' Circus through Pennsylvania and had to be a freak myself. I was put in a small den and called "Projea, the Wild Man of Mexico." I remember once when Clint Newton threw me some raw meat to eat; he hit me in the eye, and I would not look at him for three weeks, as my eyes were closed. That caused me to become tame, and someone else had to play the wild man of Mexico (*Houdini, "Houdini's Entertaining Chat" 18).

Though his experience as a circus wild man during his youth was short-lived, it is to Houdini's credit that he did not shy away from discussing the experience after he began to achieve greater fame.

Clico, the Wild Dancing South African Bushman

Though it was a common trend for wild men to behave aggressively and shock the audience with their wild antics, not all wild men acted in this manner during their acts.

---

11. In 1920, multiple news outlets ran an article about Houdini's past as a wild man, erroneously noting his character as having been called "Borjea, the Wild Man from Mexico."

In the case of popular wild man Clico, he was known for his energetic dancing during his performances.[12]

Clico's real name was Franz Taaibosh or possibly "Talbosh" ("Where the Freaks Go in Winter"). Rather than being an American made to dress up like a wild man, he was a member of the South African Korana group (Parsons 1). Taaibosh was discovered by a man named Captain Hepston, who encountered him in the early 1900s in what is now South Africa. Taaibosh was just over four feet tall and was skilled in Kohsian-style step-dancing. Hepston decided to mold him into an entertainer, and he began touring England and France around 1913. A few years later, they came to America, where Taaibosh performed with the Dreamland Circus Sideshow in Coney Island and performed with Ringling Bros. and Barnum & Bailey.

For his performances, Franz Taaibosh would dress in bushman garb, in leopard skin-style clothing, and entertain audiences with his enthusiastic dance moves. He became known by the stage name Clico for the Korana click language that he spoke. The press created several myths about Taaibosh to help add to his mystique, such as that he was 100 years old and that he left 14 wives in Africa to join the sideshow ("Where the Freaks Go in Winter").

During his career, he achieved great popularity, even posing for sculptures at museums for their anthropological studies. He retired in 1939 and passed away the following year (Hartzman, American Sideshow 134-135).[13]

Congo the Jungle Creep

Not all wild men were pressured into the role or were crafted into the character by promoters. In some instances, they were largely self-made and did well for themselves. One accomplished self-made wild man was Hezekiah Trambles, whose performances left a strong impact on his audiences.

Trambles was born in 1898 and performed his wild man act extensively throughout the 1950s and 1960s. He was born in Haiti but spent much of his life in New York City. Early in his career, Trambles was said to have been a glomming geek (Coleman). However, he

---

12. Some sources reference his stage name being spelled as "Clicko."

13. His life story is told in detail in the book "Clicko: The Wild Dancing Bushman" by Neil Parsons.

became better known for his wild man act that he performed on stages throughout New York City. He was especially known for being a regular performer at Hubert's Museum in New York City. He was mostly known by his stage name, Congo the Jungle Creep, or sometimes Congo the Witch Doctor (Coleman).[14]

For his performances, Congo would dress up in a fright wig and put on primitive garb, including a loincloth, as he assumed the role of a crazed jungle voodoo man. His act was largely a mixture of eccentric geek-like jungle theatrics and strange magic tricks, which often saw him screaming and acting threatening to the audience while in character. During his performances, he would often describe his show by telling the audience that they were witnessing "voodoo, hoodoo, and conjoo!" (Stencell 236). Some of his material throughout his career included:

- Mixing sand with muddy water into a bucket while shouting "ugga mugga," then scooping his hand into the bucket to reveal dry sand, which he would then display to the audience (Bosworth 305).[15]

- A variation on the above, only instead of sand, he would reach into buckets of water and pull out rubber snakes, with which he would then terrorize the audience (Kalver 39).[16]

- Lighting a cigarette and swallowing it, then drinking a glass of water, blowing smoke out of his nostrils, and coughing up the cigarette (Bosworth 305).

- Eating insects, particularly crickets and worms (Stencell 236).

- Ripping the feathers off a live chicken, then stretching it out until the head popped off (Stencell 236).

---

14. Hubert's Museum was a dime museum in Times Square that was known for hosting numerous sideshow freak-style entertainers over the years. It opened in 1925 and closed in 1969 (S.D.).

15. This is a version of a popular magic trick known as "Sands of the Desert" or "Hindu Sands." The trick is still widely sold and performed.

16. Early on at Hubert's, he'd done this with a live snake for his finale but was eventually prohibited by management from using a real snake because it caused customers to run out of the building in fear and hurt business (Windley).

- Taking the stage with a voodoo doll prop of himself and jabbing it with pins; each time he would stab a pin into the doll, he would scream and react as though he had just been wounded where he stuck the pin (Coleman).

- Doing the classic sideshow stunt of walking barefoot up a ladder of swords, only using carpenter saws instead of the traditional machetes, which would often stick into his feet (Windley).

- Running into the audience screaming while banging on a sheet of metal and hitting a few people in attendance over the head with it (Swiss 69).

Congo caught the attention of photographer Diane Arbus, who raved about his performances and captured his iconic imagery through her photography in 1960. Other entertainers were also taken by Congo's eccentric style. The Amazing Randi said of Congo: "Everything he did came from his soul... and the way he used his hands – they were huge, oversized, with savagely long fingernails – they'd claw the air as he performed his mumbo-jumbo" (Bosworth 305).[17]

In his youth, painter and former geek performance artist Joe Coleman recalled seeing Congo perform live at the American Theater of Magic in Times Square. The performance stuck with Coleman. "It was one of the most shocking and unexplainable acts I've ever seen," he recalled. "It blew my mind watching it. He was quite incredible" (Coleman).

Offstage, Trambles was a well-adjusted New Yorker. He made good money from his Congo performances and could be seen walking around Times Square in normal clothing, with diamond rings covering his fingers (Bosworth 305).

Outside of dime museums, Congo worked a number of seasons with traditional carnival sideshows doing his wild antics in a snake pit. He worked for Mark's Mile Long Midway, then eventually moved to Reithoffer Shows, performing at various fairs throughout the northeastern United States. Magician Charles Windley, who worked with Congo at many fairs, noted that Congo avoided southern routes because the "Southerners didn't understand his sense of humor." Eventually Congo started his own show in the early 1960s to cash in further on his caricature of a voodoo wild man. He ran his attraction as a grind show, which resulted in it being a very financially successful endeavor. Congo

---

17. Real name: James Randi. A notable magician, scholar, and skeptic.

further supplemented his income by selling scented lima beans, which he claimed had magical capabilities (Windley).

Hezekiah Trambles passed away in 1979 at the age of 80 ("Hezekiah Trambles [1898 - 1979]").

Mingo the Mud Eater

A comical tale about a wild man show gone wrong is recounted in a 1922 issue of *Illustrated World* with the story of Mingo the Mud Eater.

Early in his career, circus sideshow manager Ray Daley found himself stranded in Pawhuska, Oklahoma. Given the popularity of wild man shows in outdoor entertainment at the time, he decided to produce his own wild man show for a local Native American powwow. He pooled his resources along with another member of the circus troupe, Doc, and together they created a small, makeshift structure to house their wild man attraction.

There was just one problem: They had a performance space but no wild man. One of them would have to play the role. Doc, however, had a long and nicely groomed mustache that he refused to shave off. Realizing that this sort of refined facial hair would not befit a wild man, Daley, who was a skilled talker, resigned himself to the roles of both outside talker and the wild man, while Doc would be the ticket-taker.

Once they had gathered a crowd of the locals to their wobbly setup, Ray Daley began his talk to hype Mingo the Mud Eater to the crowd while Doc sold tickets. Once he had concluded his talk, Daley rushed inside and began frantically changing into his wild man outfit, which was a gunnysack suit, wig, and makeup. In an effort to maintain the attention of the crowd that was still waiting outside, he began yelling things like "Lie down, you beast! Get down, you bloodthirsty brute!" while interrupting himself to growl in an attempt to con the audience while he prepared.

Though he had previously indicated to the crowd not to enter until they had heard him yell "Ready" from inside the enclosure, the people outside soon grew impatient and pushed their way inside, spotting Daley while he was still changing and had yet to put makeup on his face. Fearing that all was nearly lost, in a last-ditch effort to save the show, Daley quickly produced a mixture of grape nuts, chocolate, and milk (Mingo's "mud") and began smearing it on his face and eating it while growling. The spectators were not amused. After one of them reached over and pulled off Daley's wig, Doc sprang into action and kicked over the enclosure. In the commotion that ensued, Daley ducked out of the fallen attraction and made his escape with Doc. They then headed to a circus that was playing in Tulsa the next day (Braden 9).

The Haba Haba Man

A strong example of a self-made wild man who achieved notable success was Harry Blitz, who earned great notoriety performing in circuses and sideshows during the early 1900s due to his unique take on the genre.[18] When in his wild man persona, Blitz would dress in furry clothing, wear giant prop earrings, and paint his face and head with black and white makeup. Often, he wore a large feather atop his bald head and danced around wildly pounding a drum. His appearance and persona were apelike, and he drew additional inspiration from Khoekhoe natives.[19] Though he looked quite extreme, he presented his character as a smiling and comedic wild man. When he was not performing, he was known to be a quiet and unassuming gentleman ("PETE WILL SHAVE THE LION TAMER").

Much like wild man performer Oofty Goofty, Blitz's moniker was largely a result of the nonsense speech he would make during performances. Blitz would yell things like "A-ha-a-a-a-ah! Haba-haba-haba-haba-hamababa hababab; A-h-a-a-a-ah!" during his shows; hence, he was widely known as "Haba Haba" ("DIVORCES 'MON-

---

18. Countless sources state that Harry Blitz was the son of accomplished magician Antonio van Zandt, better known as Signor Blitz (1810-1877). This is extremely unlikely. At the time of his passing, Signor Blitz had three known surviving children, two daughters named Jennie and Ada and a son named Arthur. By early 1889, Arthur was reported as having died as well ("Signor Blitz"). Signor Blitz's paternal connection to Harry Blitz may have been a myth started by Harry Blitz himself to increase the press attention for his "Haba Haba Man" character. There were also numerous Signor Blitz imitators who used his stage name to further their own careers. It is also possible that Harry Blitz may have been related to one of the imitators, making him the son of a Signor Blitz, but not the Signor Blitz that many historical sources link him to.

19. People from this southern Africa region were historically referred to as "Hottentots," which is now considered an outdated and offensive term. Because of the character he created having a backstory tied to the area, Harry Blitz was sometimes billed as "Haba Haba, The Hottentot Fire-Eater."

KEY-MAN'"). His wild man character was also known by other names throughout his career, such as Ki Ki, Monkey Man, and numerous variations on these names.[20]

HARRY BLITZ
AS THE "MONKEY MAN"

Harry Blitz in costume. The "Spokane Press" - March 18, 1910.

Perhaps a contribution to Blitz's success as The Haba Haba Man was that he performed numerous traditional sideshow feats in addition to playing the character of a wild man. These feats included glass walking, glass eating, and fire eating ("FIRE EATING REQUIRES ONLY NERVE, SAYS KI KI").

As a testament to the potential hazards of show business, there was a dangerous incident involving Haba Haba that occurred in 1910. While he was performing fire eating in front of a theater, a former member of the fire department named Edward Woods approached him and started arguing with him about fire eating. Woods then left, but returned a moment later with a bottle of gasoline. Woods then took some into his mouth, spit it onto Haba Haba, and applied a lit match to him, setting Haba Haba ablaze. Fortunately, spectators were able to help put him out, but his neck was badly burned during the incident. Woods was later arrested for assault and battery as well as disorderly conduct ("'HABA HABA' MAN BURNED BY GASOLINE").

A more lighthearted performance incident with Haba Haba occurred in May 1907 when he was hired as the entertainment for the Elk's Jubilee. His appearance was very well received, with the *Long Beach Daily Telegram* noting "The wild man is in himself a whole show and night after night has entertained the visitors by his grotesque antics. Last night he surpassed previous efforts at entertainment and made the hit of the evening." During that particular night's performance, Haba Haba was delighting the audience with his fire-eating skills. At one point in the night, however, a rival wild man dressed as a South Sea Islander showed up. When their confrontation

---

20. Some sources labeled him "The Original Haba Haba Man," likely due to other wild men using the "Haba Haba" name after his success.

occurred, Haba Haba responded with the best course of action possible when two wild men meet: He performed a medicine dance over his rival, much to the amusement of the audience ("Good Program Last Night").

Haba–Haba Eats Fire!

Most People Eat

Koehler's Malt Bread

Put Up in 10-Cent Loaves

Koehler's Pies, Cakes, Rolls, Doughnuts, Cookies, etc., are Baked Fresh Every Day and are Always Appetizing. None Half So Good.

Butter Kist Popcorn

Is all the rage--not only in Paola, but all over the civilized world. Koehler's big, new, Electric Popper puts the "POP" in popcorn.

Try Us When You are Hungry and Thirsty. We Can Fill Your Every Want.

Koehler's Bakery

OF COURSE.

Haba Haba's notoriety became so great that this bakery even referenced him in their bread advertisement. The "Miami Republican" - April 30, 1915.

Blitz's marital struggles were, somewhat curiously, a subject of intrigue for the local press. During a divorce trial in 1910, Blitz's wife discussed the struggles of being married to a professional wild man who behaved like a monkey for a living. While on the witness stand, she declared her reasoning for seeking a divorce:

> *We were happy when we were first married. For a year he was as loving a husband as any woman could wish. The change started a few months after he started imitating a monkey. He became unusually quiet, then melancholy, then irritable. I pleaded with him to get some other line of work. He kept getting more irritable until I was actually afraid to talk to him. As the years passed, in his home life he became more that which he imitated in*

public – a brute. I am sure the trouble is all due to those years of playing the monkey.

However, Harry Blitz refuted his wife's story of method acting impacting their private life and countered by saying:

Yes, I'm a "monkey man," but don't you believe that my occupation has made a brute of me. I'm an actor, and when I doff these togs, I leave whatever monkey instincts I may have in the dressing room. I'll tell you what's the trouble. My wife tried to make a monkey out of me when I was home, and she couldn't do it ("CAN PLAYING THE MONKEY MAKE A MAN A BRUTE").

Blitz continued to perform in his wild man persona right up until his death. He passed away from typhoid pneumonia in 1915 at the age of 55 ("Harry Blitz, Original 'Haba-Haba' Man, Dead").

HARRY BLITZ, in Street Attire.   KI KI, IN DISGUISE

Blitz in street clothes and in costume. The "Los Angeles Record" - April 15, 1907.

Eeka and Zoma

Just as there were wild man exhibits, there were also wild women exhibits. Two similar
and well-known wild women were Eeka and Zoma. Much like Bosco and Esau, Eeka and
Zoma were characters of their industry who were extensively promoted and played by
many.

The backstories for Eeka and Zoma were fairly standard wild person fare: They were
once primitive savages in a jungle somewhere, but they were captured and were then
exhibited to the public. Banner art for both Eeka and Zoma often portray them doing
activities like wrestling giant snakes, violently killing other people in the jungle, or committing cannibalism. Naturally, despite being crazed and uncivilized jungle savages, their
illustrations always showed them to be extremely physically attractive and scantily clad,
occasionally even topless.

Zoma predates Eeka, with documented performances of a "Zoma the Queen of the
Reptiles" performing with snakes dating back to at least 1911 ("'Queen' Accused of
Assault"). As was known to happen occasionally with geek and wild person shows, Zoma
was sometimes billed as a woman but played by a man.

In one instance during a 1948 carnival run in Alabama, the exhibit was billed as "Little
Zoma from India." However, the performer playing Zoma was actually a "grizzled little
man wearing a shabby black wig." The bally for that show was:

> *A-li-hi-hive! That pore little girl called Zoma! That strange little crea-
> ture-a-li-hi-hive. That strange little savage girl from India who lets the
> snakes crawl over her body!* (Rankin Three-B)

Zoma wasn't always portrayed as a woman, however. At the 1987 Ohio State Fair,
there was a Zoma exhibit where not only was the performer a man but the character
was also promoted as being male. During the run, a man named Gary Landow portrayed
a wild jungle man who used the Zoma moniker. For the show, Landow would wrap
snakes around his neck, occasionally placing them into his mouth. Much to the chagrin
of Landow, it seemed audiences were less entertained by wild man shows in 1987 than in
generations prior. "Sometimes the people tell me I've wasted their time or that I'm gross,"
an exasperated Landow once explained to the *Newark Advocate* newspaper. "They don't

realize how hard I have to work to be Zoma" ("Sideshow Performers Enjoy Jobs"). The previously profiled John "Red" Stuart also worked as a Zoma early on in his sideshow career. He was sometimes billed as "Zoma the Snake Boy" in the mid-1970s (Burdette 1).

The wild woman known as Eeka was the creation of Al Renton, along with his sons Bobby and Chuck, who billed their show as "Strange Eeka." The Rentons were regarded as some of the best geek show operators of their time (Meah 138). Even "The King of the Sideshow" Ward Hall once remarked that the Rentons ran the best operated geek show that he had ever seen (Fellner 14).

They were indeed very successful, especially with Eeka. During the 1954 Michigan State Fair, Strange Eeka was the second-highest grossing attraction for W.G. Wade Shows, generating more revenue than a Hawaiian unit and a Western Revue, among other attractions ("Wade Grosses 210G AT Mich. State Fair"). The following year, Eeka was the top show grosser ("W.G. Wade Chalks 207G First 6 Days At Mich. State Fair").

Bobby Renton's wife, Betty, who worked crowd control during the performances, recalled what some of the Eeka shows had been like and how the family operated them. They would pitch a show tent, then dig a pit in the ground inside, eventually installing canvas walls and floor in the pit. Once inside, they would give the Eeka character (usually male) a blanket, which he would use to cover himself when he needed to urinate and to shield himself from spectators. Eeka would aggressively move around the pit, throw pieces of innertube into the crowd, shove snakes down her pants, and occasionally pretend to escape from the pit and chase Bobby down the midway until they eventually captured and returned Eeka to the pit. The Rentons would typically go through a box of 20 snakes a week, which they had shipped to them via UPS. If it was a large crowd and they seemed to want Eeka to go full glomming geek for a particular show, the geek would first skin the snake, then bite the head off. Depending on the damage to the snake, they could make a single snake last for multiple days of shows if they kept it on ice overnight. One geek performer that the Rentons used to play Eeka was Misha Ali Bobia, who played the character with their show in the 1950s and early '60s (Stencell 232-236).[21]

---

21. For detailed information on the Rentons, including photos, see the chapter "Geek 101 for Dummies" found in A.W. Stencell's book, "Seeing is Believing: America's Sideshows."

Show producer C.M. Christ, who began
working in the sideshow industry in 1964,
notes that while most glomming geek shows
predated his entry to the business, he did
operate several wild man-style attractions.
During his career, he speculated that he must
have had at least six Eeka shows, which he ran
as what he called "roustabout snake shows."
These shows involved breakaway doors and
little people in pits of snakes, which consisted primarily of boa constrictors. He described the operations of one of the shows he
ran, called *Eeka and the Monsters*:

EEKA–Sits among the giant jungle snakes!
*A female Eeka performer among snakes at
the 1988 Heart of Illinois Fair. The "Wood-
ford County Journal" - July 21, 1988. Copy-
right 2020, Lee Enterprises.*

> *When they [customers] bought a ticket, they came in under the main ban-
> ner and we had a mirror station so the dwarves could see them when they
> came in. The first thing the one dwarf would do – depending, there was no
> real script to it – is stick a rubber snake on a balloon stick up in their face,
> and then one of them would break out of one of those breakaway doors that
> they wouldn't see and chase them out of the tent* (Christ).

An instance of an Eeka performer impressively committing to the character acting
of the role occurred at the 1957 South Florida State Fair. During the Eeka show, a
photographer from the *Miami News* stepped inside the show and took a photograph
of Eeka in the snake pit. Without missing a beat, Eeka leapt forward and began biting
the photographer's leg. The carnies working the attraction quickly intervened and broke
things up, then demanded that the photographer surrender the film from his camera.
However, once the photographer produced a letter from the public relations director of
the fair inviting newsmen to cover the opening night of the fair, the carnies, realizing
he was an authorized newspaper official, quickly changed their tune. Eeka then happily
posed with the snakes in the pit while the photographer took photos, and a story about
the incident wound up in the paper (Roberts 1).

Chapter 8
Human Ostriches

Another fringe geek act that exists within its own subgenre is the human ostrich act. Human ostriches are entertainers who eat non-food items that would appear to be harmful if swallowed, akin to how an actual ostrich will seemingly eat anything. The objects include things like glass, chains, nails, toxins, and so forth. Some may also swallow live animals, but human ostriches generally gravitate toward harmful-if-swallowed, inanimate objects.

Though there are ways to present such feats as illusions, most traditional human ostrich performers did, in fact, actually perform completely ungimmicked feats, which occasionally had fatal consequences.

There are numerous accounts of human
ostrich performers throughout history, but
the genre started to come into its own in
the 1880s. By the 1890s, human ostrich performers were quite common, finding stages in
the dime museums and street fairs of the time.
It is interesting to note that around the time
human ostrich performers were hitting their
peak in popularity, the snake-eating craze of
early geek shows was only just beginning to
take shape. Perhaps human ostriches served at
least in part as a precursor to creating public
interest in early geek shows.

There are essentially two types of human
ostriches: *digestive* and *regurgitative*. Digestive human ostrich performers were far more
common and would simply eat hazardous
objects and let nature take its course by naturally defecating the objects or, in some cases,
the hardware would accumulate in their organs over time, sometimes necessitating surgery.

*A newspaper drawing of a human ostrich
performer around the peak of the act's popularity. The "San Francisco Chronicle" -
September 23, 1898.*

Harry Houdini noted this in his own observations:

> *Eaters of glass, tacks, pebbles, and like objects, actually swallow these seem-*
> *ingly impossible things, and disgorge them after the performance is over.*
> *That the disgorging is not always successful is evidenced by the hospital*
> *records of many surgical operations on performers of this class, when quan-*
> *tities of solid matter are found lodged in the stomach* (Houdini, Miracle
> Mongers 141-142).

If the performer was a regurgitative human ostrich, however, they could expel the
objects orally at will. This is a very challenging and refined skill, though often both more
entertaining to the viewer and much safer for the performer to be able to bring objects
back up from their bodies on command rather than chance them becoming lodged in

their organs during the digestive process. Naturally, regurgitating human ostriches often had longer careers and more upscale engagements than their more common digestive counterparts.

Bill Jones

One famed early human ostrich-style performer from the late 1800s was glass eater Bill Jones. He was notable for several reasons: He was one of the first widely established glass-eating performers, achieving fame before human ostriches became commonplace in the 1890s, and he was able to achieve great success as a solo performer in the social climate of the 1880s despite being an African American.

Bill Jones was born a slave in Missouri in the 1840s. He claimed that, as a child, he and his brother would go to the ice house and bring back ice, which they enjoyed munching on. One day, they accidentally picked up some glass. Thinking it was ice, they ate it, and Jones soon discovered that eating glass was not uncomfortable to him, so he began doing it regularly. He continued to refine his self-taught technique on his own after moving to Texas. As an adult, he began performing around 1885, becoming an immediate hit with the public who were amazed by his ability. He was even studied extensively by numerous highly prestigious medical authorities in Philadelphia who all deemed him a true wonder with healthy organs ("THE GLASS-EATER").[1]

As he continued to perform, Jones even carried around with him a certificate from one of the physicians who experimented on him. He did this as a means to attest to his abilities and health ("JONES, THE GLASS-EATER").

Jones initially drew a very good salary for the strange novelty of his performances. However, as others started eating glass and competition grew a few years later, he had trouble getting large payments as a unique attraction although he was still able to make a steady living by performing regularly on the dime museum circuit ("Abnormal Appetites"). During his performances, he was known to favor eating the glass chimneys

---

1. Glass eating is still performed to this day, ungimmicked, and is much more widely understood. Those interested in learning glass eating should seek out mentorship from a working professional. Information can also be found on glass eating in books such as Joe Nickell's "Secrets of the Sideshows."

The page

from oil lamps, though he would also occasionally eat other forms of glass that audience members would bring to his shows ("Eden Musee").

Throughout his career, Jones had a strong sense of self-promotion and was part of several interesting publicity stunts, often going right to the heart of the press: the newsroom. In one instance in April 1886, while sitting in a saloon, Jones ordered a glass of milk. When it came, he drank half of it, then took a bite out of the glass and chewed it up before drinking the rest of the glass. He then proceeded to finish his meal, eating most of the physical dish that his food was placed on and then went over to the bar and drank three glasses of whiskey, eating and swallowing the individual glasses after each drink. When he then began chewing on two champagne glasses, Jones and his friends were kicked out of the establishment. They then went to several other nearby saloons to do the same. Once they had established an appropriate ruckus, Jones made his way into the local *Daily News* office, where he announced himself as "Bill Jones the Glass Eater" and proceeded to eat a glass medicine bottle. Naturally, the *Daily News* wrote a full story about him and his exploits of the day ("JONES, The GLASS-EATER").

Jones did a similar stunt a month later to promote a series of shows he was doing in the curio hall at a Bunnell's Museum. Jones went into the newspaper office at the *Times* in Buffalo, New York. During the visit, he stated that he had been eating glass for 30 years, noting that it tasted like sugar to him. He even went so far as to claim that glass eating had killed his brother, though he himself was healthy. Then he concluded the visit by eating a piece of a glass lamp chimney, letting the staff inspect his mouth before and after ("A MEAL OFF LAMP CHIMNEYS"). Jones did the same stunt for the *Review* newspaper a couple months later ("A DYSPEPTIC EDITOR").

In another instance of publicity, for a performance announcement where he was to appear at a local rink, the glass factories in the area were said to be producing extra-hard

SOUTH SIDE MUSEUM,
Clark and Madison Sts,

BILL JONES,

The Glass Eater.

Lamp Chimneys and Tumblers are Sweet Morsels to his palate, and Stained Glass Windows are his weakness. He Chews and Swallows 25 to 30 Lamp Chimneys daily, and HE HAS NO RIVALS.
Visitors can bring

THEIR OWN GLASS.
He will Bite, Chew and Swallow it.

He Lives On It!

He digests it and it agrees with him. The Medical Fraternity pronounce him a phenomenon,

Bill Jones doing his act at a dime museum. The "Inter Ocean" (Chicago, IL) - March 28, 1886.

qualities of glass to have on hand, just so that they could test the abilities of Jones during the event ("WOODBURY DOTS").

As his notoriety grew, at one point Jones was even cast in a prominent part for a 15-minute dime museum opera ("ALL SORTS"). The *Saint Paul Globe* describes an interesting anecdote regarding Jones's charisma. The paper noted that during a performance at a church, Jones "proved to be a genuine heart-smasher among the females, who admire and marvel at his feats" and that "a number of the ladies of the church were endeavoring to flirt with the young man." Sure enough, after the performance Jones ended up running off with the pastor's wife ("A COLORED HEART-BREAKER").

However, his glass-eating ways did catch up to him. At one point he was hospitalized the day after being charged with disorderly conduct and resisting arrest, as a large piece of glass had caused an obstruction in his system ("IN GENERAL").

In his later career in the early 1890s, Jones had begun incorporating the consumption of other objects into his performances, such as shingle nails and tacks. Perhaps he was seeking to reinvent himself, or maybe he was simply trying to compete with all the other human ostrich performers who were appearing on other stages at that time ("Untitled Bill Jones Act Description").

At one point, Bill Jones competed against a fellow human ostrich performer, Harry "Boy Ostrich" Harrison, in an object-eating championship contest. Harrison was a young man who ate glass as well as swallowed nails, tacks, screws, and even penknife blades, performing his act at nightclubs and private parties. When reflecting back on the contest during an interview in November 1894, Harrison remembers that Jones was doing very well with the glass-eating portion of their contest, as that was his forte. However, when the contest moved onto other objects, Harrison recalled, "When it came to swallowing screws, penknife blades, etc., he wasn't in with me" and noted that he then ended up beating Jones in the contest. During the interview, Harrison called that moment one of his greatest performances but noted that, at the time of the interview, Jones had passed away about four years prior ("THE BOY OSTRICH").[2]

---

2. There are a few references to Bill Jones performing in 1891 and 1892, but news regarding his appearances dry up after that. It is likely that Jones did, in fact, pass away prior to this interview in 1894.

Bill Jones with his glass. "Omaha Daily Bee" - April 8, 1888.

Alfonso the Human Ostrich

Another successful human ostrich of color who received notable fame was Alfonso the Human Ostrich. He was born Alfonso Hanbin in Barbados, British West Indies. Though he was known to perform some magic, his act consisted primarily of eating tacks and glass, hence his stage name. Alfonso performed in various dime museums in his career, and his success eventually led him to become a performer with the Barnum & Bailey Circus in the early 1900s (Marcelliee 324). A miniature biography of Alfonso's early performing life can be found in the promotional booklet *Life & History of Alfonso, the Human Ostrich: with Barnum and Bailey's Greatest Show on Earth, European Tour.*[3]

Though Alfonso had a lengthy performance career, according to magician John Hunniford, at least some of his human ostrich act was fakery. When Hunniford worked with Alfonso at a dime museum in 1905, he recalled watching Alfonso deceptively conceal a wad of cotton in his hand that contained various needles and tacks that he claimed to have swallowed in front of an audience. After the performance, Alfonso said to Hunniford about other human ostriches, "Kid, those guys who eat that stuff are suckers. Just a little sleight of hand does it!" (Hunniford 27).

---

3. For the full booklet, see Appendix 5.

Alfonso, the Human Ostrich. The National Archives, COPY 1/439/546.

John Cummings

An early human ostrich practitioner who met an untimely end was John Cummings, who was not a performer but rather a sailor with a competitive attitude and a fondness for alcohol.

In 1799, 23-year-old John Cummings had ported up in a small village in France. While there, he and the ship's crew attended a small theater show in which they observed a local magician presenting a knife-swallowing illusion on stage. That evening, an intoxicated Cummings, apparently not realizing that what they had just witnessed was a magic trick and wanting to best the performer he had seen, announced to the crew that he could swallow knives just as well as the French performer. He then pulled out his own knife and, after a moment, swallowed it down. Soon, three other knives were brought to him from the ship, and he proceeded to swallow those as well, much to the entertainment of the rest of the crew.

Six years later, in March 1805, Cummings was describing his previous feat to a number of other sailors. They found his claim too hard to believe, and Cummings, who was again under the influence of alcohol, decided to perform his former feat. He swallowed six knives for the skeptics that evening. Once word of his feat spread to the locals, he swallowed eight more knives for visitors the following day. That time, however, the knives took a toll on his insides and he was hospitalized. He nearly died and suffered internal pains for a month.

Nonetheless, that December while in England, a once-again intoxicated John Cummings was challenged to match his previous feat. He obliged by swallowing nine clasp-knives of various sizes over the course of two days. A few other instances followed until the total count of knives he swallowed had reached 35. He once again fell ill. The majority of the knives stayed inside his body, and John Cummings spent nearly four years in agony, with much of the time spent hospitalized, until he eventually succumbed to his injuries and died in March 1809 ("ECCENTRIC SWALLOWERS").

Henry Whallen

It wasn't simply braggadocious non-performers like John Cummings who were subject to fatal consequences, however. Sometimes even the professionals suffered the same fate.

On June 15, 1897, a human ostrich performer by the name of Henry Whallen died in Kansas City shortly after an operation to remove various bits of hardware from his system. At his time of death, Whallen was 27 years old and had been swallowing nails and glass since he was 10. He had toured all over America as a professional contortionist and human ostrich, performing with prestigious companies such as Barnum & Bailey, Sells Brothers, and Forepaugh circuses ("The Human Ostrich").[4]

After the operation, doctors had removed the following items from Whallen:

- One four-bladed knife, 3½" long

- One two-bladed Barlow knife, 4" long

- One knife blade, 3¼" long

- One knife blade, 3" long

- Two knife blades, 2" long

- One knife blade, 1" long

- 32 large eight- and 10-penny fence nails and spikes

- 34 six-penny wire nails, sharp and pointed

- 26 shingle nails, 1" long

- 16 carpet tacks and small wire nails

- One horseshoe nail

- Three large screws

- One barbed-wire staple

- Three ounces of fine glass ("'HUMAN OSTRICH' DEAD")

---

4. The majority of this information comes from death notices about Whallen. It is possible that he or someone he was with at the time of hospitalization exaggerated his resume when he was admitted.

When the anesthetic wore off, an enthusiastic Whallen inquired to the doctors if the operation was a success and was curious to know how many nails and knives the doctors had found. The surgeons concluded that all of the items had left him in an emaciated state and that he would have died within a year or two without the surgery. Though he originally seemed on the road to recovery, post-operation, his organs were badly damaged and the shock of the procedure was hard on his system. A day and a half after the hardware removal, he began to fade and passed away shortly thereafter ("The Human Ostrich").

John Fasel

Another human ostrich who experienced serious health issues from their craft was John Fasel.

German-born Fasel was a tailor living in America at the turn of the 20th century. He was unhappy with the wages he made as a tailor and yearned to be in the spotlight and to be an actor. He reasoned that perhaps the best way to get noticed would be to attempt a publicity stunt such as becoming a "freak"-style performer like those found in dime museums during the time period. So he became a human ostrich and started eating various objects such as nails, pins, and glass.

Just a few months into his quest in early 1900, Fasel, who was around 19 years old at the time, was hospitalized as a direct result of his budding career choice. During his operation, surgeons removed the following items from Fasel:

- One brass chain, 3' long

- One brass watch

- 260 common pins

- One brass chain, 1¾ yard long

- One nickeled chain, 3'2" long

- One nickeled chain, 3' long

- 10 horseshoe nails

- 12 iron nails, each 2½" long

- Six big hairpins

- Two door keys

- One large initial ring

- One brass express check

- One button hook

- One glass prism from a chandelier

- One pocketknife

- A mass of conglomerate, consisting of fine wire, needles, and pins ("HE LIVED ON METAL")

Illustration attempting to show what was removed from Fasel's stomach. The "Harrisburg Telegraph" - February 27, 1900.

Though he had yet to be discovered as an actor or even make it as a dime museum attraction, it seemed that Fasel's days as a human ostrich were over.

After he recovered from his surgery, Fasel decided to settle down and marry. Apparently still unhappy with his career as a tailor, he moved in with his father-in-law and decided to simply give up working. Once his father-in-law became irritated with him and attempted to eject Fasel from his house, a fight broke out and Fasel beat up his father-in-law, serving five days in jail ("FATE PLAYS HAVOC WITH 'HUMAN OSTRICH'").

By early 1904, 23-year-old Fasel had decided to make a comeback, allegedly after seeing another human ostrich performer in person and challenging him to an impromptu eating challenge where they consumed various knives, keys, and chains ("HUMAN OSTRICH DINES TOO FAST ON HARDWARE").

It was an ill-fated comeback, however, as on March 12, 1904, Fasel became ill and was taken to the local hospital. After giving him an X-ray, doctors concluded that another operation was necessary to remove the foreign matter from his insides to save his life. He agreed to a date for the surgery and promised the doctors that he would refrain from eating nails, chains, and knives in the meantime. However, after attending a reception later, his friends encouraged him to do his signature stunt. Though he initially refused, Fasel eventually succumbed to the social pressure and swallowed several nails, much to the amusement of the partygoers. A moment later, while everyone was dancing, he lost consciousness and was rushed to the hospital ("JOHN FASEL, HUMAN OSTRICH").

Fasel's second operation lasted four hours. When complete, doctors had removed the following items from his insides:

• Six knives

• One gold chain

• Three ring chains

• Four keys

• 12 wire nails

• Eight horseshoe nails

• A 2" metal pin

During the operation, doctors found that the primary source of the problem was that the metal pin had lodged in his intestines. Much like with his first operation, Fasel was in critical condition afterward and there was doubt as to whether he would actually survive, though he did eventually recover ("IRON DID NOT DIGEST").

After this second near-death experience, upon recovery Fasel went back to a life as a tailor. The decision was likely influenced, at least in part, by the lasting effects the trauma had on his system, as after his second surgery, he suffered from epileptic fits ("Human Ostrich's New Diet").

By 1912, an older and presumably wiser Fasel was found performing a magic act in New York ("Wyckoff Benevolent Meets"). It seems that the allure of the spotlight of show business remained strong for him. All things considered, changing entertainment paths from one based on ungimmicked danger to one centering on illusion and trickery was probably the best course of action for John Fasel's health.

Henry Harrison

One of the more extreme human ostrich entertainers was Henry Harrison from Syracuse, New York, who performed his act in dime museums and vaudeville theaters throughout the 1890s and 1900s.

In his performances, Harrison would eat a number of hazardous objects, which included pins, nails, screws, glass, and the blades of pocketknives. He first discovered his abilities when he swallowed several pins when he was six years old. His mother was alarmed and had a local physician remove the pins, but his behavior became habit-forming and did not seem to cause him harm. As a young man, he eventually ran away with a traveling circus and shifted his habit into the realm of live entertainment.

In addition to his public performances, Harrison was studied at length by those in the medical community. During one study at the Medico-Chirurgical College in Philadelphia, doctors observed him eating in one sitting:

- 40 carpet tacks

- Six pieces of broken glass

- 20 lath nails

- One glass milk pitcher

- Six horseshoe nails

- Five 2" screws

- One broken lamp chimney

- Two bone-handled pocketknives

- Three minced penknife blades

- Aqua pura (to wash it all down)

Though confident in his abilities, he did not view his skills as being extraordinary:

Any man with a good constitution and a strong nerve can do the same thing. It is simply a matter of cultivating the palate. Rusty nails are very nice when you acquire a taste for them, and glass is a particular dainty.

In order to minimize the risk of injury, he would eat a large starchy meal before each performance. In the cases of small metal objects, he would place them on his tongue individually then swallow them quickly, drinking water afterward to aid digestion. When eating larger nails, he would bend the tips so that they looked akin to a staple before he swallowed them as a means to reduce the likelihood of intestinal perforation. He also claimed to be able to drink strychnine and other poisons without ill effect.

In addition to doing private exhibitions for the medical community, he was routinely paid by surgeons to allow them to conduct operations on him for study. As a result, his body was covered in surgical scars.

Unfortunately for Harrison, not all of his surgeries were elective, and his craft eventually became his downfall. During one misadventure, after swallowing a packet of tacks, he experienced great intestinal pain after a tack became lodged in one of his organs and he had to have an operation to have it removed (Buckholder 467-470).

Last Week of
HUNGRY HENRY HARRISON
The Awful Human Ostrich

Newspaper mention of Henry Harrison. The "Times Philadelphia" - March 25, 1900.

On April 6, 1908, he was hospitalized in Seattle after one of his performances at a local vaudeville theater when one of the horseshoe nails he swallowed lodged in his intestine. Doctors operated on him to save his life, and by the following day, he was in grave condition. Though Harrison had a special technique of bending longer nails to avoid injury, in this case he had bent one of the nails to resemble more of a fishhook shape, resulting in it becoming lodged in his intestine. When the doctors opened him up, they removed the following items:

- One horseshoe nail

- 11 knife blades

- Five lath nails

- Six small screws

- Three tacks

By then, Harrison was 38 years old and had been performing his act for nearly 20 years, performing an average of 150 days a year ("KNIFE BLADES FOUND IN 'HUMAN OSTRICH"). On May 1, the *Washington Standard* stated that Henry Harrison, the famed human ostrich, had died a few days prior as a result of his injury ("MADE HIS STOMACH SELF-SUPPORTING").

MR. HENRY HARRISON, THE HUMAN OSTRICH, AT HIS DINNER OF KNIVES,
From a Photo. by] PINS, NAILS, AND GLASS. [*The Hellos, New York.*

Photo of Henry Harrison. The "Strand." 1901.

Antoine Menier

MENIER, THE "HUMAN OSTRICH."
From a Photo. by G. Sheils, Dublin.

Antoine Menier in costume, ready for the show. The "Strand." 1897

Though many human ostriches performed under their own names with the slightest hint of stage character, one performer who went the route of theatrics was Frenchman Antoine Menier, who combined the act of a human ostrich with the aesthetics of a wild man show. For his performances, Menier would wear "war paint" on his face and a large nose ring (FitzGerald 413-414).

Rather than performing in American dime museums and sideshows, Menier performed frequently throughout Scotland and England in the 1890s. In addition to being billed as a human ostrich, he was sometimes called "The Human Phenomenon." His performance diet consisted of items such as candles, charcoal, broken glass, and sawdust. In some cases, he would soak the sawdust in paraffin, set it on fire, and then eat it while it was ablaze ("THE ROYAL AQUARIUM"). A stunning visual, no doubt.

English Jack

Though not a human ostrich in the traditional sense, one performer of early note who played the same dime museum circuit as many human ostriches was a man who went by the name English Jack and whose performance prop of choice was live frogs. Intriguingly, history paints two very different pictures of English Jack.

In one version, Jack is a bearded sailor turned hermit who lived a life of heartache, largely hidden from the public eye of show business.

The sailor English Jack was born John Vialls in 1827. He was orphaned at the age of 12 but had an ambition to go to sea, even as a child. Eventually, his dream came to fruition, as he sailed to various ports all over the world.

On one tragic day, however, he became shipwrecked. During the accident, more than half the crew perished, but Jack and 13 other crew were able to make it to a nearby island.

It was there that Jack began his unusual dietary habits. Out of necessity for survival, Jack and the other survivors ate crabs, mussels, and snakes that they found on the island. By the time rescue came 19 months later, many of the remaining crew had died, including Jack's adopted father. The rescue ship picked up the few remaining crew, but by the time they got back to England, Jack was the only remaining survivor of the shipwreck.

Jack would later return to the sea and made plans to marry his childhood sweetheart upon his return. However, when he made it back to land, he found out his bride-to-be had passed away. Distraught, he joined the navy and emerged, this time, unscathed.

When he was 48, Jack joined a railroad construction project as a laborer. The build passed through Crawford Notch, located in the White Mountains of New Hampshire. Using leftover construction scraps, Jack settled into the area by creating a makeshift home for himself in the mountains, which he called his "ship." It was there that he became known as "The Hermit of Crawford Notch," and he soon became somewhat of a local celebrity, making canes and model ships for tourists. When he received visitors, he was known to entertain them by devouring live snakes and frogs for the price of a quarter, his palate supposedly accustomed to such things from his days shipwrecked on an island (Eastman).

Author James E. Mitchell wrote a short book of verse called *The Story of Jack, The Hermit of The White Mountains* that recounts Jack's life story. On developing his ability to stomach eating living things while on an island, the work stated:

> *But what we found to eat is hard to say;*
> *A snail or snake, for nothing came amiss,*
> *We ate whatever came across our way.*

On the sadness of watching his loved ones pass:

> *So I might way, "I've been in many wars,*
> *In many bloody fights I've taken part;*
> *And though at times "I show my cuts and scars,"*
> *The deepest scar of all is in my heart.*

Though he had brushes with death and watched many around him perish, Jack lived a long life, passing away on April 24, 1912, at the age of 85. Mitchell's work ends appropriately:

> *I left old England then for good and all,*
> *And do not think I ever shall go back;*
> *I've waited long for death to sound my call,*
> *But still I'm here. Your humble servant,*
> *JACK* (Mitchell).

Harry Houdini encountered English Jack in his early days and remarked that he "occasionally ran across a sailor calling himself English Jack who could swallow live frogs and bring them up again with apparent ease." The interesting implication is that English Jack not only ate frogs but possessed the skill of regurgitation as well (Houdini, Miracle Mongers 164).

Advertisement for English Jack the Dime Museum Performer. The "Boston Globe" - September 26, 1886.

The other historical picture of English Jack shows him as a young, well-dressed public performer who began his career in the mid-1880s and continued into the early 1900s. He performed in dime museums and theaters with an act that consisted of eating live frogs out of a tank, sometimes consuming up to 30 in a single day. Though frogs were his preference, occasionally he would eat other small animals as well, such as mice ("Ostrich Stomachs").

Given his dietary choice, Jack was occasionally billed as "Frog Man" and regularly received press coverage for his engagements. Regarding the liveliness of his subjects, Jack was once quoted by the *Boston Globe* as saying "I haven't any objections to swallowing 'em dead; but, you know, I prefer to swallow 'em alive and kicking" (Austin & Stone's Museum Advertisement).

The two life stories of English Jack seem to correlate in certain ways but differ in other ways. One wonders if English Jack led two very different lives at different points in his life or if there were actually two English Jacks who ate live frogs during the same time period. Variety entertainment imitators were common during that time (and continue to be), with imitators attempting to cash in on the success of other popular performers. In referencing various newspaper mentions, English Jack the hermit would have been in his 60s during Frog Man's heyday in dime museums, though he is depicted as looking much younger, which implies two different people. Though it seems that there would be little to gain from using the same name and dietary habit of a local hermit, it is possible that a young public performer was inspired by the stories of the Hermit of Crawford Notch and decided to use the English Jack moniker for his own act. It is also possible, albeit highly unlikely, that there were two unrelated frog-eating Englishmen that came to America and went by the same name during about the same time period, completely unbeknownst to each other.

English Jack with a frog. The "Boston Globe" - October 5, 1886.

English Jack The Hermit of Crawford Notch. Image courtesy of the New Hampshire Historical Society.

English Jack the dime museum performer, pictured with his aquarium and frogs. TCS 7, Box 1 folder 10, Houghton Library Harvard University.

Mr. McKenna

Newspaper depiction of McKenna. The "Daily Palladium" (Benton Harbor, Michigan) - August 16, 1890.

Another performer who made a living performing unusual eating feats at dime museums in the late 1800s was a man known as Mr. McKenna.

For his act, McKenna's ate glass, carpet tacks, live frogs, and occasionally other household items. During one exhibition in 1890, a reporter observed him eating six 10-penny nails, a handful of assorted carpet tacks, a pocketknife, a piece of fork, four frogs, and a glass tumbler, all within the span of a half hour.

McKenna was billed as "The Human Ostrich" and sometimes "The Man Ostrich." His showbills occasionally pictured him as a literal ostrich with a human face. The *Daily Palladium* out of Benton Harbor, Michigan, said of him on August 16, 1890, "McKenna is proud of his swallowing ability and quite looks down upon a professional rival." The paper goes on to mention English Jack (the Frog Man performer) by name as McKenna's professional rival ("Ostrich Stomachs"). Their tendency to both eat live frogs in their respective shows likely also contributed to their rivalry.

McKenna was said to be surprisingly slim, and his strange diet did not seem to impact his physical health. Once, when questioned about the cause of his unnatural appetite, McKenna simply stated, tongue no doubt firmly in cheek: "Cigarettes!" ("Abnormal Appetites").

McKenna dime museum ad. The "Times" (Philadelphia, Pennsylvania) - January 17, 1889.

Mac Norton

A performer who was more of a regurgitating purist was the Frenchman Claude Louis Delair. He was born in 1876 and performed for the majority of his career under the name Mac Norton. Initially, his career in show business began in 1894 with singing in music halls. However, that pathway did not last long as he soon found a much more unusual and memorable career path as a swallower of strange things in unusual quantities ("Claude Louis Delair, Aka Mac Norton").

For his act, he would frequently consume large quantities of water, beer, and bread onstage. However, he was best known for his regurgitation abilities which saw him swallow fish, turtles, frogs, and snakes whole, then bring them back up again at will. He was especially well known for the frogs, which became his trademark with promotional photos and posters depicting him holding them up over his gaping mouth. His unique ability to swallow aquatic creatures and allow them to dwell within him for a period of time before regurgitating them led him to become known as "The Human Aquarium."[5]

Promotional poster from 1913 featuring Mac Norton. Unknown artist. 1913. https://upload.wikimedia.org/wikipedia/commons/8/8d/Mac-Norton_-_buveur_d e_bi%C3%A8re_et_avaleur_de_grenouil les_et_de_poissons.jpg

One of his non-animal acts included drinking 30 to 40 glasses of beer onstage. His secret to achieving the feat was both deceptive and skillful; he would drink the glasses of beer by the handful and when he would turn away to obtain more full glasses from the back of the stage, he would quickly and secretly expel the beer he had just drank into a hidden receptacle, just out of the audience's view.

Despite the seemingly gross nature of his profession, Norton was an incredibly classy and prolific performer. He was well dressed in formal clothing and performed in large theaters all over Europe. The notoriously anti-geek Houdini even went so far as to remark

---

5. This is opposed to the frog eaters discussed previously who simply relied on swallowing and digesting live animals. The refined skill of regurgitation no doubt brought much greater "class" and more deserved fame.

that when it came to frog swallowers, "Norton was the only one I ever saw who presented his act in a dignified manner" (Houdini, Miracle Mongers 162-164).

Doctors studied Mac Norton and wrote about his abilities. A promotional pamphlet from 1922 noted their findings.[6] When spouting water, Norton never forced his stomach muscles. If he was spouting a water jet and felt resistance, he would end that stream, wait a moment, and comfortably begin a new stream without any strain. When swallowing solid objects, medical examination found that small objects would travel down slowly and larger objects would go up and down several times before settling into the stomach. The objects would typically stay toward the surface of the liquid inside the stomach. When Norton wanted to bring objects back up at will, he would contract his muscles and they would come up very quickly, within a second or so. Outside of its extraordinary abilities, Norton's stomach was found to be healthy and of normal size and orientation (Pares).

Norton continued to perform well into his 70s, retiring in 1950 and passing away in 1953.

Mac Norton poster from 1920. Susanlenox.
1920. https://upload.wikimedia.org/wikipedia/commons/a/a8/Ci
rcus_Busch%2CMac_Norton_%281920%29.jpg

6. For a full translation of this text, see Appendix 6.

Photograph of Mac Norton. From the author's private collection.

The Great Waldo

Another impeccably dressed, gentlemanly regurgitator of live vertebrate animals was a man known as The Great Waldo. Like Norton, Waldo was capable of swallowing frogs and housing them in his stomach after drinking water and regurgitating them unharmed. However, Waldo's preference and signature act involved live white mice.

The Great Waldo's real name was Dagobert Roehmann (Sherman, Part 2, 1), and he was from Germany. He was Jewish and was an outcast as a child. In his youth, he would frequently attend traveling carnivals that came through Europe and took a liking to the freaks he saw in the sideshows.[7] It was there that he first saw several performers regurgitating small objects and began to learn the trade himself. As an adult, he studied medicine in his native land. Once the Nazis began to take power, however, Waldo migrated to Switzerland to escape the anti-Semitic politics of the time. There, he began to perform his regurgitation act in nightclubs. During this period, he caught the eye of a booking agent for American road shows, who offered Waldo a contract. Waldo accepted and made his way to the United States to establish himself as a performer there (Mannix, Memoirs 86).

In his book *Memoirs of a Sword Swallower*, Daniel P. Mannix wrote about befriending and performing with The Great Waldo.[8] At the time, Waldo was performing as "The Human Ostrich" and had briefly joined the same show Mannix wrote of working with, "Krinko's Great Combined Carnival Side Shows."[9] In the book, he describes several of Waldo's routines in detail.

---

7. Some sources erroneously state Waldo's real name as Dagmar Rothman.

8. There is debate regarding the authenticity of some of the firsthand experiences Mannix writes about in his book. He did indeed work sideshows in his youth, though it is believed that some of the stories he tells were likely received from other showpeople and incorporated into the work to make a more entertaining read. At the least, the information he presents about real performers such as Waldo is likely accurate, even if he did not experience it firsthand.

9. Some contemporary biographies on Waldo also refer to him as "The Regurgitating Geek."

With the sideshow, Waldo would begin his act by borrowing small objects from the audience. He would then swallow the objects and get several volunteers to examine his mouth to prove that he really did swallow them all. Once those in attendance were convinced, he would regurgitate the items with ease and return them to their owners. One of Waldo's favorite variants of his act was to swallow a watch borrowed from the audience, then allow people to put their ears up to his chest so they could hear it ticking inside of him before bringing it back up (Mannix, Memoirs 86).

Waldo also did a human fountain/water spouting act. It involved drinking 20 glasses of water quickly, then slowly regurgitating the water back out in a steady stream while music played in the background (Mannix, Memoirs 107).

His technique for his signature trick of swallowing live mice was one of calculated caution. He preferred white mice, which he kept in an aquarium that he traveled with. He would first produce them from the aquarium and clean them using a toothbrush (Mannix, Memoirs 84; Thompson 88). If the mice were moving around excessively, he would utilize a specially made cigarette that was soaked in nicotine, which he would smoke and blow into the mice's faces. This smoke would make them groggy, a state that made them easier to swallow. He would then swallow them completely and regurgitate them completely unharmed before placing them back into the aquarium (Mannix, Memoirs 107).

Though an impressive act, it wasn't without risk. Mannix wrote about one mishap during one of Waldo's performances. After his captive mice had perished in a rainstorm, adhering to the show business adage of "the show must go on," Waldo ended up doing his act with some large wild rats that the show owner had captured that day. After swallowing one, Waldo found that he was unable to regurgitate it. The unruly rat had grabbed onto the lining of Waldo's stomach. After a short panic, Waldo drank a large quantity of water, which flooded his stomach, causing the rat to let go, at which point Waldo successfully made the regurgitation (Mannix, Memoirs 107).

Very early on in his career, magician John Thompson worked with The Great Waldo during a series of amusement park shows in Chicago at Riverview Park. Thompson described Waldo as "almost dwarflike. He had an extended sternum – what they called a chicken breast – and a humpback, warts, eczema... and a Viennese accent." Thompson also recalled another instance where Waldo's act went seriously awry. During one performance, after swallowing a number of objects, including a mouse, coins, and a lemon, Waldo attempted to bring the items back up to finish the show, but the lemon became lodged in his throat and he began to choke. In a panic, Thompson ran next door to the fire department, where one of the personnel was able to get to Waldo and pump his stomach, saving him but killing the mouse in the process. Rather than being grateful to Thompson for helping him, Waldo was irate. Apparently, the mishap was common, and Waldo told Thompson that he should have done what everyone else does when he gets the lemon stuck in his throat. When Thompson inquired as to what that was, Waldo simply replied "Hit me on the hump." Thompson, taken aback by such an unusual response, began laughing. Waldo, irritated by the teenage Thompson's reaction, had him fired the following day (Thompson 88).

Another Waldo anecdote comes from the late 1940s, when Waldo sent promoter Milt Robbins a letter looking for work. He introduced himself in the letter, indicating what his act was with swallowing rats, and stated that for his terms he was looking for $75 a week with cookhouse meals provided, and that his wife at the time, who did not work but traveled with him, would need to receive cookhouse meals as well. Taken aback by his terms, Robbins wrote back to Waldo: "If you can find a show that will give you cookhouse for you and your wife and your wife doesn't work and $75 a week, I'll swallow the rat!" (Christ).

Waldo achieved some real success in the United States. In addition to performing at carnival sideshows, he also performed at notable venues such as Robert Ripley's Odditorium, Hubert's Museum, and with the Ringling Bros. and Barnum & Bailey Circus. During his time on the sideshow circuit, sideshow manager Fred Smythe used the following bally to promote The Great Waldo:

> *Stop! Pause a moment in your mad rush toward the grave. If you have never had the extreme pleasure of seeing a man swallow a live mouse, a treat is indeed in store for you within. The Great Waldo... Ugh! How does he do it!*
> (Sherman, Part 2, 1)

Incredibly, some video footage of Waldo exists performing his act. The brief video (which can be found scattered around the Internet in various forms) shows a grinning Waldo swallowing a lemon, drinking a glass of water with a goldfish in it, and performing his signature mouse regurgitation.

Sadly, The Great Waldo committed suicide in 1952 at the age of 62.[10] Waldo, who was living in an apartment in New York at the time, had lost track of a woman that he was in love with ("Great Waldo Is Dead By His Own Hand, Love Sick"). Heartbroken and unable to find his lost love, Waldo wrote two suicide notes, one in Hebrew, one in German, filled his apartment with gas from his stove, and ended his own life ("'The Great Waldo' Found Dead of Gas").

Hadji Ali

Perhaps of all the notable regurgitator performers throughout history, the most extreme was Egyptian entertainer Hadji Ali, who was born between 1887 and 1892 (Underwood).

Hadji Ali was said to have been born of Egyptian parents on a small island off of the west coast of Africa ("Hadji Goes Whale One Better"). While playing with his friends as a child, he would frequently swim in the river. Over time, he discovered his ability to consume then expel water on command ("Hadji Ali, Miracle Man, Coming Here").[11]

Over the course of his career, Ali performed in a wide variety of events all over the world, including performing for royalty throughout Europe ("Hadji Ali, Miracle Man, Coming Here"). He was especially popular on American vaudeville stages during the 1920s and 1930s. In the USA, he was billed as The Human Fountain, The Human Ostrich, The Human Camel, and The Human Volcano (for his finale).

He became known for several distinct acts that he performed based on regurgitation. In one, he would swallow dozens of hazelnuts and a single walnut, and then bring them

---

10. Numerous websites and books list Waldo as having been born in 1920, which would have only put him in his early 30s at the time of his passing. However, newspapers from the time announcing his death, including the ones sourced here, list Waldo as being 62, stating that the pamphlet he was found with notes him as having been born in Berlin in 1889. The author of this book is inclined to believe the period newspapers that indicate Waldo as being older. Further supporting evidence can be found in John Skoyles's memoir "Secret Frequencies: A New York Education," where the author recalls encountering Waldo at Hubert's Museum in New York and describes him as "an old man in a three-piece suit." (Skoyles 111).

11. Though Ali made the news frequently throughout his career, much of his early life remains a mystery, and some of the claims about his background conflict, including his birth year. The details of his exact origins should be taken with a grain of salt.

up for the audience, being able to separate and bring up the outlier nut on command. For his human fountain act, he would drink upwards of 40 glasses of water in front of the audience, then expel the entirety of it in the form of a single continuous stream. In another stunt, he would swallow three handkerchiefs of different colors, then bring the colors back up in whatever order the audience indicated. His signature stunt, and most dangerous, was his finale. In this act, Ali would drink another large quantity of water. Then he would drink a bottle of kerosene. Internally, the two fluids would separate. Due to the lower density of the kerosene, it would float to the top of the water. Ali would then stand in front of a small preset structure or a pile of rags. Either there would be a small flame on the object he was facing, or he would hold out a small flaming object in his hand as an ignition source. Then he would proceed to regurgitate his stomach contents at the object. Since the kerosene floated to the top inside his body, it would naturally come up first, and he would spit out fire blasts at the target. Once he had exhausted all of the kerosene inside his body and the object before him was ablaze, Ali would then regurgitate the water and extinguish the flaming object with a single stream of water, bobbing his head up and down to completely saturate it ("Orphans Doubt If Elephant Can Duplicate Feats of Hadji Ali").

Ali was said to, on occasion, swallow objects such as nails and pocketwatches. Numerous physicians also studied him over the years. During a stint in Buenos Aires, Argentina, Ali swallowed live frogs during a demonstration for some local medical students. Allegedly, he accidently swallowed a live scorpion at one point, but after one of the students informed him, he was successfully able to bring it back up without harm ("Does Tricks Before Staff").

Despite his extensive prestigious engagements and the dangerous nature of his act, Ali was a humble and friendly individual, occasionally doing small shows for good causes. In 1926, he performed his full act for underprivileged children at the Home for Friendless Children in Reading, Pennsylvania ("Orphans Doubt If Elephant Can Duplicate Feats of Hadji Ali"). In another instance, he was made an "Honorary Member of the Los Angeles Fire Department" in 1935. A smiling and laughing Ali performed his human volcano finale act for a small group of local firemen to mark the occasion (Hadji Ali, the "Human Camel"). In 1927, he summed up his philosophy to the *Charlotte Observer*: "I don't want money; I want friends." He continued with, "You might be broke or I might be broke, and then we would need our friends" ("Hadji Goes Whale One Better").

Ali was filmed on several occasions, most notably for the 1931 feature film *Politiquerias*. In the film, he does water spouting, regurgitation of nuts, and his Human Volcano act. He wore sheik garb, which he was known to dress in for many of his performances. Fortunately, the video as well as several other clips of Hadji Ali's performances have survived the ravages of time and can be easily found and enjoyed on the Internet.

Hadji Ali passed away on November 5, 1937, while on tour in Wolverhampton, England. He died of heart failure after coming down with bronchitis. Curiously, it had been said that in life he had signed a $150,000 con-

Hadji Ali spouting water in 1926. National Photo Company Collection. 1926. https://upload.wikimedia.org/wikipedia/ commons/2/2a/Hadji_Ali_demonstratin g_controlled_regurgitation_Crisco_edit.j pg

tract to the Rockefeller Institute in exchange for his body to be studied when he passed away ("Ostriches Out of Picture As Hadji Ali Eats"). Not only did the study not come to fruition after he died, being an apparent false claim for publicity, but after his death his assistant, Princess Almenia, offered his body to Johns Hopkins University for examination, but they declined (Soboleski).

Hadji Ali's unusual legacy left a strong impact on several notable performers. Judy Garland, who worked with him on the vaudeville circuit, was very impressed by Ali's performances and even described watching his Human Volcano act decades later on *The Johnny Carson Show*. Street magician David Blaine noted Hadji Ali was one of his favorite historical performers of all time and said that of the footage of Ali's Human Volcano act from the film *Politiquerias* that he had "been obsessed with this clip since I was a kid" (Underwood).

There is also the more recent full-time performing regurgitator Stevie Starr from Scotland. Starr performs feats similar to Ali, particularly swallowing various household objects and bringing them back up in different sequences at the command of the audience. He tours extensively and has been featured numerous times on "Got Talent" television shows around the world.

Poster of Hadji Ali performing his water spouting. Text translates to "Ali, the mysterious Egyptian." Anonymous artist. Adolph Friedländer company. 1913. https://upload.wikimedia.org/wikipedia/commons/c/c2/Hadji_Ali _-_water_spouting.png

HADJI ALI

Hadji Ali ingesting a large quantity of water, preparing to spout. Grant Schmalgemeier Century of Progress Collection. https://upload.wikimedia.org/wikipedia/commons/4/47/Hadji_Ali_%28NBY_416058%29.jpgIMAGE: Hadji_Ali_demonstrating_controleld_regurgitation.jpg

Kanichka

One regurgitative human ostrich who had a
strong sense of showmanship was the Spaniard
Alvarez Kanichka, who often performed simply
as Kanichka in the 1930s.

Kanichka's performances saw him swallowing
objects such as pocket watches, lightbulbs, billiard balls, Spanish coins, and live goldfish, then
regurgitating them at will. The fish, he would
bring back with them still alive. For his coins act,
he would swallow several coins at a time, then
ask spectators how many to bring back up. He
would then regurgitate the number specified by
the audience followed by the rest. His most difficult and signature feat involved swallowing an
electric lightbulb still plugged in. With the bulb

*Kanichka with light bulb and pocket
watch. Image courtesy of Rhett Bryson.*

attached to a power source when he swallowed, the light emanating from the bulb was
visible as it made its way down Kanichka's throat.

Kanichka performed his act at venues such as the Birmingham Empire Theatre in
England in 1932 ("SPAINIARD EMULATES OSTRICH"). The following year, he
made his way to the United States, where he performed at Ripley's Odditorium at the
1933 Chicago World's Fair ("Ripley's Outrageous Oddities").

Zorita Lambert

Female human ostrich entertainer Zorita Lambert performed with various productions
of Ripley's Believe it or Not Shows in the early 1940s. At her performances, she would
eat glass and razor blades.

During a stint with Ripley's Odditorium at Treasure Island in 1940, she was asked
by a reporter how she got started in her profession, to which she replied "I used to be a
bookkeeper," continuing, "but I was out of a job and had to get something to do." When
pressed further about how she got this idea, she just shrugged and stated, "Well, you see

I started in by chewing cigarettes and matches and worked up to glass and razor blades." (D. Wood).

Footage of Lambert eating razor blades at Ripley's Odditorium can be found on the Internet. Her image is also circulated on a reproduction postcard along with sword swallower Edna Price. Of Zorita Lambert, the postcard reads "The Fearless Woman. Eats whole electric lightbulbs with the ease of an apple."

Chaz Chase

An entertainer who incorporated a strong comedy element in his performances as a human ostrich was vaudevillian Chaz Chase.

Chase was born in Kiev, Ukraine, in 1901 and moved to the United States with his family when he was young. After his family immigrated to Chicago, he began studying ballet (Jones).

Though trained as a dancer, he soon moved over to the vaudeville circuit after developing an unusual pantomime act, with which he toured the world for over half a century. For his act, Chase would walk out smoking a cigar while wearing dress clothes that were far too large for his small frame. He would then eat his lit cigar and engage in a series of comical dance moves in his floppy clothing. A moment later, he would produce a cigarette, which he would light with a match before eating it. He would then go on to light the matches individually and eat them one at a time before eventually eating the matchbook itself. Eventually, he would move to eating other things on his person, such as a small prop harmonica, his front shirt bib, and the flower that he had pinned to his coat before concluding his act.

Once the vaudeville era passed, Chase continued in show business touring Europe, playing nightclubs, and doing theater. Some of his notable career engagements included working at the Latin Quarter in New York, an eight-year performance run at the Crazy Horse Saloon in Paris during the 1950s, and appearing in notable theatrical productions such as *Ballyhoo of 1930* with W.C. Fields and performing alongside Mickey Rooney in *Sugar Babies* (Cullen 215-216).

In 1975, Chase starred in an interesting theatrical production called *The Cooch Dancer* by John Kenley. The production was a comedy with a carnival setting, and it even featured a geek as one of the characters. Though the *Dayton Daily News* gave the production a poor review, they did note that "The only bright spot[s] in the otherwise murky evening were the random appearances of Chaz Chase, former vaudevillian and nitery [nightclub] entertainer, who pantomimed his merry way through several vignettes based on his hilarious nightclub routines" (B.W.).

He also made a number of television and movie appearances during his life. In 1928, he appeared in a short film called *Chaz Chase: The Unique Comedian* that showcased an early version of his act. That same year, he appeared in an uncredited role in Tod Browning's *West of Zanzibar*.[12] Chaz Chase's television appearances included numerous late-night shows, such as *The Ed Sullivan Show*, *The Tonight Show Starring Johnny Carson*, and *Late Night with David Letterman*.[13]

Regarding the authenticity of his methods, the pantomime style that Chaz used for his act, coupled with his tendency to give facetious answers to the press, makes it somewhat challenging to ascertain exactly where to draw the line in terms of what he actually consumed in his act. In 1932, the *Cincinnati Enquirer* made the claim that Chase actually spit out his cigars that he chewed up after he had left the stage but noted that he did actually swallow the lit matches and his shirt front, the latter of which was specially made of paper ("Chaz Is The Name, Says Chaz Chase; So 'Chaz' It Is!"). Chase told the same newspaper in 1941 "Sure, it all goes down. People think I'm faking, but I cross 'em up. My act is genuine." Though he then went on to note that he does have to be careful because "Bad cooking upsets my stomach!" (Stegner). In 1981, he told the *Tyler Morning Telegraph* that since he began in 1919, he had likely swallowed around four million cigars but noted that he doesn't actually swallow the tiny harmonica in his act because "I tried it once, but it didn't go down right." Naturally, he also concluded the interview in a tongue-in-cheek manner, saying "But cigars don't bother me; matches don't bother me. I get heartburn from food" ("Chaz Chase Diet A Lighted Cigar For Lunch").

Chaz Chase continued working into his 80s and passed away in 1983 at the age of 82, leaving behind a daughter, three grandchildren, and an unforgettable legacy in show business (Jones 7).

---

12. Browning directed several sideshow-themed films during his career, including the cult classic "Freaks" in 1932.

13. Many of his television and movie appearances, including the short film "Chaz Chase: The Unique Comedian" can be found online.

Monsieur Mangetout

One commonality between both digestive and regurgitative human ostrich performers is that they stuck to relatively small household objects that could be ingested either at once or over the course of a single performance. However, one notable figure who was very much a human ostrich-style entertainer but preferred to focus on eating exceptionally large objects over longer periods of time was Michel Lotito, most commonly known as "Monsieur Mangetout" (translates to "Mr. Eat-all").

Lotito was born in France in 1950. As a young boy, he developed a general fondness for eating pieces of glass and metal. Interestingly, doctors determined that he had an extraordinarily resilient digestive system and suffered no ill effects of his appetite. Eating regular soft foods such as eggs and bananas actually made Lotito feel ill. His behavior was later attributed to him having a psychological disorder known as pica, which results in a craving for non-food objects (Littlechild).

When he was a schoolboy, he noticed that he also had a high tolerance for pain, so he would let his peers jab him with needles or hit him with baseball bats for amusement. As a young adult, he decided to take the skills to the stage and began performing sideshow-style torture acts for audiences. The acts would consist of him allowing audience members to throw darts into his back, light matches under his fingernails, and pinch his skin with pliers (Tiede).

Though his pain-proof acts no doubt left lasting impressions on young Mangetout's body and his audiences' minds, he eventually became known for his extraordinary eating. For encores in his shows, Lotito would eat pieces of a bicycle. He would eat the whole thing over a period of several days, limiting himself to eating three bicycles per year. Eventually, he focused exclusively on eating large items, over time moving onto bigger and more extreme objects.

His technique was to take large objects apart and break their metals and various components down into small pieces to consume, slowly chipping away at the object as a whole over time until he had completely finished it. He would lubricate his throat with a mineral oil, he claimed, to help prevent internal cuts and abrasions from the sharp edges on the items he ate.

The items he consumed ran the gamut of large household appliances and everyday objects. Occasionally, he performed paid publicity stunts, such as in one instance in 1981 when he was paid $5,000 by Lifestyles Bedrooms to eat an entire queen-size waterbed as part of a store promotion ("This 'Nut' Ate a Waterbed to Get His Name Recorded for Posterity"). However, his greatest achievement was eating an entire Cessna 150 airplane, a feat of consumption that he started in 1978 and finished in 1980.

Notable items that Michel Lotito ate throughout his lifetime include:

- 18 bicycles

- Seven TV sets

- Two beds

- 15 supermarket trolleys

- A computer

- A coffin

- A pair of skis

- Six chandeliers

- An airplane

By 1997, he had eaten nearly nine tons of metal over the course of his life. The *Guinness Book of World Records* featured him in their publication numerous times for his eating stunts, and, at one point, they officially deemed him the man with the "strangest diet." His unusual habit never seemed to have any short or long-term effects on his health throughout the course of his life. Lotito passed away of natural causes in 2007 ("Strangest Diet").

Chapter 9
Headless-Chicken Wonders

In the realm of sideshow, many geek shows used live chickens as props. Often, the geek mutilated or decapitated them to bring the shock factor to the act. Over time, the stereotype of a geek biting the heads off chickens became a standard motif in regards to what a geek show attraction was all about. Ironically there are several instances where headless chickens weren't merely discarded props but rather sideshow attractions themselves. They were also very much alive.

Headless Chicken Mania

An early occurrence comes from the spring of 1869, when a man by the name of N. Benedict purchased a headless chicken from his neighbor. The chicken had lost its head when Benedict's neighbor had decapitated a number of chickens in their yard, preparing them for market. The neighbor left for a moment and found that when she returned, one of the chicken corpses was missing. Upon searching around, she eventually located the chicken in the corner of her yard, standing upright despite having no head. Benedict heard about it and made his way over to see the chicken. Upon viewing it, he was so intrigued by the curiosity that he purchased the headless chicken to see how long it would live. He fed it with a syringe into the hole in its neck and exhibited it in the Blue Wing saloon in San Francisco. Benedict later ended up selling the chicken to the owner of a sideshow for $250. After changing hands again, the owners of the headless chicken formulated a plan to travel and attempt to sell it to P.T. Barnum. However, the chicken died on a steamboat after six weeks of transport, during which time it was not properly attended to ("The First Headless Chicken").

A year prior to that, in 1868, a man named Harmon Edgar, who worked as a cook at a hotel, exhibited a headless chicken. After chopping the heads off two chickens and throwing the bodies into the woodshed, he later discovered that one of the chickens had survived its decapitation after he found it walking around the barnyard. Edgar took the chicken, covered the wound with a sweet oil lubricant, and took to feeding the chicken by pouring food from a spoon directly down into what remained of its throat. He then began exhibiting the chicken. The *Columbian* newspaper on June 19, 1868, wrote of the occurrence, "Such cases have occurred before, but the chicken is a curiosity nevertheless" ("HEADLESS, YET ALIVE AND WELL").

Though the sight of a living chicken without its head might sound like a real novelty, we can find a number of such exhibitions taking place throughout history.

In the 1880s, Randolph Warrick and Henry Irving were arrested and charged with animal cruelty for exhibiting a headless rooster in public. Their defense was that it was an "ordinary curiosity" that they had merely purchased from a man in Richmond, Virginia, for $25. However, the judge stated that any creature without apparent brain had no doubt suffered, and, therefore, exhibiting it constituted cruelty. Irving was discharged and Warrick was fined $50 for the incident. After the case was over, Irving stated that they had previously hoped to sell the rooster to Barnum for $1,000 ("A Headless Rooster Alive a Year").

The exhibition and demand for headless chickens became so great at one point that the September 26, 1879, edition of the *Pantagraph* newspaper of Bloomington, Illinois, ran an article noting that a number of headless chicken sightings had been made of late, going so far as to call it a "mania." Morbidly, the article stated that rather than headless chickens occurring through happenstance, "various other parties in McLean county have devised every means to reproduce the wonderful curiosity." It then noted several success stories of those who succeeded in creating their own headless chickens. On the future of the attraction, the article concluded by saying, "The headless chicken mania no doubt will continue until the curiosity becomes a drag in the market and a chicken without any head is no more of a curiosity than a dog with his left ear gone" ("The Headless Chicken Mania").

Though the idea of a chicken with no head living for weeks or months on end may sound improbable, they were very much a real thing and quite popular. In such instances, a chicken is decapitated in a way where it does not bleed to death and just enough of the brainstem is left intact at the top of the spinal column for the chicken to remain living. Since the brain stem controls involuntary processes needed to sustain life, such as breathing and digestion, the chicken can, in some cases, survive. The chicken is able to move, as the small portion of the remaining brain is able to accommodate basic motor function, even though it no longer has the higher mental capabilities to care for itself ("A Headless Chicken").

This "headless chicken mania" of the late 1800s and the money paid by curious audiences led some people to devise some of their own techniques as they attempted to create their own living headless wonders.

In one 1879 instance, a cook named Albert Spacy saw a headless chicken on display at a local exhibition. He was so taken by what he saw that he examined the chicken up close, then went home to experiment on live chickens to see if he could replicate what he had seen. After six unsuccessful attempts, Spacy's calculated blow to his seventh chicken saw the animal flop around for a moment but then stand back up and begin walking around. He immediately plastered the chicken's neck with tar to prevent it from bleeding out, and the chicken remained alive for 24 hours. Curiously enough, the news stated that the local spectators in attendance that watched Spacy's work were so impressed that they "voted him a genius" for his efforts and temporary success. Spacy described his practice technique as trying to sever the head just right so that the brain stem and jugular vein were not cut, believing those were the key technical components to achieving the feat ("Headless Chickens").

As the desire for headless chicken exhibits spread, some desperate for their own attractions began to formulate techniques to create "gaffed" or phony headless chickens. Some media outlets also refused to believe that the exhibitions were completely authentic. A skeptical *Weekly Marysville Tribune* article from 1879 stated that that the technique for creating a headless chicken attraction was as follows: "We are told that the eyes are taken out and bill cut off. The head is then skinned back, bent around, and the skinned parts tarred over so as to give the appearance of being headless." The article went on to state that "We think it may safely be set down that a chicken cannot live after its head has been decapitated" and concluded that in regards to all the headless chicken exhibits popping up, "There must be some cheatery about these headless chickens" ("Live Headless Chickens").

When speaking to the *Times - Philadelphia* in 1883, showman W.F. Crowley discussed popular dime museum attractions of the time. He commented that "The headless chicken is a great fake." Crowley discussed a technique to create a fake headless chicken: "Pull the skin over the head and sew it there and feed it into the drop. If it lives a week, it will for months and be worth $50." The attraction was not only popular but quite lucrative at the time. "It's pretty well played in this part of the country," stated Crowley, "but if I was broke, I could take a headless chicken under my arm and start across the country and make my living" ("A MARKET FOR FREAKS").

Before they became highly successful circus entrepreneurs, even the Ringling Brothers exhibited a headless chicken as one of their attractions back in their early days ("Ringling Railroad Owner, Art Collector").

Mike, the Headless Superstar

Though the headless chicken mania of the 1870s and 1880s saw numerous exhibitions and media coverage, all of it was dwarfed decades later by the legacy of Mike the Headless Chicken, the most famous headless chicken of all time.

On September 10, 1945, farmer Lloyd Olsen was decapitating chickens while his wife cleaned them, as they routinely did. After he had finished decapitating a number of chickens, he noticed that one was still standing, though it had no head. Confused, he put the chicken in an old apple box so that it might expire on its own overnight. However, the next morning the chicken was still very much alive. Soon word spread about the bizarre creature, and Lloyd was approached by a sideshow promoter named Hope Wade. Wade visited Olsen and proposed that they all go on the road with the marketable attraction.

The chicken was soon rebranded as "Miracle Mike the Headless Chicken" by Wade and was taken on the road on the sideshow circuit, where he was a huge hit. The novelty also received extensive media coverage, such as being featured in *Life* magazine ("The Chicken That Lived for 18 Months without a Head"). Perhaps part of Mike's appeal came, in part, because an entire generation had passed since the prior headless chicken mania, lending to the perspective that Mike was more likely to be viewed as the first of his kind by the general public.

While on the road, Olsen would display Mike's head in a bottle of preservative fluid and talk about Mike while the chicken strutted around for the audience to see ("HEADLESS ROOSTER STRUTS HIS STUFF").

Mike and His Head.
https://upload.wikimedia.org/wikiped
ia/commons/b/bc/Mike_headless_chic
ken.gif

To keep Mike alive, his caretakers fed him with an eyedropper that released liquid food directly into his esophagus, and a syringe was used to clear mucus from his throat. While on the road, Mike actually gained weight and seemed in good health.

In early 1947, about a year and a half after Mike had lost his head, he began choking in the middle of the night while staying at a hotel in Phoenix, Arizona. The Olsens had left Mike's syringe at the sideshow that night and, despite their best efforts, they were unable to save him. He died that night ("The Chicken That Lived for 18 Months without a Head").

Decades later, Mike's legacy remains strong not only through the media coverage he has received but also with a major annual celebration. His hometown of Fruita, Colorado, hosts an annual festival in his honor.[1] The event features a 5K race, disc golf tournament, merchandise vendors, and various

---

1. www.miketheheadlesschicken.org

other attractions, all honoring the memory of Mike the Headless Chicken. Though the population of Fruita is only about 13,000, the festival averages about 18,000 attendees per year (Casal).

American rock band The Radioactive Chicken Heads also recorded a song about Mike called "Headless Mike." The accompanying music video features a rock-and-roll retelling of Mike's life story featuring the band members. Professional wrestler and sideshow entertainer Sinn Bodhi makes an appearance in the music video as well. In turn, the band has also appeared in events put on by Bodhi's professional wrestling organization, Freakshow Wrestling.

Quite an impressive run for a chicken without a head.

Statue of Mike the Headless Chicken in downtown Fruita, Colorado. Image courtesy of the City of Fruita.

Chapter 10

Professional Wrestling and Geeks

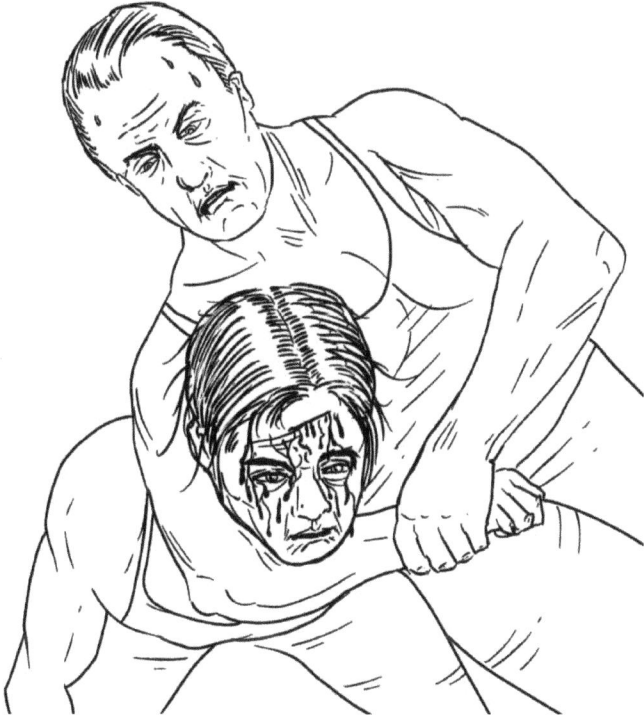

T hough it may sound surprising, professional wrestling has historical ties to and lasting subcultural commonalities with the carnival sideshow, particularly geek shows.

Professional wrestling in America started shortly after the Civil War as a form of live entertainment held at carnivals beginning in the late 1800s (Hester). Wrestling events often shared the fairgrounds with a number of sideshow attractions that were on the midway. Much of the operations were very similar– going from town to town, setting up, selling tickets, and providing a loosely scripted visual spectacle for the locals. There is a strong similarity in the entertainment type as well, with an over-the-top performance and a marketable gimmick accompanying mostly staged and exaggerated displays of entertainment. Both genres frequently use real and implied theatrical violence as a selling point. There was direct crossover at times, as there were sideshows that would sometimes have attractions that would allow locals to participate in challenge matches against touring professional wrestlers (Bodhi). In some cases, the locals even fought against animals, such as chimpanzees (Lewis 127-149).

Much of the language used among carnival workers and those in the professional wrestling business has intermingled, too, both in terms of the slang words used as well as the cant, or industry-specific dialect. In terms of slang overlap, there are words such as *mark*, which refers to a customer or fan who is highly prone to suggestion and hence easily able to manipulate into parting with their money. There is also the concept of *kayfabe*, which was used in both circles. *Kayfabe* is a somewhat complex philosophy that involves protecting the secrets of the business and its perceived realism. It is said to have started in the carnival, possibly as an inverted derivative of the word "fake." For wrestlers, *kayfabe* often means maintaining their characters and the storylines around the general public, even when not in the ring, to protect the credibility of the business and illusion of reality. If someone steps out of character or references the nature of the matches being "fixed" in some way, they are said to have broken *kayfabe*. The word is also said aloud in situations to indicate when people should stop talking about industry inside information when outsiders are present. To *kayfabe* someone means to withhold information from them ("Torch Glossary of Insider Terms"). Though the term is still in use to this day, the mainstream rebranding of professional wrestling as performance-based sports entertainment in the late 20th century coupled with the rise of social media in the early 21st century has made the concept of *kayfabe* less guarded than in generations past.

Regarding the cant, some career carnival folk adopted their own way of speaking that was unique to their subculture, which was known for its pronounced Z sounds. It was less a standalone language and more a distortion of American English, somewhat akin to Pig Latin. The cant is known by different names, most commonly carny, czarny, z-talk, or z-latin. There are variations on the carny way of speaking, but the common theme is inserting pronounced Z sounds into words, like "earz" before the first vowel sound of a word. In some cases, this sound is inserted into each syllable of a word (Winter

15-21).[1] When spoken fluently in conversation, it was difficult for outsiders to interpret what was said, allowing carnival workers to speak freely in front of the marks. The dialect also bled over into the locker rooms of pro wrestling and became common in certain professional wrestling territories (Blassie 16). During this period, the perception of professional wrestling being authentic was more veiled than it is today, and so some wrestlers would use carny talk as a means to call their matches and communicate with each other in the ring without the fans being able to decipher what was being said (Bodhi).

Playing off the sideshow geek's association with drawing blood and shocking audiences with gore during the climax of their performances, the term *geek* was used in professional wrestling as a verb to describe when a wrestler cut himself. To add excitement and brutality to big matches, a common practice among wrestlers was to conceal razorblades on themselves during matches and to inconspicuously cut themselves on the forehead to add blood as the matches picked up. When a wrestler did this to himself, he was sometimes said to have "geeked himself" ("Torch Glossary of Insider Terms"). A few years into the 21st century, this practice fell slightly out of favor in most mainstream wrestling circles. When it is utilized now, it is more commonly known as "blading."

Though the two forms of entertainment have largely drifted apart in recent decades, there are still wrestling promotions that hold events on local fairgrounds and occasionally utilize carnival/sideshow elements. Wrestlers utilizing unkempt wild man gimmicks have been common for generations, for example. In addition, there are also more direct crossovers in recent history that remind viewers of the shared interests and histories of the fan bases and entertainment genres.

During the late 1990s, touring sideshow revivalist Jim Rose shifted the direction of his show, The Jim Rose Circus, moving slightly away from modern interpretations of traditional sideshow feats and instead including more provocative acts like "Mexican Transvestite Wrestling." The professional wrestling shows were not always well received, however, as in one instance when the troupe was arrested after a show in Lubbock, Texas, on the grounds that the Mexican transvestite wrestlers' simulated sex acts on stage were a violation of local decency laws ("Lubbock police determine touring side show too freaky").

---

1. Example: "How are you doing today?" Becomes "Hearzow earzarearze yearzou dearzoing tearzodearzay?" Try out the carny speak generator: http://www.mapvi lle.com/carny/carny.php

Mainstream professional wrestling company World Wrestling Entertainment (WWE) has even integrated sideshow characters into their brand on several occasions. During the late 1990s, the WWE introduced a stable of wrestlers called The Parade of Human Oddities, a group that consisted of carnival freak show-style wrestlers who would dance around and come to the ring while a montage video of Tod Browning's *Freaks* played in the background. The group had numerous members come and go during its brief existence but lasted only about two years in the WWE.

Additionally, there have been a number of wrestlers throughout history that have all had careers related to or paid homage to the sideshow geek in some notable way.

"Classy" Freddie Blassie

Perhaps the most notable professional wrestler who relates to the carnival geek is "Classy" Freddie Blassie. Born in 1918 with a wrestling debut in 1935, Blassie made a career out of being a major heel in the professional wrestling business.[2]

Throughout his career, Blassie would frequently insult those he looked down upon by calling them "pencil-neck geeks." If a wrestler were to call his opponent a "pencil-neck geek" today, it would largely go unnoticed, the implication being that the wrestler was referring to his adversary as a scrawny dork, talking down to them and insulting their athletic prowess. Blassie, however, developed the catchphrase very early on in his career and was using it decades before the word *geek* had evolved linguistically. He was not using it from the standpoint of a jock condescending to a nerd; rather, he was using it as a means to equate the person with the lowest of the low on the carnival lot – a sideshow geek.

When Blassie started wrestling, he began by working wrestling shows at the local carnivals. He was immersed in the culture of the carnival and regularly encountered sideshow performers. During one wrestling show early in his career, one of his friends suggested that Blassie go check out the geek tent while he was waiting for his match. When he went in, he saw an emaciated geek biting the heads from live animals, stabbing himself with pins, and driving nails through his hands. After the show, Blassie's friend asked him what he thought of the geek show, and Blassie remarked, "Did you see what that guy looks

---

2. In professional wrestling, a heel refers to a wrestler who portrays a bad guy character. This is opposed to a babyface character, who plays the good guy ("Torch Glossary of Insider Terms").

like? He's got a neck like a stack of dimes. He's what you'd call a real pencil-neck geek." The "pencil-neck geek" line stuck and became his trademark (Blassie 17). It was said that the date in which Blassie coined the phrase was April 27, 1953 ("Phrase 'Pencil Necked Geek' Is Devised").

During his matches, Blassie even engaged in geek-like behavior, often drawing blood on his opponents and biting them on their heads. During promotional segments, he could be seen sharpening his teeth with a file. Some fans began calling him "The Vampire" because of these actions ("Freddie Blassie, Pro Wrestler Popular as Villain, Dies at 85").

Blassie also dabbled in music. In 1974, he went so far as to record a song called "Pencil Neck Geek," which received regular radio play on the *Dr. Demento Radio Show*. In the song, Blassie, in full character, sings about his extreme disdain for geeks and his desire to rid the world of them. Incredibly, the song and the airplay it received may have been at least partially responsible for shifting the meaning of the word *geek* away from the sideshow connotation and toward that of an insult of a socially inept weakling, as the word began shifting to its current meaning in the early 1980s (Patrin). In 1983, Blassie released a full-length album called *I Bite the Songs*.

His love for portraying a bad guy in wrestling and his professional adherence to *kayfabe* sometimes resulted in all-too-real occurrences. He was attacked on multiple occasions by enraged wrestling fans, stabbed more than 20 times, and even had acid thrown on him (Ryan). None of the attacks were successful, and Blassie stayed involved in the wrestling business as a manager and personality after retiring from in-ring competition. He passed away at the age of 85 in 2003, the same year that his aptly titled biography *Listen, You Pencil Neck Geeks* was released.

Abdullah the Butcher

Making his wrestling debut in 1965, Abdullah the Butcher (real name Lawrence Paul Shreve, born 1941) was known as a largely silent but incredibly violent adversary to his opponents in the ring ("Abdullah the Butcher Profile").

Though from Windsor, Ontario, Canada originally, he soon adopted the persona of a Sudanese wild man. Often called "The Madman from the Sudan," Abdullah weighed nearly 400 pounds during his career and was known for his extremely bloody battles. During his matches, he would brawl with opponents all over arenas and attack them with his weapon of choice: a fork. Abdullah's forehead is a testament to his violent career. It had been cut open with razorblades so often (from "geeking" himself) that deep grooves of scars prominently decorated the top of his head.

Frequently, his matches would not stay confined to the ring, as a bloody Abdullah and his opponent would brawl around the venue, often resulting in audience members fleeing in fear as the carnage migrated toward them, not unlike how audiences fled from bloody sideshow geeks running toward them during a roust.

Abdullah also demonstrated his taste for blood and madness during promotional opportunities. Playing up his madman character, he would occasionally eat raw meat and lightbulbs (Gervais 76). He also claimed to have also eaten live chickens and snakes throughout his career (G. Wood). In addition to a long career as a professional wrestler, he once owned a restaurant in Atlanta, Georgia, appropriately called Abdullah the Butcher's House Of Ribs & Chinese Food.

Abdullah the Butcher bloodying up his opponent, Andy Ellison, during a match in 2004. Marty555,CC BY-SA 3.0 <https://creativecommons.org/licenses/by-sa /3.0>. 2004. https://upload.wikimedia.org/wikipedia/co mmons/0/00/AbdullahTheButcher.jpg

Kamala

Born in Senatobia, Mississippi, James Harris (1950-2020) is best known by the name he used in the professional wrestling business: Kamala. For his wild man character, he wore a loincloth and had primitive "jungle symbols" painted on his face and body. He portrayed a hulking wild man from Uganda, frequently billed as "The Ugandan Giant." On his way to the ring, he would typically wear an exaggerated tribal mask, and one of his trademarks during his matches was to slap his belly while facing off against his opponents.

Kamala had many managers throughout his career but worked with "Classy" Freddie Blassie during the 1980s. During his time with Blassie, Kamala made an appearance on the World Wrestling Federation's talk show, *Tuesday Night Titans*, where he ate a live chicken during the program. In actuality, the chicken was not hurt, as the segment was scripted and carefully edited to make it look as though Kamala had eaten the chicken alive (Laroche).

The Wild Samoans

A notable pro-wrestling duo that used long-standing wild man gimmicks were The Wild Samoans. This tag team consisted of the real-life brothers Arthur "Afa" Anoa'i and Leati "Sika" Anoa'i. They started their wrestling careers in the early 1970s and gained popularity through the 1980s.

The two brothers very much fit their gimmick as intimidating wild men as they took the wrestling world by storm. Both weighed over 300 pounds, had large afros, and grew shaggy facial hair. To further cement their personas, the brothers did not speak when in character and their mannerisms included grunting, picking their noses, and eating raw fish. The duo made it to the WWE where they were managed by Captain Lou Albano, who would speak on their behalf during interviews. They had a successful run as a tag team, winning the WWE tag team championship multiple times before splitting up.[3]

After going solo, Sika enlisted the managerial services of professional wrestling manager Mr. Fuji. In one memorable televised segment from 1987, just before a match against Hulk Hogan, Sika stood in place with a dead chicken and began taking bites out of it, feathers and all, while Mr. Fuji cut a promo that sounded very much akin to the bally of what an outside talker would say at a geek show:

> *This is Sika! The Wild Samoan! Like all my men, he's a savage and he'll eat anything! And tonight, he'll devour Hulk Hogan. Eat! Eat! Eat! Eat!*

After retirement, the brothers opened up a professional wrestling training center in Florida, appropriately called The Wild Samoan Training Center. The brothers were inducted into the WWE Hall of Fame in 2007 ("The Wild Samoans").

---

3. At the time, the WWF. The World Wrestling Federation (WWF) changed its name to World Wrestling Entertainment (WWE) in 2002

Sinn Bodhi

For professional wrestler Sinn Bodhi, aka "The Warlord of Weird," carnival sideshow and wrestling are two genres that he has worked in both independently and in combination.

Ever since he was a child, Sinn Bodhi (real name Nicholas Cvjetkovich, born 1973 in Ontario, Canada) always loved circus and sideshow. Explaining how he spent his childhood, he said, "I spent a lot of time in this little ranch house, just kind of in my own brain reading comic books, watching pro wrestling – which, to me, was the real-live version of comic books, and I loved circus and I loved movies. Anything that would just really kind of let my imagination go wild, and I always was enamored by the whole running away to join the circus [idea]."

Bodhi would indeed go on to train and become a professional wrestler. Early in his wrestling career, he did stunts and acting in the film *Zombie Beach Party* (2003), where he met Scott McClelland, who also had a small role in the film. McClelland, who is perhaps better known by his stage name Nikolai Diablo, ran a successful sideshow in Ontario called Carnival Diablo. McClelland was in the market for a new strongman to add to his show, as his previous strongman performer was retiring. After hitting it off with Bodhi on set, he offered to bring Bodhi aboard his sideshow as the new strongman performer.

Though promoters billed him as a strongman, many of Bodhi's performances were more like pain tolerance acts. During his stint with Carnival Diablo, Bodhi performed feats such as smashing cinder blocks on himself, sitting in electric chairs, bending iron bars in his teeth, and acting as a human dartboard.

In 2008, Sinn Bodhi joined World Wrestling Entertainment on their *SmackDown* brand. Befittingly, he was given a carnival character gimmick and was known as Kizarny. His nationally televised promotional videos leading up to his debut even featured him speaking in carny, which Bodhi had learned how to speak years prior under his original wrestling trainer Ron Hutchison in Toronto. His stint in the WWE was short-lived, however, as he was released from the company in March 2009.

Right after his release from the WWE, Bodhi received a call from Jim Rose of The Jim Rose Circus, who pitched the idea of collaborating for a show. They teamed up with profession- al wrestling legend Jake "The Snake" Roberts in fall 2009 and went on tour with a show called "The Jim Rose Circus vs. Jake 'The Snake' Roberts," which pitted sideshow against profes- sional wrestling. The promotional release for the tour stated "When Legends Collide Tour: Pretty Girls, Wrestling, Amazing Circus Stunts, and... a FIST FIGHT!" ("The Jim Rose Circus vs. Jake the Snake Roberts").

Sinn Bodhi. Image courtesy of Karen Kreep and Sinn Bodhi.

Also in 2009, Bodhi fused profession- al wrestling and sideshow with a four-person troupe called the Dynamite Death Monkeys, which played at a number of concert venues, opening for bands. The performances consisted of comedy wrestling stage shows that incorporated various magic tricks and sideshow feats. Bodhi said the shows would start with some comedy magic and sideshow among the performers, then shift into a conflict that ultimately reached a climax with a wrestling brawl onstage. He described the show with his fellow entertainers:

> *I would show them a few different things to do and then at some point we would piss each other off and we'd have this very Tom and Jerry-esque kind of hardcore battle on stage. It wasn't in the ring; it was on a stage, and we would cap our set off with that. We would use very avant-garde wrestling weapon props, stuff that you wouldn't see on a wrestling show but stuff that we could morph into "oh, I haven't seen that before."*

Bodhi explained that rather than using the traditional tables and chairs that are com- mon in hardcore wrestling shows, they would use creative weapons that matched their brand, such as an eight-foot wooden staff they would produce out of thin air and use it as a bludgeoning weapon. Another move he utilized during the shows was a sideshow-inspired attack of hitting an opponent in the face with a whipped cream pie – filled with thumbtacks.

Bodhi found that the term "geek magician" was a good tongue-in-cheek way to describe his unusual style and blending of genres.

> *I refer to myself as a geek magician because a lot of the feats that I would do technically might not have fallen into the strongman pocket. Some stuff that I would do would fall into magic, some stuff would fall into sideshow, some stuff would fall into mentalism. So I just found it a key way to refer to myself as a geek magician because that was kind of cobbling up all sorts of little bits and pieces of circus, pro wrestling, sideshow, magic, and so forth.*

In addition to a catch-all term to describe what he did, he found it also worked well as a means to arouse curiosity.

> *I think that term just sounds like an ornier, more elusive term like "'What does it mean? What is he going to do?" So I kind of use that term as sort of a hook to make you the fan, the mark, the rube, the punter, curious of what I am going to do. So maybe when you see my face on a poster, you're like "Oh, I got to go see this. This guy is crazy! I know he always does weird stuff!" I kind of want you always on the tips of your toes.*

In 2011, Sinn Bodhi evolved the brand of the Dynamite Death Monkeys into his own Las Vegas-based independent wrestling promotion. Appropriately called Freakshow Wrestling, the promotion features both professional wrestlers and established sideshow performers/variety entertainers making appearances during live events. Occasionally, sideshow feats are even used as moves during matches in the ring as wrestlers battle one another. Bodhi calls it a "tornado of creativity and collaboration between cousin mediums," explaining:

> *Freakshow [in the beginning] was sort of a half-variety show, half farce. It was a farce in the sense that I would make fun of things I did not like about pro wrestling and then I would combo that with adding a variety of bur-*

lesque, magic, sideshow, music, things like that. Then somehow sometimes tie it all together, so some of it was very skit-ish.

Ultimately, Sin Bodhi continues to blend different genres into unique presentations for his professional wrestling career. He summed up his creative process as a performer by saying:

As a performer I think it is good to be a student of your industry and other cousin industries so you can sort of see what came before you and help you be inspired to, not plagiarized by any means, but be inspired, and take and borrow little pieces. If you borrow too much, you're a thief; if you borrow fractions of pieces and smash them together with other fractions of pieces, combo-ed with, I dare say, some original thought, there is true artistry (Bodhi).

The Boogeyman

Another contemporary wrestler who played the role of a modern geek-inspired performer is Martin Wright, who wrestled as The Boogeyman. During his matches as The Boogeyman, Wright would come to the ring wearing bizarre face paint and had bands of hair around his neck and arms. For his entrance, scary music played while he creepily made his way to the ring. In some instances, he would materialize in random places and scare those nearby. His appearance and character behavior was very much akin to that of a sideshow wild man.

However, what made him the most geek-like was his tendency to eat live worms before matches and sometimes even in the ring. He would carry them in a satchel with him to the ring and pull the worms out in large quantities, shoving them into his mouth by the handful. Wright appeared in the WWE off and on for several years throughout the mid-2000s before semi-retiring and settling into making occasional appearances at independent promotions, including Sinn Bodhi's Freakshow Wrestling.

Chapter 11

Geek Magic

There is an entire subgenre of magic known as "geek magic." This style of magic relates to doing shocking illusions intended to gross out spectators, eliciting a response much like that of a traditional geek show. These acts typically involve the presentation of the performer doing something destructive or disgusting to themselves, though as the name implies, geek magic primarily utilizes skilled trickery to achieve these effects rather than the literal physical execution found in many traditional sideshow feats. There was even a popular instructional DVD called *Geek Magic* released by magician Tomas Medina.

Theater professor and magician Rhett Bryson offers a concise perspective on what constitutes geek magic by saying, "It's unusual and repulsive magic" (Bryson, Interview).

Toronto magician Andy Blau, who performs as Zoltan the Adequate, often uses the term "geek magic" to describe elements of his performance style. As a veteran practitioner, he offers this definition of the phrase:

> *If you're presenting sideshow geek stunts and accomplishing them by trickery (rather than in actuality), I'd call that geek magic. More broadly, I'd define anything that makes the audience squirm as geek magic.*

As it relates to the thematic bleed-over between a traditional sideshow and geek magic, Blau states:

> *There is absolutely bleed. If I jam an icepick in my nose or I simulate jamming an icepick in my nose (with an icepick where the metal part slides into the handle), from the audience standpoint, is there a difference? And perhaps more importantly, does it matter? Most sideshow purists I know HAAATE people who simulate actual geek stunts – the worst seems to be people who fake sword swallowing (perhaps because it's particularly difficult to learn). They're okay with geek magic if it's obviously ridiculous (like cutting off a head, hopefully gorily, and then restoring the person to life), but regarding geek magic that simulates effects that are possible in actuality... the debate continues. (And a lot of that debate is around how it's presented: If I say up front I'm a magician and this is a magic show, I get a lot more latitude) (Blau).*

There are magicians who do violent acts with actual live animals, like Bartolomeo Bosco. Techniques exist that present these types of tricks with similar visuals but do not involve actual animal harm.

Dedi

What is widely regarded as the first ever instance in the recorded history of magic involved a geek-like Egyptian magician named Dedi (sometimes known as Djedi or Teta), who would decapitate animals and then restore them, bringing them back to life. The story of Dedi comes from the Egyptian Westcar Papyrus and dates back to 2500 BCE, where it recalled the time that he was brought to the pharaoh Khufu to perform his wonders. Dedi was purported to have a gluttonous appetite and consumed 500 loaves of bread, a shoulder of beef, and 100 jugs of beer every day. When he was summoned to perform for the pharaoh, Dedi was said to be 110 years old.

During the performance that the papyrus recalled, Dedi was asked to decapitate the heads of one of the prisoners. He refused, noting that ethically he could not perform the severed head restoration on "the noble herd." Instead, Dedi opted to perform with a goose. After severing its head, Dedi placed the body and head on separate sides of the temple, spoke some magic words, and soon the goose was restored. He then replicated the same feat using a pelican, concluding the performance by severing the head of an ox and restoring it as well (Christopher 1; "Westcar Papyrus: Khufu and the Magician").

Though the tale of Dedi has been an influential one on the history of magic, the nature of the story and lack of any additional evidence of Dedi's existence has led many to believe that his story is one of pure fiction ("History - American Museum of Magic").[1]

Donba Jutsu

In the history of Japanese magic, there exists an unusual trick called *Donba Jutsu*, which means "the technique of eating a horse" – that is, the magician eats a fully grown live horse onstage.

呑馬術

Donba Jutsu written in Japanese.

The exact origin of *Donba Jutsu* is one of ambiguity and debate. It is said to have first been performed by a magician named Chojiro Shioya, who performed the trick in various small theaters in Japan from 1688 until 1704 (Matsuyama 11).[2]

Intriguingly, very little information about Chojiro Shioya actually performing the act exists. An early program indicates that Chojiro was an accomplished coin magician (Matsuyama 35), though most early references to *Donba Jutsu* are based primarily on

---

1. Dedi is in the Society of American Magicians Hall of Fame.

2. Sometimes known as "Chojiro the Salt Vendor" (Marshall 51).

hearsay rather than firsthand accounts. The most notable comes from an essay titled "Kankonshiryo," which was written in 1826, well over a hundred years after Chojiro was said to have performed the act. The text of the essay noted that "Chojiro Shioya was a conjurer, of whom word had it that he excelled in deceiving people by swallowing not only various sizes of swords, but even a cow or horse" (Matsuyama 12).

There is a Japanese folktale that first appeared between 1288 and 1293 about a man named Choji Shiono who had a farm where he would butcher and eat horses. According to folklore, over time he began having nightmares about a horse that would force itself down his throat and inhabit his digestive system. Over time, Shiono died from the visions. There is speculation that perhaps when the magician Chojiro Shioya began performing centuries later, he either adopted a name similar to the character in this folklore on purpose or those who heard of him associated him with the folktale and created rumors about what his act entailed (Matsuyama 41-42). After Chojiro Shioya's death, the act fell into relative obscurity, but talk of its execution became that of legend.

In October 2009, traditional Japanese magician Shintaro Fujiyama brought the act into the modern era, performing the feat during a stage performance in Tokyo. After opening the show with traditional Japanese magic tricks, Fujiyama brought a live horse out on stage. He spent a moment petting the horse, then he said "I don't have to eat every day. Instead, I must eat a whole horse once every twenty days. I feel kind of bad, but I need to eat you so that I can live on." He then stretched the horse's head out, put the end of it into his mouth, and began to suck it in like a noodle. When he reached the neck, he broke it off, decapitating the horse. Fujiyama then moved on to consuming the other portions of the horse until the animal was gone (Marshall 48-51).

Though Fujiyama's reenactment certainly made waves in the magic community, there was no earnest revival of the act beyond that single exhibition. Nonetheless, the sheer strangeness of *Donba Jutsu* coupled with its vague historical context continues to fuel its mystique.

Dufour

Harry Houdini wrote about a Frenchman named Dufour whose act was described in Martin's *Naturliche Magie* in 1792. Dufour made his debut in Paris in 1783, and his act consisted of strange comedy magic involving eating large quantities of unusual things.

During his performances, Dufour would sit on stage and eat while brass musicians played background music. He would consume hot coals, large amounts of beef, and live animals. For dessert, he would eat the silverware and dishes. He also employed trained cats on stage that would be obedient during his show. However, he would have one of the cats misbehave during the performance, then during the end of his show, he would snatch the offender, tear it limb from limb, and devour the carcass. At that point, his musicians would stop playing and beg him to bring the cat back. Dufour would then dine on soap and water, pull the tablecloth from the table, cover his head briefly, then bring the cat back alive.

Houdini also noted a skit that Dufour performed using a live dog:

> *A dog had come in with a farmer, who was probably a confederate, and now began to bark. Since Dufour could not quiet him, he seized him, bit off his head, and swallowed it, throwing the body aside. Then ensued a comic scene between Dufour and the farmer, the latter demanding that his dog be brought to life, which threw the audience into paroxysms of laughter. Then suddenly candles reappeared and seemed to light themselves. Dufour made a series of hocus-pocus passes over the dog's body; then the head suddenly appeared in its proper place, and the dog, with a joyous yelp, ran to his master* (Houdini, Miracle Mongers 34).

Le Roy, Talma & Bosco

A successful touring magic show around the turn of the 20th century was a troupe consisting of Belgian-born magician Servais Le Roy, his wife Mary Ann Ford (stage name Mercedes Talma) (Caveney 25), and comedian Leon Bosco.

Servais Le Roy was born in 1865 and toured extensively in Europe. He was also quite popular in American vaudeville theaters with a show that consisted of big stage illusions, many featuring grand human and animal disappearances and reappearances. Le Roy's early signature style featured his assistants dressing up as imps, and he himself would occasionally dress as a devil for his performances. As a result, he would go on to adopt the nickname "The Devil in Evening Dress" (Caveney 28). Though he was part of numerous touring shows during his lifetime, the group of Le Roy, Talma, and Bosco proved to be among one of the most successful.

Servais Le Roy in 1915. Hartsook. University of Washington: Special Collections. 1915. https://upload.wikimedia.org/wikipedia/c ommons/9/92/Servais_Le_Roy%2C_vaud eville_entertainer_%28SAYRE_5307%29 .jpg

The supergroup was sometimes known as "The World's Monarchs of Magic" and "The Comedians de Mephisto Co." During the run of Le Roy, Talma, and Bosco, though, Le Roy and his wife Talma remained in the production consistently, there were actually up to nine different performers who played the role of the buffoonish Bosco character over the years throughout the troupe's lifetime (Caveney 58).

The original Bartolomeo Bosco, the influential Italian conjurer, he was known for several of his illusions, one of which involved removing and swapping the heads of different colored birds. Due to the multi-performer character association of the name Bosco, it is fitting that many years later, with the production of Le Roy, Talma, and Bosco, they also had numerous people assuming the role of bumbling Bosco and using the same moniker after the original Leon Bosco departed from the troupe.

Another tie-in was that in their Le Roy, Talma, and Bosco stage production, Bosco performed the same head-swapping trick with birds that Bartolomeo Bosco had done generations prior. In fact, it became one of the signature tricks of their production. However, the Le Roy, Talma, and Bosco presentation was a comedy act and was executed using a completely different and much more humane technique than the bird-killing Bartolomeo Bosco used. Their version involved dummy heads and concealing the actual birds' heads so that they were not harmed during the effect. Servais Le Roy first picked up the trick from magician Imro Fox, with whom he had previously toured. Imro Fox would do the trick by swapping out the heads of black and white pigeons. With Le Roy, Talma, and Bosco, they originally did the trick with black and white ducks, then later found a way to execute the trick with different types of birds, using a duck and a rooster. The much more extreme pairing greatly increased the comedic effect of the otherwise morbid illusion. Regarding the absurd visual, Le Roy himself noted, "They were unusually funny to look at and when we tried it out at the Empire Theatre, Sheffield, England, even I and my assistants had to laugh with the audience" (Caveney 68-69).

Though the company did not use fatal techniques with their birds, they were not immune from accusation. In 1917, when performing at the prestigious Palace Theater in New York, the American Society for the Prevention of Cruelty to Animals, who received an anonymous tip indicating that Le Roy and company had been killing birds during their shows, paid them a visit. Le Roy was outraged, but after the ASPCA inspector examined the animals backstage, he concluded in his report that the animals were well cared for and the charges against Le Roy were groundless (Caveney 187-188).

Their version of the illusion became so popular that even though Le Roy was protective of his methods, he later sold rights to the "duck and rooster effect" to the highly accomplished stage illusionist Howard Thurston. Though a popular effect, Thurston was the only man to whom Le Roy ever sold the rights of the illusion (Caveney 162; 230).

The particular version of the trick done with a duck and a chicken being decapitated and switching heads continues occasionally to this day. American stage magician David Copperfield has performed it, notably during his 1988 television special *David Copperfield X: The Bermuda Triangle Challenge*, and British magician Ali Cook performed it on the first episode of *Penn & Teller: Fool Us* in 2011.[3]

It's interesting to note the evolution of the name "Bosco" in show business through a relatively short time span, beginning with the accomplished Italian conjurer Bartolomeo Bosco and the imitators in magic that adopted the Bosco name to further their own careers, then onto Bosco the snake eater and his countless imitators. Eventually, the name became more associated with the bumbling comedian Leon Bosco and his ensuing replacements in a touring magic show. As for the bird head-swapping trick, not only has it largely become a much more lighthearted comedy act in tone, but the standard methods are now fully simulated with no harm coming to the birds themselves.

---

3. Interestingly, Ali Cook would later return to "Fool Us" in season seven, where he executed a mentalist trick that involved the old snake girl carnival illusion of a live woman's head on a snake's body.

Fielding West

Magician Fielding West (born 1949) does an act with doves that involves several illusions. After displaying a live dove, he crushes it down so that he can fit it into the palm of his hand. After reproducing the dove alive, he pulls on the dove's head and stretches out the neck until the head breaks off. He displays the head in one hand and the body in the other momentarily before restoring the bird to its living state. West has performed the act on numerous recorded television specials.

Harry Anderson

A notable entertainer who was vocal about his fondness for the sideshow geek was Harry Anderson (1952-2018). His legacy is one of a talented comedy magician and actor.

Anderson moved around a great deal as a young boy and developed a love for magic and the allied arts at an early age. As a young man, he frequently performed street shows, often under the guise of a street hustler parody persona called Harry the Hat. After graduating from high school, he opened up a magic shop in Ashland, Oregon, and began performing his unique blend of shocking comedy magic at bigger and more notable events as word of his name and skills spread (Hill).

Anderson was a fan not only of magic but also unusual entertainment, such as the sideshow geek. He would occasionally even reference the geek act specifically both in performances and in media appearances. In a 1986 interview, he noted that while he still attended carnivals and circuses on occasion, he was disappointed that geek shows had fallen the wayside, noting, "It's not like when they still had sideshows... when they still had geeks. There's nothing like seeing a guy bite the head off a chicken" (Devault).

As a practitioner of geek-style magic, he also occasionally used the "geek" moniker himself due to the shocking nature of some of his magic effects. However, he made a point to educate his audiences on occasion about the history of the sideshow geek. During one of his signature acts, he addressed the audience by saying "Let's talk geek..." then went into an explanation about the wild man biting the heads off of chickens or swallowing snakes on a sideshow midway. When he'd set the tone for shock, he'd then state that he was going to show the audience a geek trick. He'd then proceed to do a signature illusion of his where he appeared to stick a large needle through his arm (Anderson).

He later shifted gears in show business and became a successful actor, making numerous television appearances, most notably playing the character Judge Harry T. Stone on the show *Night Court*, which ran from 1984 to 1992.

Anderson also made several appearances on *Saturday Night Live*. During a hosting appearance on the show on February 9, 1985, Anderson parodied his transition from a geek magician to a television star. When he started his opening monologue, he stated that he was no longer "Harry the Geek" and noted that he was now a respectable television actor and had cleaned up his act as a result. A moment later, he concluded the monologue by pulling out a live guinea pig from a box, then proceeded to eat it in front of the studio audience ("Saturday Night Live - February 9th, 1985").

Anderson wasn't just interested in doing shocking illusions in the same thematic vein of the geek show but also in performing illusions based on exactly what a true sideshow geek would do with live animals. That particular illusion is known as "The Guinea Pig Box" and was first created around 1945 by Loyd Made, a magic company owned by inventor Edward Loyd Enochs (1897-1968). The version that Harry Anderson used and popularized throughout his career is a refined design produced by Viking Mfg. Co (Robinson Jr.).

Other entertainers have gone on to perform The Guinea Pig Box illusion as well, perhaps most notably Las Vegas magician Mac King, who also performs another geek-like illusion involving feigning to eat a goldfish made of carrot, then spitting out a live goldfish into a glass of water. King has performed both tricks during national television appearances.

Around the turn of the 21st century, Harry Anderson largely stepped away from acting and moved to New Orleans. While there, he and his wife Elizabeth opened a magic shop called Sideshow as well as a nightclub called Oswald's Speakeasy, where he regularly performed his magic show. Shortly after the devastation of Hurricane Katrina in 2005 and the ensuing economic impact, he and Elizabeth relocated to Asheville, North Carolina, where he lived out his final years (Hill).

Magic Brian

There are also some entertainers who perform contemporary parodies and tributes to the geek act without using any live creatures at all. One such example is variety performer

Magic Brian (born 1971), who has a comedy magic geek routine involving a unique presentation on the classic "torn and restored" magic trick. Brian describes his act thusly:

> *My act is a comedy homage to the traditional act. I give a brief description of what the actual act was, say I am going to be doing my tribute to this classic act using a rubber chicken. I make a big deal that it's a "real rubber chicken" and if they do not have strong stomachs, they should look away. I proceed to bite off the head with blood pouring out, I then drink the blood from the head and neck, then I say, because I am a magician I will restore the chicken back to its former state. I do this by chewing up the head and spitting it back up on to the neck. The rubber chicken is completely restored as good as new... aside from all the blood* (Brian).

David Blaine

Magician David Blaine (born 1973) is primarily known for his street magic television specials, where he does close-up magic for passersby on the street. The specials are very hands-on with the people he interacts with, and he has done several tricks in his specials over the years that contain very geek-like illusions. In one, Blaine referenced the ancient Egyptian magician Dedi and how he was able to remove and restore the heads of birds. Blaine then reproduced the act with a chicken for passersby on the sidewalk, much to their horror. In another special, Blaine presented an illusion where he acquired a live snake and seemingly ate it alive. A moment later, the snake reappeared unharmed in a spectator's backpack.

He has also gained much attention as an endurance artist, engaging in numerous high-publicity and very real stunts. They have included:

- Being buried alive for a week

- Encasing himself in a block of ice for 63 hours, 42 minutes, and 15 seconds

- Standing on a 22"-wide pillar 100 feet in the air for 35 hours, then concluding the stunt by jumping off into a stack of cardboard boxes

- Fasting for 44 days straight while living in a plexiglass box suspended 30 feet in the air

- Holding his breath for over 17 minutes

- Floating up more than 20,000 feet into the air by way of holding 52 helium-filled balloons, then releasing himself from the balloons and parachuting down to the ground

Though his performance style is not restricted to magic tricks and feats of endurance, Blaine has been greatly influenced by several notable historical performers, whom he has successfully been able to emulate. One is "The Human Aquarium," Mac Norton, and another is "The Human Volcano," Hadji Ali. David Blaine read about Norton through an account written by Houdini and had seen footage of Ali from the film *Politiquerias*. He then endeavored to learn the internal control needed to replicate the unique regurgitation acts. It wasn't until Blaine saw viral footage online of a man water spouting with extreme force that he was able to finally push toward his goal. After putting out a number of posters to search for the man in the video, Blaine eventually tracked the man's location and traveled to Africa to meet him. The man's name was Winston Carter, and he worked as a security guard and lived in a small village in Liberia. Carter met with Blaine and showed him secrets to developing stomach control. After training with Carter, Blaine returned home and was eventually able to develop the skills needed to spout water. Blaine's quest and footage of him training with Winston Carter can be seen in Blaine's 2013 special, *Real or Magic*. After continuing to refine his new internal control with spouting, he moved onto learning it with frogs, like Mac Norton. Blaine has gone on to perform the "Human Aquarium" act, regurgitating live frogs in numerous television appearances and during his live stage show. When interviewed, Blaine makes a point to credit Mac Norton as the originator and his inspiration for the unusual performance piece (Wright).

Blaine then went on to master Hadji Ali's "Human Volcano" feat. For this, he drinks copious amounts of water, then drinks kerosene and blows a fireball to ignite a nearby object. A moment later, he spouts out a constant stream of water to extinguish it. Blaine performed the full replication of the trick on *Jimmy Kimmel Live* in 2013. During his touring show, he wisely modified the trick slightly so that he held the kerosene in his mouth and executed a traditional fire blast by spitting it out rather than swallowing it completely before spitting it back out (Rogan).[4]

In addition to learning Mac Norton's "Human Aquarium" regurgitation act with frogs and Hadji Ali's "Human Volcano" act, David Blaine has learned and performed a number of other sideshow-style shock stunts, such as sword swallowing, sewing his lips shut, and sticking an ice pick through his hand. However, unlike traditional geek magic, Blaine does many of the feats for real rather than through means of illusion, blurring the lines between magic and reality. He has also been known to occasionally post geek-like content on his social media channels, such as showing live bugs crawling out of his mouth. It seems that even when one is highly successful in show business, a little geek flair now and then can help keep things lively.

---

4. Much of the danger involved with oral-based fire arts is not just the immediate hazard of potentially being burned but rather the long-term ramifications of exposing the body's mucus membranes to highly carcinogenic fluids. Naturally, having kerosene just in the mouth, while still potentially very harmful to the body, is much less harmful than actually drinking it and allowing it to sit in the stomach for a period of time.

Chapter 12

The Collegiate Goldfish Swallowing Championship of 1939

These days, it is not uncommon to see gross-out challenges sweeping the nation. Fueled by viral Internet videos and reality television shows, the ability to view and participate in such challenges is simple. However, there was one major geek-like challenge that predated such technology and bizarrely swept college campuses across the nation, including Ivy League institutions. Over the course of about a month, it repeatedly made national news and evolved into an intense and popular competition – The Collegiate Goldfish Swallowing Championship of 1939.

It all started on March 3, 1939, when a Harvard University freshman by the name of Lothrop Withington Jr. boasted that he could eat a live goldfish. Soon, a bet was made; if he could do as he claimed in front of his peers, he would win $10. Withington made good on his promise and won the bet by eating a live goldfish in the dining hall while spectators looked on. As a means to put an exclamation mark on his victory, he started drinking water out of the bowl from which he had obtained the fish, remarking that "Fishbowl water is good, too" ("Swallowing Live Goldfish Wins $10 Bet at Harvard"). He stated afterward that "...the scales caught on my throat a bit as it went down" ("HE SWALOWED LIVE GOLDFISH").

Word of Withington's unusual feat soon spread not only among the Harvard campus but across national news outlets. Before long, other college students thought to not only try the feat themselves but attempt to best one another in terms of the number of goldfish they were able to consume in a single sitting. Soon, the phenomenon exploded into an intercollegiate competition.

The first to receive credit for besting Withington was a Franklin and Marshall College student named Frank Pope, who swallowed three live goldfish on March 20, 1939. When asked for his motivation for outdoing Lothrop, Pope said, "I did it to show up those Harvard bums and sissies" (Brubaker 10).

Rather than defend his crown, Lothrop Withington Jr. respectfully bowed out of the competition early on. After hearing of Pope's achievement, Withington told the press, "This is getting to be too big a snowball for me to push. He can have the title" ("Harvard Student Quits Goldfish-Gulping Race").

Frank Pope's victory was short-lived, however, when on March 22, 1939, a fellow Franklin and Marshall student named George Raab took the title by swallowing six live goldfish. When asked to comment on his new title, Raab snarkily stated, "I did it just to show Frank Pope how simple his stunt was and to show him that he is a sissy." He also noted that he ate his fish completely naturally, alleging that Pope had salted and peppered his to make them easier to stomach ("F. & M. Wrestler Downs Six Live Goldfish And Becomes New Champion Of Gulpers"). However, Raab did fall ill after his achievement and ended up in the hospital ("Goldfish Gulper's Condition Fair; College Head Denies Suspensions").

Harvard soon took the title back when sophomore Irving Clark Jr. took the lead four days later, swallowing 24 live goldfish.[1] University of Pennsylvania's Gilbert Hollandersky then bested that with 25 the following day. The University of Michigan's Jules Aisner promptly beat that with 28, then Donald V. Mulcahy of Boston College set the bar with 29 (Sann 42). Albert E. Hayes of the Massachusetts Institute of Technology made the front page of the school newspaper on March 31 for setting a new record with 42 fish ("Albert E. Hayes, Jr. '42, Crowned New Champion"). At that point, new records were set nearly daily from colleges across the United States as the competition heated up and the press ate up the mania and one-upsmanship of the unusual challenge.[2]

As one might expect, the behavior and the widespread popularity it was receiving was not taken well by college administrators, who often sought to punish students who participated in the craze. In the case of Howard Francis, a freshman at Kutztown State Teachers' college, who (very briefly) held the record at 43 goldfish, he was actually suspended from school by the dean for "conduct unbecoming a student in a professional preparation course." Not only was the school upset by his actions, but the goldfish-swallowing competition had become such a source of interest among students that when word got out that Francis was going to attempt to break the record, numerous students skipped class to witness his attempt, nearly emptying some classrooms. The dean took this campus-wide learning interruption into account when issuing the suspension ("GOLDFISH GULPERS SUSPENDED BY SCHOOL").

The fad became so noteworthy that it received coverage in *Life* magazine. A new dance move called "Doing the Goldfish" that involved pantomiming swallowing a live goldfish even emerged ("Collegiate Goldfish Eaters").

By the end of March, things had gotten so out of hand that the state of Massachusetts brought forth legislation as a means to put an end to the competition. The bill authorized investigating instances of live goldfish eating and was written as a means to "preserve, conserve, and protect the breeding grounds of goldfish and protect them from cruel and wanton consumption" ("Seek Legislative Probe For Goldfish Protection").

---

1. Years later, Irving Clark Jr. made the claim that after his initial feat, Robert Ripley of Ripley's Believe it or Not offered him $250 a week to compete in goldfish-swallowing contests in New York, but Clark opted to stay at Harvard ("'Gobbler' Recalls Goldfish Swallowing").

2. No pun intended.

The "Doing the Goldfish" dance, created by college students Ruth Allen and Jay Jerome of the Massachusetts Institute of Technology.

Step 1: The Gulp - Swallowing the fish.

Step 2: The Interview - Discussing the fish-eating feat.

Step 3: The Moaning Low - Showing the wriggly after-effect.

Illustration based on photos and descriptions found in the April 9, 1939 edition of The "St. Louis Post-Dispatch."

The bill was not enough to end the competition, as shortly after that, a women's division materialized. Marie Hansen of Missouri University was the first to claim the title of the women's division champion after downing a goldfish and making headlines. She was soon bested by Mary Monroe, a sophomore at State Teachers' College in Springfield, Missouri, who was reported to have consumed two (Hutsell 2). The *Des Moines Register* later noted, however, that "A coed in West Texas claimed the girl's title by downing three goldfish," and indicated that a zoologist had been consulted projected the maximum amount of possible goldfish consumption by estimating the physical limit of the human stomach at 150 goldfish ("A Few Fads and Follies of an Earlier Day"). The women's division title ultimately went to Scottie Hunnicutt of the Texas College of Mines for her achievement of swallowing three live fish. Hunnicutt achieved the title during an organized "fishathon" that was held in the college gymnasium on April 5. While her male counterparts were busy downing goldfish, she casually walked onstage, said "Give me one," smiled, and proceeded to eat three fish. Her calm demeanor resulted in her being called the "dark horse" of the competition, as she secured the win for the women's division ("Dark Horse Co-Ed Grabs Goldfish Swallowing Title").

The craze also gave some a taste for other creatures. In one instance, a 17-year-old named Elmer Brunner, no doubt taking advantage of the mainstream news coverage of the recent collegiate goldfish swallowing, made news for swallowing a live cockroach and boasting to the press that he would attempt to swallow 25 of them during a public exhibition if he could locate that many ("HERE'S ANOTHER! YOUTH SAYS HE'LL EAT 25 ROACHES"). Over at the University of Illinois, a freshman named John Poppelreiter swallowed five white baby rats, dipping them in mayonnaise and eating them in front of his fellow Pi Kappa Phi fraternity brothers ("Goldfish, Angleworms, Now It's White Rats").

Just about a month after it had begun, the overall intercollegiate competition had escalated to absurd heights and its participation began to wane. As the novelty wore off and the dust began to clear, it was time to settle upon a champion. A pre-veterinary student from Middlesex University named Gordon Southworth pulled to the lead and took the intercollegiate title after he consumed an incredible 67 live goldfish during a demonstration. After word of his achievement spread, the University's president issued a statement that Southworth would be punished for his stunt. Ultimately, in early April 1939, the college officials were so intrigued by what he had done, however, that as a means to productively discipline him, they made him into a human guinea pig to study his digestive capabilities. A test was conducted where scientists (among a crowd of 90 students) inserted tubes from his mouth to his stomach to take gastric samples of his fasted and fed stomach states at different intervals. When they were done, they concluded that Southworth's digestion was nearly twice as rapid as that of the average person, and that likely contributed to his ability to consume such a high number of goldfish in a single sitting ("DIGESTION IS FAST, THAT'S WHY HE CAN SWALLOW GOLDFISH").

On March 31, 28 days after the craze began, over at the Wyomissing Polytechnic Institute, a student came forward to break the goldfish-swallowing record but became nervous before making the attempt. Fortunately, one of his peers, a 19-year old student named Neil Keim, stepped up as his stand-in and managed to swallow 74 live goldfish in 22 minutes while at the office of a local newspaper. After he set the new record, Keim remarked, "Now the boys in the big-league colleges have something to shoot at." His mother, however, was less than enthused. When asked about her son's achievement, she stated, "I'm very much disgusted, and my faith in higher education is crushed" ("GOLDFISH GULPING TITLE NOW AT 74").

As seemingly unbeatable as Keim's feat was, however, his record was beaten by Clark University student Joseph Deliberato one day later, who was ultimately dubbed the final Collegiate Goldfish Swallowing Champion of 1939 after winning the contest with an astounding 89 goldfish ("Gold Fish Eating Athlete Sets New Gulping Record"). However, controversy soon arose.

Though numerous news outlets reported Joseph Deliberato as the winner and some contemporary reports of the goldfish-eating craze of 1939 also indicate him as the victor, Deliberato didn't eat any goldfish. Rather, it turns out that his victory (which was reported on April 1), was actually the result of an April Fool's joke that got out of hand. Some in the press were noble enough to issue a correction to the competitive standings, such as the *Paducah Sun-Democrat*, which stated in their April 4, 1939 edition that "Southworth regained the intercollegiate championship when Joseph Deliberato's record of 89 proved a myth" ("Looks Like The Press Ate A Lot More That Day Than Deliberato").[3]

There was also the case of the surprisingly underreported achievement of Oather Morper, head cheerleader at New Mexico State College. In the April 3 edition of the *El Paso Herald-Post*, Morper bragged that he could swallow 75 fish in 20 minutes, claiming

---

3. The "Paducah Sun-Democrat," apparently not privy to Neil Keim.

that his previous feats included eating four salt wafer crackers in 30 seconds, drinking four quarts of milk in 12 minutes, and drinking 15 bottles of soda in seven minutes ("Cheer Leader At N. M. College Challenges Mines Fish Gulpers"). Morper allegedly ended up swallowing 101 goldfish to obtain the championship title ("Remember?").

Intriguingly, yet somewhat unsurprisingly, the fad became so popular that it gained participation from beyond the campus quadrangle. In one case, a 50-year-old World War I veteran named Sam Copenheaver announced to the press his intention of participating in a public goldfish-swallowing exhibition "just to put those college boys in their place" ("Yorker To Try For Goldfish Eating Title").

The event occurred on April 3, 1939, at the York Court House steps in Pennsylvania. The public interest for the show was so strong that an estimated 2,000 people showed up to watch Sam Copenheaver. The audience was so massive that it overflowed from the courthouse sidewalk onto the street, causing traffic delays. The city enlisted law enforcement officers to assist with getting Copenheaver into position and to keep the crowd under control. He was able to consume 55 goldfish before the large crowd became so unruly that he had to stop and make his escape by hailing a taxi. Copenheaver later remarked, "I could have consumed a lot more if I had not been hampered by the crowd" ("2,000 See Goldfish Gulping Show On Court House Plaza").

Evidently unimpressed by the college students and laymens' attempts, there were a few professional human ostriches and geek-style performers who stepped up to the plate.

On April 11, 1939, at the Silver Dollar Bar nightclub in Boston, Massachusetts, professional glass eater and razorblade swallower Lou Ascol decided to set a new gold-fish-swallowing record on stage. During the performance, he was able to consume 127 fish total, often expertly eating up to three at a time, salting and peppering them before chasing them down with beer.[4] Ascol bragged that he could have eaten up to 200, then promptly concluded the performance by swallowing pieces of a photographer's lightbulb ("Goldfish Swallowing 'Goes Pro,' Night Club Performer Gulps 127").

The fact that competitive goldfish swallowing was not just being done by college students anymore and now had serious performers such as Ascol led the *Boston Globe* to note on April 12 that "Goldfish gulpin' went professional" ("Goldfish Swallowing 'Goes Pro,' Night Club Performer Gulps 127"). The *Lansing State Journal* echoed the tongue-in-cheek sentiment by agreeing that after Ascol's show, "Goldfish gulping became

---

4. Some newspaper sources indicate his final number being 128.

a professional sport" ("Goldfish-Gulping Professional Now"). At that point, competitive goldfish swallowing had transcended being a mere fad and morphed into a cultural zeitgeist of sorts.

The very next day, another professional eater named Cyrus Gingrich outdid Lou Ascol. Gingrich had made a reputation for himself by staging unusual eating performances throughout the 1920s and 1930s, often at the local Lebanon fairgrounds in Pennsylvania ("Cyrus Gingrich Dies From Heart Attack Saturday Evening"). During these exhibitions, Gingrich did human ostrich performances, eating unusual things such as razorblades, electric lightbulbs, and cigarettes. He was said to also perform the feat of bending dimes with his teeth ("ACTIVITIES At ATTERBURY"). Gingrich also did eating challenges, not only eating strange things but also consuming large volumes of food. Some of his highlights included allegedly eating 120 eggs in 33 minutes, eating 300 oysters in 40 minutes, and eating 100 frankfurters in 52 bites. He claimed to train by chewing glass to help enhance his appetite and by sharpening his teeth to help bend coins more easily ("ATTERBURY HAS EATING WONDER").

During his goldfish-eating attempt, Gingrich ate a whopping 140 goldfish in front of more than 200 people at a local taproom in Lebanon, Pennsylvania.[5] It took him two hours and 35 minutes. He seasoned the fish with salt and pepper and drank orange juice, beer, and water during the spectacle. Halfway through the attempt, he also ate bread, his logic being that it would prevent the fins and scales from sticking to his stomach. Gingrich, who was 37 at the time, gave his thoughts on the goldfish-swallowing craze that had been sweeping university campuses. "These college boys are sissies," he said, further remarking, "Why, fifteen years ago, I ate fifteen goldfish in a taproom, then drank the water from the bowl and started to eat the bowl when the proprietor stopped me" ("'Unemployed WPA Worker' Swallows 142 Fish at Lebanon").

Gingrich died of a heart attack in 1951 at the age of 49. In his death announcement, the *Daily News* in Lebanon noted that he was a World War II veteran serving with the 72nd General Hospital and that he previously operated a local roadside market. The announcement reflected on his extraordinary eating feats and noted that when it came

---

5. Some newspaper sources indicate this figure at 144. The article cited here indicates the number 142 in the title, but 140 in the body text. In any event, it is safe to say that his final number fell somewhere within the low to mid 140s.

to goldfish eating contests, he "at one time was a claimant to the world's title" ("Cyrus Gingrich Dies From Heart Attack Saturday Evening").

Like many novelty trends, the appeal of the competition was short-lived. By mid-April 1939, the participation and news coverage of competitive goldfish swallowing began to dry up. However, even though interest in continuing with the competition had passed, the memories of the competition and press coverage of the participants remained in recorded history – which, in some cases, was a point of frustration later on for the competitors.

Collegiate Regret

Thirteen years after the collegiate craze ended, in 1952, the *Daily News* in New York ran a story reflecting on the impact and interviewed a number of key participants.[6] Somewhat unsurprisingly, a number of them, then older and settled into professional careers, did not reflect on their involvement in the fad with fondness.

Irving Clark Jr., who was practicing law in Seattle, commented "I am hesitant to go into that" when asked about his past goldfish consumption, further remarking, "Naturally, it has been the cause of some embarrassment" (McHarry 64).

Women's Championship participant Marie Hansen looked back on her involvement and noted "I guess I'll never live it down." She commented that she "wouldn't dream of eating one of those little things today" (McHarry 64).

Erroneously credited overall champion Joseph Deliberato noted that he never had any desire to actually eat a live fish and was nearly expelled for his fabrication of saying he consumed 89. "It was another student's idea of a publicity stunt, and the dean was ready

---

6. Curiously, the "Los Angeles Times" featured an article in 1969 profiling a teacher named Fletcher Flynn who claimed to have started the craze at Harvard back in 1931, when he wrote a stage production that involved one of the actors pretending to eat a live goldfish on stage, which was actually a carrot. Flynn told the Times that people thought it was real, and the fad caught when Yale students tried to best them and it spread. However, the report predates the actual competition by eight years, and Flynn's own claim of the origin seems to be the only source. It was most likely an unrelated incident that did not influence the later craze ("Teacher Inspired Fad of Gulping Goldfish").

to throw me out. I had to prove that I was home visiting my mother at the time," he said (McHarry 64).

The article does contain several interesting bits of information, however. In doing their diligence to track down Lothrop Withington Jr., the man who kicked off the craze, the reporters were able to find his father, Lothrop Withington Sr., who was rather upset that his son's goldfish-eating days were about to be brought back up into the public eye. He reluctantly gave the reporters the information needed to track down his son. As it turned out, Lothrop Withington Jr. had left Harvard just a year after the craze, in 1940, and joined the Air Corps. Upon leaving that in 1945, he settled down and started a family. While his goldfish-eating days were behind him, he was still willing to discuss the whole phenomenon and even admitted to eating a couple live goldfish at a party right after he had joined the Air Corps. At the time of the interview, he was still receiving a considerable amount of fan mail about his goldfish-eating days.

Withington noted that he felt his achievement was more authentic than many of his imitators as he didn't just simply swallow the fish whole like the others. Many of those who were vying for the record simply swallowed the fish as quickly as possible, as indicated by many of the competitors themselves.

One of the previous swallowers going for the title was a Boston College junior named Donald V. Mulcahy, who briefly held the record at 29 fish, a feat which he set in front of 300 spectators. In looking back on the achievement, Mulcahy described the swallowing technique he used to accommodate so many fish: "It's very simple. You lay the goldfish well back on the tongue, let it wiggle forward till it hits the top of the throat, then give a big gulp. It is almost the same as eating a raw oyster."

Withington, however, used a much different technique. "I chewed them," he said. "Stayed down better that way. Not very pleasant to taste. Rather slippery and very bitter."

Modern sideshow performer and former goldfish eater Reggie Bügmüncher also noted the superiority of the chewing technique, particularly when working with larger goldfish. "As they are going down your throat, they will start to panic if you swallow them whole, and their gills are very sharp and they will start opening," she explained. "I got my throat cut up pretty bad one time, but from then on I just chewed before I swallowed" (Bügmüncher).

During the 1952 interview with Withington, the reporters offered him a live goldfish to see if he would be willing to relive his college days and consume the goldfish for their story. He declined (McHarry 64).

Withington's popularity for originating the strange fad during his college days stuck with him throughout his life. In another interview in 1967, when explaining his feat, he said that it was "Mind over matter," continuing, "I didn't mind and the fish didn't matter" (Sann 42).

Ultimately, with no central source of reporting, conflicting declarations of a victor, non-collegiate participants later joining in, and instances of false claims, it is difficult to ascertain exactly who was the undisputed champion of The Collegiate Goldfish Swallowing Championship of 1939. However, given the nature of the competition and the nearly universal regret felt by the student competitors later in life, it could be said that, in the end, none of the participants emerged as any sort of victor.

Competitive Goldfish Swallowing in Later Years

Though no subsequent occurrences could possibly match the media frenzy of 1939, competitive goldfish swallowing has since been revived in a few isolated instances and organized record attempts.

On May 1, 1968, during a goldfish-swallowing contest at St. Joseph's College, Dan Cavuto of Philadelphia consumed 269 fish ("Goldfish Supply Wiped Out By Swallowing Contestants").

The following year, in early 1969, a 19-year-old college student from Texas named Charles Winfield downed 210 goldfish in one hour and 40 minutes as part of an activities week stunt at St. Mary's University ("Good Old Goldfish Swallowing Revived").

On April 28, 1974, the Century Square shopping center in Los Angeles held an event called the "Oddball Olympics," where a 24-year-old man named John Parker consumed 250 goldfish.[7] Some press promoted this as a new record, indicating that the previous record was 225 ("Oddball Olympians Perform").

In early April 1973, a Bennett Senior High School senior in Salisbury, Maryland, named James A. Hill swallowed 250 live goldfish during an All Sports Night held at the school (Cooper 1).

---

7. Many sources indicate the figure as 300 fish. This is possibly due to the fact that he succeeded in breaking the alleged record of 225 after announcing his intention of eating 300.

On October 12, 1975, a 24-year-old store clerk from Oakland, California, named Leonard McMahan swallowed a seemingly improbable 501 live goldfish in just under four hours. The event was a part of an organized world record attempt with multiple participants and was sponsored by Oakland's Tropical Fish Hut, which donated around 3,000 goldfish to the contest. The contest ended when the organizers ran out of fish. The top five finishers were Leonard McMahan (501), Steve Collins (441), Terrance Keenan (315), Tom Grace (247), and John Burnaford (225) (Waugh 5).

However, several years earlier on April 7, 1972, a 22-year-old DePaul University graduate student named Bob Gries is said to have set the world record by swallowing an unbelievable 601 goldfish. During his achievement, Reggi Nowak and Linda Levi also set the new women's record by each downing 155 ("Goldfish Eating Record Set By DePaul Student").

Though they had officials on hand at some of the early organized competitions, Guinness World Records no longer recognizes attempts at goldfish swallowing.[8] Their last official recognition of the record came from the 1973 edition of the book, where they list the official record as 225 set by Roger Martinez at St. Mary's University in San Antonio, Texas, on February 6, 1970 (Guinness World Records).

Much like the challenges associated with declaring a winner to The Collegiate Goldfish Swallowing Championship of 1939, it is also difficult to ascertain what the current world record is for live goldfish consumption. Conflicting record claims, exaggerations, lack of consistent reporting, elimination of official recognition, and changing public acceptance on such record attempts make determining the actual current world record of live goldfish swallowing difficult. Perhaps the history surrounding the record is more intriguing than what the final number may actually be.

---

8. When writing to Guinness for information on their last official recognized figure on this record, they made a point to emphatically preface their response by stating in bold that "This title is no longer monitored by us due to a stronger policy on the welfare and better treatment of animals."

Chapter 13
Controversies and Decline of The Geek Show

W hile it seems obvious that modern audiences would reject the notion of a traditional glomming geek show, it would be erroneous to say that geek shows were
widely accepted and without controversy even during their peak. Though geek shows
were quite common on carnival midways during the early to mid-20th century, they were
often closed down by local city authorities, and many carnival managers refused to book
geek acts due to their vile nature (Boles 29). But even when they did manage to get
booked, controversies occasionally arose at every stage of the act's development as a staple
of carnival entertainment.

Despite the popularity of his character, even performers portraying Bosco the Snake Eater found themselves at the center of controversy. In 1902, a Bosco was eating snakes in a tent in San Bernardino, California. When authorities heard of his performance, they decided to charge him with animal cruelty. However, Bosco caught wind of this and left town before the warrant could be issued ("Warrant Out for Snake-Eater"). The following year, Kansas (Bosco's place of origin) passed legislation which prohibited eating snakes. This was a direct result of public "Bosco" demonstrations happening in the area ("Snake Eating in Kansas").

Interestingly, a show by Snake-Oid resulted in a legal debate over the legislation. While in Kansas in 1911, Snake-Oid was performing his act where he would swallow live snakes. The sheriff caught wind of this, obtained a warrant, and confronted the performer. However, Snake-Oid's style differed from his snake-eating counterparts in that he did not actually eat and kill the snakes. Rather, he would swallow them then regurgitate them back up while leaving them still alive. He was eventually taken before a justice of the peace and fined $25, though he argued that he was technically only swallowing snakes momentarily and not actually eating them ("IS SWALLOWING SAME AS EATING?"). Though there was some question regarding the spirit of the law compared to the letter of the law, after considerable debate, the show was allowed to resume at the local carnival with new performance restrictions in place to ensure compliance ("Snake-Oid in Toils of Law").

Not only was the act appalling to many (even for the time) and quite dangerous to the performers themselves, its popularity also had other unfortunate results. In 1903, a 12-year-old girl named Allie Fairchild suffered life-threatening injuries after being bitten by several snakes while attempting to eat them. Fairchild had recently seen a Bosco performer doing snake-eating at the carnival and had been inspired to attempt the feat herself ("Pure Clean Grit").

A rather heartbreaking tale of a Bosco show took place in Minneapolis, Minnesota, in 1901, when a man, allegedly suffering from a mental disability, was put on display as a "wild man of Borneo." This person was strapped in a cage and set up for spectators to pay money to see. His back was covered in welts from being beaten by his handlers, and it was said that he remained chained through the night. A local resident saw the attraction, expecting an entertaining theatrical presentation, but was horrified by the apparent realness of it: "I paid my money to see a fake wild man. I expected and wanted to see a fake. The more ingenious the fake, the better I am pleased. But 'Bosco' is a horror utterly inimitable, a sight that no women or children should ever be permitted to witness. The men exhibiting him should be put under arrest immediately and the unfortunate given proper care." The resident filed a report with the Minneapolis Humane Society to help save the man being exhibited, but by the time the report was received, the show managers had already made their escape along with their "wild man" ("Humane Society Missed Good Chance to Relieve Bosco's Suffering").

In 1911, a legal case made headlines when a man dressed as a "wild woman" going by the name Zoma, the Queen of Reptiles, was performing with a circus sideshow in Waterbury, Connecticut. At one point during the performance, the young man playing Zoma threw a live snake into the audience, striking a woman. As it struck her face, the snake wrapped itself around the woman's arm and shoulders, prompting her to go into hysterics that led to her being committed to a physician's care. The Queen of the Reptiles was arrested for assault and battery ("'Queen' Accused of Assault"). Zoma, whose real name was Littlefield, was jailed for a week over the incident, then released ("NO PROSECUTION FOR THROWING A SNAKE").

Four years prior, in 1907, a man named Frank Jones, who performed as Youno the Snake Eater, was arrested and sentenced to serve 60 days in jail for slapping a woman in the face with a rattlesnake. Though Jones said that he didn't mind serving his time, he indicated to police that he was looking forward to resuming his career as a snake eater upon his release ("SNAKE EATER WAS SATISFIED").

Other instances that occasionally made the news demonstrate public perception of the geek shows that turned up in certain areas. In one example, during the fair season in 1951, a traveling carnival that featured a geek act made a stop in Nyack and Spring Valley, New York. The local residents were so appalled at "the indecent spectacle of a so-called 'geek' chewing off the head of a live chicken" that the Spring Valley community created a cease-and-desist petition to stop the performance. The local press also put down the appearance of the carnival, stating, "Under the circumstances, it is obvious that the traveling carnival is held in no particularly high regard" ("More Knocks").

Also in the summer of 1951, a geek show in Henryetta, Oklahoma, caused controversy when a drunken carnival man was arrested after getting into a brawl with the geek at the wild man show. The geek in question was an African American man with a peg leg who spent his days at the attraction eating the intestines of live chickens and biting the heads off of snakes. The carnival man claimed that he had heard the geek curse out a female ticket seller, so he attacked the geek, later justifying his actions by saying, "I couldn't take that, even if he was drunk and had a wooden leg," further stating, "I slapped him out of the tent, and I'd do it again, even if they give me sixty days." Further cementing his bravado, he made a point to also mention that "I'm not afraid of any wild man." The same carnival featured a "half-man, half-woman" show, which had a gender-bending performer doing and saying lewd things behind a curtain. After parents complained that both shows were inappropriate for children, coupled with the fight at the geek show, the local police decided that the productions were not family-friendly and were not helping live up to their motto of "The Cleanest Midway in America," so they intervened and put a stop to both attractions ("Police Stop Two Carnival Exhibits").

In June 1941 in Aliquippa, Pennsylvania, a sideshow called "Feed-the-Wild-Man" was broken up by a local humane agent. The show consisted of a wild man tearing snakes apart with his teeth. The owner of the attraction was fined $10 for the display, and the humane agent who shut it down commented on the situation by saying, "Women and children were watching the ghastly sight. What's the use of spending our money teaching children not to be cruel if they are to be allowed to see such things?" ("Side Show Halted In Aliquippa").

A somewhat comical controversy came from an occurrence in Calumet City, Illinois, during the summer of 1950. The local citizens committee was attempting to relieve a financial deficit, with the goal of raising funds to send underprivileged youth to summer camp. To help them achieve this goal, the local police chief made the decision to allow a carnival to appear in town as a means to generate funding. The local community, apparently expecting a family-friendly affair, was taken aback when the carnival featured both a glomming geek show and an attraction featuring nude women. During the geek show, a man came out and ripped a live chicken apart with his teeth, then proceeded to eat its innards. Reports say this caused at least one woman in the audience to cry out and faint. The geek show caused such an uproar among the citizens committee that the Police Chief publicly assumed personal responsibility for the event and formally apologized for allowing the carnival to appear. He also assured the community that he would personally see to it that no more shows of that nature would ever happen within the city's limits again ("Wleklinski Takes Blame For Carnival").

A darker and more tragic incident involving a geek show transpired at the White County Fair in Sparta, Tennessee, in August 1959. At the fair, an ex-Marine named Roy Deal was geeking at a wild man attraction on the midway in a show called the Congo Show. While he was eating a live chicken, a spectator threw acid into his face and fled the scene. Deal was badly injured during the attack. To add to the tragedy, the commotion resulting from the incident caused the 68-year-old midway manager J. W. Campbell to have a heart attack, and some of the acid splattered onto several snakes in the geek tent, killing three of them. Police theorized that the attacker's motive was that he was so revolted by the geek's performance that he sought to inflict harm upon the wild man ("ACID TOSSER HITS SPARTA SHOWMAN").

The *Atlanta Constitution* described a strange geek occurrence in their September 28, 1960, edition. A man named Ken Williams, who happened to be the executive director of the Atlanta Humane Society, was passing through the local carnival and decided to pay 50 cents to buy a ticket to the geek show to see what it was all about.

Once inside the tent, Williams found himself standing around a pen with a pig and several live chickens in it. After a moment, the geek, clad in only a plaid bathing suit, entered the pen and addressed the crowd. "I am from the West Indies," said the geek in a British accent. "I am not an alcoholic, nor am I a dope addict. The only thing which ever touches my stomach is warm blood and raw meat." He then stated, "Now I will eat a live chicken." At that point, the geek laid down flat on the floor of the pen and stared at the chicken a moment, as if to hypnotize it, before snatching it up and biting its neck and chest. After a moment of chewing on the chicken, he then reached inside it, pulled out its heart, and ate it in front of the stunned onlookers. Williams was so shocked by the display that he took action against Johnny Portemont of Johnny's Side Shows, the man who had produced the geek show.

Portemont, who was under a $500 bond due to the charges, was not concerned about the accusations against him. "It's a trick," he said. "Sleight of hand. Now figure this: How could a man do a show every hour and eat that many chickens? It's an illusion, like most everything else on this earth is an illusion."

Williams, however, was not convinced. "Three feet away, and I saw him pluck out the heart and eat it," he remarked (Barker 5). Though he likely killed the chicken and tore it apart with his hands and teeth, it's probable that theatrics made the act seem more gruesome and extreme than it otherwise was.

An oddly amusing incident of spur-of-the-moment geeking took place at the Walter L. Main circus in 1937. While one of the snake shows was taking place in the sideshow tent, one of the roustabouts entered the tent and inexplicably went berserk, jumping into the snake pit and biting one of the snakes in two. This resulted in the circus having to bury their show's best snake and the roustabout being laid up for a week ("Untitled Walter L. Main Circus Paragraph").

Sideshow performer and historian Todd Robbins once recalled reading about an old geek-like routine with a cannibalistic theme simply known as "I will eat a live human being." For this act, a sideshow performer would come out on stage and declare to the crowd that for their performance, they were going to eat a live human being. The performer would then ask the audience for a volunteer to come on stage to be eaten alive. Naturally, the vast majority of the time, no one would volunteer, so the performer would simply say "Well folks, I was prepared to eat a live human being but since nobody volunteered, we will move on." Hence, it was presented as a joke, and the show would then go to the next act. However, in the rare instances where someone would actually volunteer to be eaten alive, the performer would bring them on stage and ask them to confirm that they were okay with agreeing to be eaten alive and that they would absolve the sideshow from any legal responsibility. The performer would then bring out a contact, and have the volunteer sign it, indicating that they were agreeing to be eaten alive by their own free will. With the formalities taken care of, the performer would then ask the volunteer to stick out their thumb, at which point the performer would then shake a little salt on it. Once seasoned, the performer would then bite down hard on the volunteers thumb. The volunteer would then run off stage bleeding and screaming in pain, at which point the performer would conclude the performance by remarking to the audience "Well, you almost saw me eat a human being, but he left just as I got started." A comical routine no doubt, but no longer performed for obvious reasons (Corsaro).

By the mid-20th century, geek shows had moved away from street fairs and circuses and had become more consolidated, primarily finding homes on carnival midways at various fairgrounds across the United States. However, they were also starting to fall out of favor socially. Their exploitative nature coupled with their cruelty to animals was becoming increasingly unacceptable and uninteresting to the general public as generational perspectives changed.

The *Billboard*, which had previously featured comments praising the popularity of snake eaters as early as 1900 was a publication commonly used to connect show producers and geek performers, but it gradually started to reflect society's changing perception. In July 1935, they printed a letter from the president of the Michigan Federation of Humane Societies saying that Michigan was no place for carnivals featuring geeks that bite the heads off chickens. The magazine reiterated this sentiment in the following issue, summarizing her comments and adding "Our opinion is there shouldn't be a place anywhere for such 'attractions' as they are a disgrace to the carnival profession" ("'In Our Last Issue' Section").

Though the general insider perspectives were continuing to shift, want ads for geek show performers and operators continued in the publication's classified section throughout the 1930s, 1940s, and 1950s. By the 1960s, however, the number of want ads were dwindling rapidly. Some of the advertisements actually specified "no geek shows" as a means to emphasize that they were professional, clean, family-friendly entertainment outfits. Soon the magazine branched off into several smaller publications, then eventually moved away from the outdoor amusement business altogether, ultimately becoming the review of popular music that it is today.[1]

Sideshow operator Dick Best reflected on the decline when he was profiled by The *Tampa Times* in 1959 as part of a promotion for their winter shows at the fairgrounds. Best noted that geek shows used to draw large audiences and people would pay good money to see a man rip apart a live chicken, but he said that many fairs, including the one he was being profiled for, wouldn't allow geek shows anymore on the grounds that they were not family-friendly. At that time, Best indicated that he had not seen or heard of an actual geek show occurring in about 15 years (Bayle 10).

The *Fresno Bee* ran an article in 1970 that posed the question of "Whatever happened to the Wild Man from Borneo?" They spoke to longtime carnival worker Wayne Palm, who said that he no longer saw sideshow attractions at fairs as he had in his younger days. "They were here and then one day I looked up and they weren't no more," he explained. When asked about the wild man act specifically, he offered a thoughtful perspective: "Well, he wasn't a wild man at all. He was just a lonesome soul crying out for another drink or some attention. You don't see him in a carnival tent no more. No sir. But you can see him everyplace else. In the towns and in the cities and everywhere you look. He's still in his cage and you can hear him screaming for somebody to kill the chicken" ("Shed A Tear For Wild Man Of Borneo").

---

1. One of their spin-off magazines, "Amusement Business," was created in 1961 and continued to cover outdoor entertainment until the publication folded in 2006.

Geeks and the Horrors of Drug Abuse Shows

In what was perhaps a collective last-ditch effort to save the geek act amid changing public sentiment, a widespread rebranding of geek shows occurred beginning around the early 1970s. Instead of geeks being portrayed as wild men captured in a savage jungle, they were promoted as victims of drug abuse. Much of the new presentation was no doubt fueled by Richard Nixon's war on drugs campaign, which began in 1971. Many showmen shifted the geek presentation to play into this social climate as a means to continue finding profitability with a geek show under the guise of performing a social good. The idea was that geek attractions were now educational shows that warned the audience of the horrors of drug addiction by displaying the consequences in the form of a filthy drug-addicted geek (Meah 138).

Much like how Bosco and Esau, the snake-eating geeks, had become archetypes portrayed by many during their popularity in the early 20th century, a new geek character emerged in the form of Billy Reed. The backstory for Billy Reed was typically that of a previously normal young man who had tried recreational drugs either due to peer pressure or as an attempt to cope with a social trauma. The experience of drug use had caused him severe brain damage, and he was now in a near-catatonic state, his life forever destroyed because of his experimentation with drugs. As a result, he was put on display at carnival shows as a warning for others. Often, he would be placed in a wheelchair and have medical equipment in his cage, typically along with a reptile. Though he would not commit glomming acts with animals, he would still do unusual things and behave in a geek-like manner by trying to invoke feelings of shock among onlookers. The wild man trope was gone, but the geek show's underlying intent to shock audiences remained with the catatonic gimmick.

The first Billy Reed show was promoted by showman Jack Constantine. Originally, Constantine booked his drug abuse show back in 1973 using a female character named Kathy Reed. After things didn't work out with his actress and he was forced to replace her with a male performer, he renamed the show Billy Reed. It eventually became a hit and the name stuck, spawning numerous imitators using the Billy Reed namesake. Jack Constantine credits Randy Rosenson and Mickey Saiber as the first showmen to combine the geek with the drug abuse angle (Stencell 236-238).

This new incarnation of a geek show received a degree of financial success. However, the educational angle was often ineffective with the public, as many failed to see any redeeming social or entertainment value in the act itself.

The *Hope Star* newspaper echoed this sentiment when a geek, billed as a drug addict, appeared at a carnival in 1977. The police department received numerous complaints, and the chief of police ultimately concluded, "It [the geek act] may be rare and unusual, but it is offensive to some people. As an educational program, it doesn't fit" ("Carnival Act Here Brings Complaints").

In 1988, Coleman Brothers Shows featured a Billy Reed geek show exhibit during a tour through Connecticut. This "Horrors of Drug Abuse" show featured a Billy Reed performer sitting in a wheelchair inside of a cage holding a snake. On the wall, there was a sign stating that after Reed saw his friend die in a train accident, he took 70 LSD "pills" to ease his tormented mind. As a result, he went insane and now believed that the snake was a reincarnation of his friend. As patrons would walk by inside, he would hit the side of the cage with a club in an attempt to startle them. Don McConnell, the executive director of the State Alcohol and Drug Abuse Commission, condemned the attraction, viewing it as an exploitative and inaccurate portrayal of how actual drug addicts are treated. "We don't put people in cages anymore. We don't treat addicts like animals," McConnell stated to the the *Hartford Courant* before adding, "We're trying to treat people with diseases. Would you put someone with a traumatic brain injury in display in a carnival?" The *Hartford Courant* also expressed distaste for the display, writing, "Billy has got to go. What's next, an 8-year-old rape victim?" (Condon C1).

Another documented instance of a Billy Reed show was at the Prince William County Fair in Manassas, Virginia. The event made news in 1991 for its midway attraction, which featured a sign saying, "See Billy Reed. This Student is a Shocking Example of the Horrors of Drug Abuse." Once inside, people saw Reed in a wheelchair with various intravenous tubes hooked to his body. The actor portraying Billy would convulse and roll his head back as people passed by. Many were disgusted by the attraction and formally complained to the fair manager. The attraction was presented by Bobby Brooks of Brooks Side Shows, who argued that "...the main thing is to keep the kids away from using drugs." Brooks even went so far as to claim that former first lady Nancy Reagan had endorsed the display as part of her *Just Say No* campaign with the war on drugs. After word of the attraction spread, Reagan's spokeswoman Cathy Goldberg issued a statement to clarify that Nancy Reagan had not, in fact, endorsed the exhibit (Thomas-Lester).

Showman Rick Dennis (aka "Dr. Blood") also ran a drug abuse attraction for a few seasons, which he called Willie Wright Went Wrong. The show followed the typical format, with the character being promoted as having done an excessive amount of drugs and displaying erratic behavior. During a run at the Allentown Fair in Pennsylvania in 1989, a female performer playing the part of Willie would throw rubber snakes at customers that had paid a dollar to step in to see the show. When asked about his reasoning for having a show of this nature, Dennis told the local paper, "It's something the kids will remember long after the fair is gone. Education saves lives; drug abuse is serious." When pressed about if that was the case, then why was there a price of admission, Dennis added that his show was indeed "first and foremost a business" (Jackson B3). The following year, his Willie Wright Went Wrong attraction returned to the Allentown Fair. During this run, his Willie performer was made up to look dirty and sat with a snake around his neck and would put a drill in his nose periodically while those in attendance looked on.[2] Dennis reiterated to the same paper during this 1990 run that "The object is to keep today's youth from experimenting with drugs" (Snyder B3).

The Downswing of Sideshow

Gradually, longtime showmen began to notice of the death of the glomming geek show. The *Arizona Republic* profiled a retired sideshow promoter in 1980 called "Side Road Shorty." On the subject of geek shows, Shorty remarked, "You don't hardly ever see a decent geek show no more," lamenting, "It looks like geeks are going out of style" (Ives C11).

Similarly, in 1983, the *Boston Globe* reviewed the just-released book *New England Country Fair!* by writer and former sideshow talker Phil Primack. In discussing fair attractions, Primack briefly recalled glomming geek shows of years past. "Crowds lined up to see the glomming geeks eat live snakes, chickens, and other animals," he reflected. "People paid hard cash to be publicly disgusted." Primack was relieved that there were no longer geek shows around for him to have to write about. The *Globe* echoed his sentiment

---

2. This behavior is a variation of the popular sideshow feat known as The Human Blockhead, which involves sticking an object such as a nail or drill straight into the sinus cavity. It was originally brought to the sideshow stage and popularized by entertainer Melvin Burkhart (1907–2001).

by stating that, by this point, glomming geeks had "mercifully disappeared from fairs" (Murphy 60).

Career showman Bobby Reynolds indicated that he had worked as a geek briefly in his sideshow life, recalling that they used to kill chickens by slitting their throats and squeezing the bodies so that the blood would hit the ceiling of the tent and rain over the audience during the performance. After the show, they would simply take the dead chickens, give them to the cookhouse, and then have chicken for dinner. Though the corpses were put to good use, Reynolds noted in 2001 that "[if] you did that today, they'd carry you away to the SPCA and beat the shit out of you" (Nickell 205).

But it wasn't just geek shows that were in trouble. Sideshows themselves were rapidly falling out of favor. There were a number of factors causing the change in direction.

Longtime showmen, including Ward "King of the Sideshows" Hall, attributed much of the downward spiral in the second half of the 20th century to the increased innovation and implementation of carnival rides at local fairs. From a practical and financial perspective, large carnival ride attractions require fewer people to operate and are often more lucrative than sideshow attractions with performers (Hall 39-40).

There was another innovation that was taking place in entertainment as well. Television sets were becoming more and more common. The new technology made going out to pay for local entertainment less appealing to the average consumer when they could enjoy a new form of entertainment in the comfort of their own home.

Social attitudes had changed a great deal, too. Not only were geek shows seen as cruel toward humans and animals alike, but even displaying performers with physical abnormalities in general was seen as exploitive. Some states even adopted penal codes against displaying physically abnormal individuals for any reason other than scientific purposes. Pennsylvania, for example, enacted a statute in 1972 regarding a "public exhibition of insane or deformed person" as part of their ruling on public indecency. The statute reads:

A person is guilty of a misdemeanor of the second degree if he exhibits in any place, for a pecuniary consideration or reward, any insane, idiotic or deformed person, or imbecile (Statutes of Pennsylvania).

Michigan has had a penal code in place since 1931, though the wording was amended slightly in 2015. It states:

A physician or other person who exposes or exhibits any human being who is disabled or disfigured, except as used for scientific purposes before members of the medical profession or medical classes, is guilty of a misdemeanor punishable by imprisonment for not more than 90 days or a fine of not more than $500.00, or both (Michigan Legislature).

Massachusetts law says:

Whoever exhibits for hire an albino person, a minor or mentally ill person who is deformed or a person who has an appearance of deformity produced by artificial means shall be punished by a fine of not more than five hundred dollars (Massachusetts General Laws).

It should be noted that these state laws are fairly minor and weren't necessarily earnestly enforced. In the great scheme of sideshow history, the laws themselves were not a major contributing factor to the downfall of the American sideshow. Rather, they are more of a reflection on the evolution of social perspectives that related to this form of exhibit.[3]

Still, many performers that fell under these legal provisions were consenting adults that had made good money working in sideshows. Additionally, due to advancements in medical technology, preventative testing, and prenatal care, births of those with notable physical abnormalities were becoming less and less common (Wall and Clerici).

The Usage of Geek in Other Forms of Entertainment

Though geek shows were quickly waning in popularity, acceptance, and occurrence during the last half of the 20th century, there were several notable geek activities that occurred

---

3. Showman Ward Hall and his associates Stanley "Sealo, the Seal Boy" Berent and Pete "Poobah, the Fire-Eating Dwarf" Terhurne once challenged a Florida law which prohibited exhibiting for profit "any human being that is deformed, malformed or disfigured." They felt that the law discriminated against such people who wanted to willingly display themselves in sideshow in the state for work. After being escalated to the Supreme Court for the State of Florida, the case was ruled in their favor and the law was stricken and removed from the books (Hall 29-31).

in popular culture during the time period, especially within the music industry. Professional wrestler "Classy" Freddie Blassie's influential 1974 music single, "Pencil Neck Geek" was only one instance, though an early one. References to traditional sideshow geeks were also found in more mainstream music. Perhaps the most noteworthy of these was the 1965 song "Ballad of a Thin Man," by Bob Dylan, which contains the following verse:

You hand in your ticket
And you go watch the geek
Who immediately walks up to you
When he hears you speak
And says, "How does it feel
To be such a freak?"
And you say, "Impossible"
As he hands you a bone.

Other sideshow performers, such as a sword swallower and a "one-eyed midget" are also referenced in the song. The lyrics are very symbolic, as the geek is also a metaphor for the emerging counterculture of the 1960s, presenting a juxtaposition between the concept of who is the outsider and who is the traditionalist. In the song, the mainstream character of "Mr. Jones" struggles to cope with his surroundings and soon realizes that despite all the unusual things he is experiencing, he is the one who has become the outcast, someone left behind by society.

During live performances, Dylan occasionally commented on his experiences with the sideshows of his youth and geeks. In one 1978 tour, he stated:

Remember those carnivals that they used to have? I guess they must have had them here in the '50s. Anyway, most of them usually always had what they called a geek in them. You know what a geek is? A geek is a man who eats a live chicken. He bites the head off, eats that. Then he eats the rest of it, heart, blood, everything else but the bone. Sweeps all the feathers up with a broom... I was talking one day with the bearded lady, at breakfast, and she was telling me, "The geek, stay away from him. He is the pits. Awful low down, you don't want to get near him. He's got his own way of life, he don't bother with nobody else." I said, "Oh, well. Maybe you can tell me a little more about him?" She said, "Well, of all the people in the carnival, freaks and everybody, this man thinks he's the only straight person. He look at everybody else as being freaks." I said, "Uh-huh." It didn't make much sense to me at the time, but years later when I was wandering around making my rounds, all that came back to me when people started looking at me in strange ways for doing things which might not be too common ("Still On The Road: 1978 World Tour: US December").

In 1969, Alice Cooper was playing at the Toronto Rock and Roll Revival and during the set, a live chicken made its way onto the stage. Not having been around chickens previously, frontman Alice Cooper picked up the chicken and threw it into the audience, thinking it would simply fly off over them. The chicken quickly plummeted into the audience. The rowdy crowd then tore it apart and threw the chicken pieces back at the band. After the festival, rumors quickly spread that Alice Cooper had ripped the head off the chicken on stage and drank its blood. Cooper later remarked, "What should have been incredibly horrible press for anybody became the thing that put us on the map" ("Supermensch: Alice Cooper and the Infamous Chicken"). Many years later, Cooper would go on to record a song called "Sideshow," which features the lyric:[4]

Alice Cooper performing with a snake in 2012. Kreepin Deth, CC BY-SA 3.0 <https://creativecommons.org/licenses/by-sa/3.0>, via Wikimedia Commons. https://commons.wikimedia.org/wiki/File:Alice_Cooper_with_snake_2012-10-28.jpg

I pay to see the freaks
Some finger-lickin', chicken-eating geek
Hey, that sounds cool to me

---

4. This track can be found on Alice Cooper's 1994 album, "The Last Temptation."

Alice Cooper frequently performs onstage with a live boa constrictor wrapped around his upper body, much like a modern-day snake charmer.

Perhaps the most infamous examples of geek activity in the music world occurred on two separate instances during the early 1980s with shock rocker Ozzy Osbourne.

The first instance occurred in 1981, when Osbourne was meeting with some record executives. His plan was to give a speech, then release some doves into the air, which he had brought with him. He reportedly had several drinks before the meeting, and when he became annoyed with the public relations executive from the label, he decapitated two of the doves with his teeth, right there in the conference room. Reflecting on the incident later, Osbourne told his publicist, "[I] pulled out one of these doves and bit its [expletive] head off. Just to shut her up. Then I did it again with the next dove, spitting the head out on the table. ... That's when they threw me out" (Mansfield).

The following year, when Osbourne was performing in Des Moines, Iowa, a fan threw a bat onto the stage. Thinking it was a toy, Osbourne promptly picked it up and bit its head off. Quickly realizing his misjudgment, he sped to a local hospital for rabies shots after the show (Mansfield).

In 1987, there was a news story about a radio station in Indiana holding a contest at a local nightclub. The contest posed the question "What's the most outrageous act a person would do for $1,000?" They were clearly in for more than they expected when a young man showed up to the event and proceeded to bite the head off a live chicken (Gartner C2).

There was also punk rock musician GG Allin, who terrorized audiences throughout the 1980s and early 1990s with his wild behavior. During his shows, Allin would often strip naked, beat himself bloody, and rush toward his audiences, grabbing and swinging at them, effectively rousting them like a geek. He was also known for defecating onstage and eating the feces during his performances, sometimes flinging it into the audience as well. These extreme, gross antics and physically confrontational style are similar to shocking motifs found in a traditional geek show. The outrageousness of his performances resulted in a similar public intrigue for those who attended his concerts.[5]

Picture, if you will, a warm summer night in 1973. Outside, somewhere in the southern United States, off a side street, a small crowd is forming. The locals bump into one another, swear, and laugh at the thought of what they are about to witness. They are

5. There was also a rock band in the late 1980s and early 1990s called Glomming Geek.

collectively gathered outside to watch what is about to take place before them: a street battle between two geeks. Though the setting sounds almost absurd, it was actually a very real scene from the 2005 documentary film *Stranded in Canton*. After the crowd settles in, the talker holds up two live chickens and gives the following introduction: "Ladies and gentlemen, representing for your amusement and entertainment tonight from the St. Phillip Amusement Society, a real, live carnival geek. He is going to severe with his teeth the head of this live, writhing chicken and he will then proceed to drink its blood!" A shaggy-haired young man then takes the chicken, strokes its feathers for a moment, then places its head in his mouth and bites it off while the crowd cheers phrases like "Geek! Geek! Geek!" and "Geek power!" He then makes good on the talker's promise by tipping his head back and drinking blood from the stump before throwing the body on the ground. A second talker then steps forward and introduces the local hometown geek. "He says he's as good a geek as our geek that we brought in here. One of your own hometown people!" A second geek, with shining fake front teeth, then takes the second chicken, bites the head off in a similar manner, and drinks the blood while the headless chicken flaps its wings. As the scene draws to a close, the second geek smiles for the camera, blood and gristle on his chin, as the film's narrator remarks: "I'm not so fond of the geek scene. Too many other people were involved. It was not nearly as personal [as the rest of the footage in the film]. Like a circus act."

By the final quarter of the 20th century, a true geek show was virtually unheard of. The once-thriving sideshow business was reduced to just a handful of outfits that hung on to capitalize on what little nostalgia was left for the art form.

Chapter 14

Geek in Popular Culture After Its Decline in Sideshow

T hough the carnival sideshow had nearly fallen into extinction by the last part of the 20th century, something interesting occurred in the early 1990s.

Fueled by the Generation X grunge music scene and interest in retro culture, sideshow entertainment saw a revival of sorts among youth when groups like the Jim Rose Circus, which toured with the 1992 Lollapalooza festival, began performing as modern-day sideshow troupes, spearheading a new era in sideshow. Instead of cramming into tents along the midway at the local carnival, sideshow now had a new setting: rock concert venues.[1]

Many types of sideshow acts translated smoothly as new performers learned the acts. Fire breathers, sword swallowers, and human pincushions found a new niche and appreciation with the edgy attitudes of rock music audiences.

Some acts, however, did not age as well. By the 1990s, both having tattoos and being obese were becoming increasingly common among the general populace. As a result, acts relating exclusively to those selling points were less common and less interesting to the public.[2]

However, though some acts were lost in translation as the new era of sideshow unfolded, many routines were still taken in this new tradition. The geek act, both in terms of glomming geeks and ordinary geeks sitting in pits with animals, however, was completely gone.

For numerous social and legal reasons, not only did many geek shows cease operating but they simply couldn't attract enough paying customers to be worthwhile. Audiences wouldn't stand for them, and those promoting them would likely be arrested. Though animal rights organizations have existed for generations, groups such as PETA (which was founded in 1980) came into prominence and began to have strong social influence as well. Between the lack of interest of the public and the lack of motivating factors for showmen, geek shows became extinct.

Similar acts, such as human ostriches and wild men, have also diminished greatly in popularity. Many of these shows were a product of their times. Mercifully, much like minstrel shows, the civil rights movement and the evolution of social perspectives have made race-based "jungle savage" acts a thing of the past. Though even with racial elements removed, we live in a world of technological innovation and fast-paced, on-demand en-

---

1. The early Jim Rose Circus featured a sword swallower originally stage-named Slug who would also eat live worms and bugs during shows. Shortly after joining the circus, he had his body completely covered with puzzle piece tattoos and reinvented himself as a tattooed man known as The Enigma. In 1995, he appeared in a carnival-themed episode of "The X-Files" ("Humbug"), playing a character known as The Conundrum who engaged in geek-like behavior.

2. There are some exceptions, obviously, though modern performers generally have to take tattoos to a much greater extreme or also learn working acts in order to be marketable.

tertainment. Would an attraction whose sole concept revolved around seeing a performer acting crazy within the confines of a cage and/or pit alone be appealing enough to modern audiences to be a lucrative venture? It seems unlikely.

Human ostriches were largely a fad during the height of dime museums in the 1880s and 1890s. The more common the act became, the less unique they were to medical researchers and the less interesting they were to audiences. Dime museums, once a common entertainment venue, became the roadside attractions and small "oddities" museums that are much less common. However, there are some regurgitative human ostriches working to this day, and glass eating has become a staple among many modern sideshow performers. But one is unlikely to see a human ostrich eating screws, knife blades, and so forth.[3] Perhaps modern aspiring entertainers have better education, interests, and caution in regards to digestive processes compared to the human ostriches who paid the price of their acts over a century ago.

However, some sideshow performers from our era do occasionally engage in geek-like performances that involve eating insects. It is slightly less offensive to modern audiences to utilize bugs without a central nervous system in comparison to the traditional, pain-feeling snakes and chickens from years gone by. This era's interpretation of the geek act became known as the "insectivore" act. While these types of acts do touch upon the same grotesque feelings of a geek show with the consumption of something alive and unsavory, the performances are lacking many of the traditional elements found in geek shows, such as a pit show setup, the use of vertebrate animals, portraying themselves as wild, and rousting the audience during the show.

For some, this rebranding of the act from geek act to insectivore act isn't simply a matter of differentiating the creatures used but also of differentiating verbiage for the sake of audience interest. By the 2000s, the term "geek" had become so associated with "nerd" that some spectators would hear the term and instantly make that association, whereas, "insectivore" is much more logically descriptive in a contemporary setting (Bügmüncher). Surely, for many of those who would attend a sideshow-style event, the idea of watching a bug-eating show sounds far more appealing than watching a nerd-show.

---

3. There are, however, some magic effects that are popular to this day that are visually akin to human ostrich acts. One example is the illusion of the performer swallowing a string and razorblades independent of each other, then reproducing them from the mouth with the blades tied to the string.

Some notable recent insectivore sideshow performers include Coney Island's Insectavora and Olde City Sideshow's Reggie Bügmüncher.

Insectavora began performing at Coney Island in 2002 after being recruited by
Sideshows by the Seashore performers who saw her performing at the New York City Tattoo Convention. Her repertoire for creatures consumed includes live crickets, grasshoppers, mealworms, maggots, and nightcrawlers. She also performs other sideshow working
acts, such as walking on a ladder of swords (Hartzman, American Sideshow 259-260).

Reggie Bügmüncher started out her sideshow career doing bug-eating, geek-style acts
as a means to get her foot in the door to sideshow entertainment before moving on to
learning other sideshow skills.[4] Reggie describes her early insect act as follows:

> *When I started out, I was doing an entire three-course meal. So, crickets,*
> *mealworms, and nightcrawlers, and the presentation really depended on*
> *our booking. Sometimes it was set up as like a little dinner date between*
> *myself and another person in the show, and that was a big surprise, and*
> *there was a pretty girl eating disgusting animals. And sometimes it was*
> *presented with my talker talking the act about my interesting diet.*

Bügmüncher retired the insect act after several hospital stays in 2007 when she discovered that she had developed a shellfish allergy that was manifesting when she ate live
crickets. After that, she performed her eating act with goldfish but ended up later retiring
that as well, citing difficulty in obtaining creatures on the road coupled with occasional
negative reactions from people seeing her working with live creatures onstage. "I don't
know that there is even room for me to do the geek act most places," she reflects. "I
think there are some people that are really into it and there are people that are really into
sideshow or circus and things like that, but the climate has changed so much." When
pondering on the historic evolution of the geek act, Bügmüncher says:

> *On one hand, I'd like to think that 100 years ago, if traditional sideshow*
> *acts had the Internet, they'd be eating some wild animals, like crazy stuff*
> *that they could just order online from someplace. They weren't eating*

---

4. Pronounced "boo-moo-shay" – a clever and appropriate play on words.

Madagascar hissing cockroaches unless your sideshow was close to someplace where they could get Madagascar hissing cockroaches. So on one hand, we can get so much cooler stuff now, but society just isn't cool with it. I think the evolution is that the performances have gotten better but the actual gross-out act isn't as gross.

Though she no longer does geek-style acts, Reggie Bügmüncher continues to perform various working acts as an active sideshow entertainer (Bügmüncher).

Occasionally, in recent times, events billed as geek shows arise at events like haunted attractions around Halloween. However, they are more small-scale theatrical reenactments than actual geek shows, usually involving fake animals and stage blood capsules with a caged geek who rattles the bars of his cage while people walk by (Stuart).

Reggie Bügmüncher eating nightcrawlers in 2009.
Image courtesy of Paul Szauter.

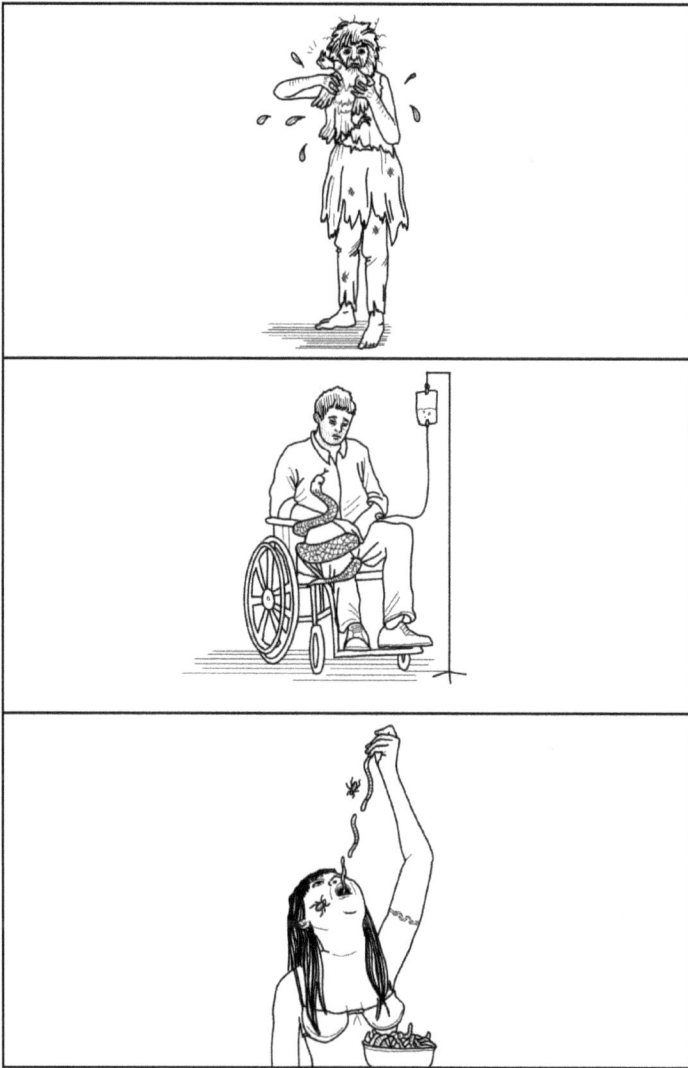

The cultural evolution of the geek act through generations.

Panel 1: The Wild Man Geek (Early 1900s)

Panel 2: The Drug Show Geek (1970s)

Panel 3: The Insectivore (1990s)

As carnival geek shows slowly disappeared in the latter half of the 20th century, the word continued to evolve. Starting around 1983, *geek* had caught on as a word to refer to "a person who is extremely devoted to and knowledgeable about computers or related technology" ("geek, n." OED Online).

There are smatterings of the word *geek* used in similar contexts before it assimilated into mainstream vernacular in the 1980s. One of the first widely recognized usages of the term with a more contemporary meaning occurred in 1952 when author Robert Heinlein published a short story called "The Year of the Jackpots." In the story, Heinlein refers to a technologically focused character as "the poor geek" (Roeder).

Another notable example is DC Comics 1968 comic book *Brother Power the Geek.* The comic follows the adventures of a mannequin brought to life by a bolt of lightning. He then becomes a hippie-superhero known as Brother Power the Geek. At one point, Brother Power gets kidnapped by a "Psychedelic Circus" and is forced on display in their freak show. The comic only ran for two issues and was allegedly originally called "Brother Power the Freak" but DC executives were concerned that "the Freak" might be perceived as a drug reference at the time, so they changed it to "the Geek" (Shaw).

As sideshow had reached one of its most absent decades during the 1980s, the term *geek* as a means to describe a socially inept yet passionately focused person slowly exploded as a term used in popular culture. In many ways, the linguistic shift was appropriate. The sideshow geek was the outsider among mainstream variety performers and only focused on things like biting the head from an animal's body, so it made sense that modern geeks were outsiders who focused on their passions for a particular hobby or interest in which they excelled. By the time the computer support company Geek Squad was launched in 1994 and the term was being used on a corporate level, the word had reached completely grand heights of usage and acceptance beyond that of adolescent slang.

Geek also has modern connotation to another word: *nerd*. Intriguingly, the etymologies of these two words are actually not that far removed from each other. The word *nerd* originated in the 1950 Dr. Seuss book *If I Ran the Zoo*. In the book, this line appears: "And then, just to show them, I'll sail to Ka-Troo / And Bring Back an It-Kutch, a Preep, and a Proo, / A Nerkle, a Nerd, and a Seersucker too!" Much like *geek*, by the last couple decades of the 20th century, the word *nerd* had become widely known in modern English to describe a certain type of person.

To some, the word *geek* is interchangeable with the word *nerd* in American vernacular. However, especially since the early 21st century, the two terms have become increasingly more distinct from one another. The general consensus based on their current incarnations is that geeks tend to be enthusiastic fans of certain things which exist as part of a greater community of like-minded individuals, whereas, nerds tend to have a more specialized technical knowledge that relates to serious study of a subject matter (Trota).[5]

The social perception of *geek* has also changed from one of a pure insult from the 1980s to one of community pride since the 2000s. Often, people are proud to call themselves geeks as a means to associate themselves with a certain core interest and/or community based on the interest.

Much in the way the word was applied in the context of a sideshow performer, its contemporary usage can also be both as a noun and a verb, either to describe the individual as a geek or the act of behaving as a geek. That is, if a person were to "geek" using this modern connotation, then they have suddenly become overexcited about a specialized subject or activity, or talk about it with excessive enthusiasm. This usage is usually followed by the word "out," as in when someone enters into this enthusiastic state, they are said to "geek out" ("geek" Dictionary.com).

Even throughout the sideshow revival of the 1990s, the term *geek* as it relates to a sideshow performer became confusing. The media and performers alike began using the catchphrase "Freaks and Geeks!" in promotional copy and reviews, despite there usually being no actual geeks in their shows.[6] The phrase likely caught on due to both words rhyming and being associated with the sideshow. It is easy to envision a journalist, mildly privy to the fact that both words have some sort of connotation in the sideshow realm, putting them together for the sake of a snappy headline.

In the variety entertainment realm, the meaning shifted somewhat to become a not-completely-accepted but commonly used term to describe any type of act that had the visual of a traditional sideshow feat (sword swallowing, bed of nails, Human Blockhead, etc.) that contained a shock factor. Even accomplished sideshow revivalist Jim Rose was known as "Jimmy the Geek" early in his career (Japenga E8), though he did not ever per-

---

5. Using this differentiating factor, perhaps Geek Squad should have gone with the more appropriate "Nerd Squad" for their company name. Then again, that doesn't quite have the same ring to it.

6. "Freaks and Geeks" was also the name of a television show that ran on the NBC network from 1999 to 2000. The show was a teen drama and did not actually feature any animals getting their heads bitten off.

form as a literal sideshow geek. For some, simply being associated with any sideshow-style type of performance made them susceptible to the geek label. It was around this time that the term "geek magic" started being used to describe gross-out illusions, which complicated the terminology further.

To illustrate how much the terminology had changed in the sideshow, the term "glommer," which was previously used to describe a geek that actually bit/ate animals, is now used in some modern sideshow performer circles to describe sword swallowers who perform their acts for real rather than using a gimmicked technique (Taylor, "(After Tonight's about) Geek Shows."; Blau).

Geek shows, however, did continue to receive periodic references in popular culture. While the traditional act had been largely dead for years, it was still recent enough that many in the general public had heard of geek shows and had a general idea as to what they were. As such, references to sideshow geeks began appearing in entertainment media as jokes and satire to emphasize absurdity, often focusing on the seemingly ridiculous concept of biting the heads off chickens for money. Popular television shows such as *The Simpsons*[7] and *The Ren & Stimpy Show*[8] made such jokes during their runs in the 1990s. Troma Entertainment also released a horror film in 1990 called *Luther the Geek* about a geek-show obsessed antagonist who eventually goes on a killing spree, biting his victims to death.

There were also several notable books published in the mid-to-late 20th century that relate to the sideshow geek, such as Katherine Dunn's National Book Award finalist, *Geek Love* (1989), and Craig Nova's *The Geek* (1975).

The mainstream shift of the word *geek* from a negative connotation to one of pride was further fueled by Internet culture of the early 2000s. The term exploded into areas outside of computer culture to refer to proud, self-described "geeks" and their various fandoms, including subcultures relating to things like comic books, Japanese animation, and collectibles such as playing cards and action figures. Conventions that catered to these

---

7. "The Simpsons," Season 9, Episode 12 - "Bart Carny." Original air date: January 11, 1998 – "Now, this geek bit is pretty straightforward. You just bite the heads off the chickens and take a bow."

8. "The Ren & Stimpy Show," Season 4, Episode 8a - "Double Header." Original air date: January 7, 1995 – "Hmmm... You know, you guys look like a couple of GEEKS to me!"

markets grew in popularity and leveraged "geek pride" as both a tool for promotion and a legitimate moniker. Soon cosplay became popular and modern geeks were receiving major media attention. Now if you search the word *geek* on the Internet, the search results are completely overtaken with hits relating to modern geek fandom and technology. You are unlikely to find anything related to sideshow geeks unless you search through historical usages or add associated keywords relating to the circus, sideshow, or carnival.

Even the term *snake eater*, which was used to describe the literal act of snake eating in the late 1800s and early 1900s, prior to the popularization of the word *geek*, has also changed in connotation. Starting in the early 1960s, the term *snake eater* began as a nickname to describe military special forces.[9] This usage is said to have started when a Green Beret unit came to Fort Bragg in 1961, and the men caught and ate a snake. The term caught on after that (Onion).

In the 2000s, pop culture still occasionally referenced the traditional geek show, though the context had changed. By that point, geek shows had become so far removed from variety entertainment that, unlike the 1990s, any jokes or references to a sideshow geek would have been likely lost on audiences. As such, most references to traditional sideshow geeks in modern popular culture reflected on a historical presentation to give context. They explain what a geek show is in a period-piece format to the audience and present it in context as an example from that area. This type of example was seen in shows such as *Carnivàle* (2003) and *American Horror Story: Freak Show* (2014), as well as in films like *Carnies* (2010).

In 2016, Mezco Toyz released a sideshow carnival-themed line of their popular Living Dead Dolls series. They included a sideshow geek doll, known as Lucy the Geek, depicted with a gaping mouth and blood splattered all over her face. The doll's date of death was listed as 10/28/1947, with the death certificate reading:

> *Lucy was the Sideshow's resident Geek*
> *She would bite the heads off of chickens for the crowds each week*
> *But soon when the audience demanded more*
> *She bit off their heads and showered them with gore* (Lucy the Geek).

---

9. There is also the critically acclaimed 2004 video game, "Metal Gear Solid 3: Snake Eater."

Jay Bliznick's Sideshow Gelato shop in Chicago, Illinois, serves a variety of artisan gelatos based on traditional sideshow acts and performers. These illustrations from the shop's menu showcase stylized and cleaned-up versions classic sideshow acts. One flavor is "The Wildman of Corneo" which is sweet corn gelato with a ribbon of buttered caramel. Another flavor known as "The Geek!" (illustration inspired by one of Russell Lee's photos of the Donaldsonville, Louisiana, State Fair Geek of 1938) features blue raspberry, mascarpone and gummy worms. Images courtesy of Sideshow Gelato and David Gilleran.

There are also shades of geek acts that exist today and are seen in other cultural settings. In 2003, magicians Penn & Teller released a three-part documentary series called *Penn & Teller's Magic and Mystery Tour*. In each episode, they go to a different country to explore that country's magic and variety entertainment scene. In the China episode, they encounter a magician performing on the street who takes a live snake, inserts it into his nose, and pulls it out his mouth. In Egypt, they see a human ostrich-style performer who eats glass and nails and chews on a brick. Later, they go looking for a street performer named The Great Bafa of Alexandria, who is a snake swallower. When they encounter Bafa, he demonstrates his skill of swallowing a live snake then letting it slowly emerge from his lips after a moment. While in India, they attend an interesting magic show that climaxes with a performance of tug-of-war that features two wild men tied to the middle of the rope. The two men are dressed in minimal clothing, adorned in feathers and leaves along with body paint, and were snarling and clawing at the audience while tied to the rope. After a moment, they went into full glomming geek mode, with one picking up a live chicken and one picking up a live pigeon and proceeding to tear them apart with their teeth while the tug-of-war match continued. After the experience, Penn & Teller spoke to the magician who put on the show, who noted that due to the intensity, he always finished the show with that act, also noting that the wild men were actually his brothers-in-law. Later, in speaking to any Western viewers who may have been offended by the footage of the geek part of the act in their documentary, Penn Jillette eloquently commented, "It's a goddamn chicken! Tough it up! It's just a chicken. How many chickens are killed a day in just the U.K.? Self-righteous son of a bitch. It's just a chicken!"

More Recent Media Coverageof Geek-like Activity

Regardless of one's religious path or the sheer number of animals killed commercially for human consumption, the overall public perspective has become more critical in the 21st century and the consequences for geek offenders are much greater. In many cases, the previous perspectives of simply being grossed out and personally offended have been replaced with focused outrage and collective calls for retribution, which is evident in numerous cases from the 2010s.

In 2012, YouTube personality Louis Cole, who had gained a following by posting videos of his eating strange things such as live scorpions and giant ragworms, found himself in serious legal trouble after posting a video of him eating a live goldfish. Cole, who was based in the United Kingdom, received a letter from the Royal Society for the Prevention of Cruelty to Animals indicating that he may have violated animal cruelty laws that cover all vertebrate animals, including goldfish. He was facing a potential £20,000 fine and up to six months in prison for his alleged crime of eating a single goldfish. After obtaining a lawyer and having a trial date set, Cole was able to settle out of court by admitting "guilt" and being officially cautioned, hence avoiding a costly trial and criminal record for his actions (Thring).

During spring break 2015, University of Mississippi fraternity Phi Delta Theta member Brady Eaves, 18, was recorded biting the head off a hamster at a party. After the video made its way online, the fraternity removed Eaves from their organization and released a statement condemning his actions. As a result of the incident, his parents withdrew him from school and released a statement to the media announcing their intention to have him professionally assessed as a means to explain his behavior (Apel).

In March 2018, a 17-year-old Florida high school student named David Andrew Jiminez snuck into his school's chicken coop at night and bit the head off a chicken. He was arrested two days later and, when asked why he did it, he simply told the deputies, "I have violent outbursts." Numerous news outlets ran stories with outrage headlines regarding his actions. Jiminez was given a felony charge of animal cruelty in addition to trespassing (Cohen).

Geek activity on social media caused a controversy with French athlete Bixente Larralde. In 2019, online video emerged of Larralde biting the head from a live rooster at a small, private party. Larralde, who was the Basque Pelota World Champion, was met with outrage over his actions. An online petition for Larralde to be sacked by the French Pelota Federation gathered nearly 11,000 signatures, and the animal rights group The Brigitte Bardot Foundation announced that they were taking him to court over the incident (Terrell).

Geek's Got Talent

There are several instances of geek acts somehow making it onto national television during talent contests in various parts of the world during the 2010s.

During a live 2010 broadcast of the Pakistani talent show *Entertain If You Dare*, one of the participants walked out and bit the head off a live snake for his act. He then peeled off its skin and ate everything but the bones. After the show mistakenly aired in Britain, a complaint was filed against the show indicating that the performance was "clearly unsuitable for children and had the potential to cause offense to viewers in general" (Metrowebukmetro).

During a 2013 recording of the show *Arabs Got Talent*, a contestant named Ahmed Al Dousary started his performance by eating glass and lit charcoal. He then proceeded to eat a scorpion and bite the head off a live snake. Though his performance enraged local animal rights activists and the female judge hit her elimination buzzer and walked off in disgust, the two male judges, apparently intrigued by the unusual nature of the act, both voted their approval (Collis).

In 2017, news and video broke regarding a woman who appeared on a major talent show in Chongqing, China. She took the stage wearing traditional wild woman-style jungle attire and proceeded to bite the head off a live snake, then peeled the skin off of the body while the judges and audience looked on in horror. When interviewed, the woman noted that she had been eating various live animals with no side effects, saying, "Bullfrogs, pigeons, eels – I don't discriminate" (Webb).

In 2021, Texas snake handler Jackie Bibby made two appearances on the TBS talent competition *Go-Big Show*. A veteran snake performer, Bibby began handling snakes in 1969 and has made numerous television appearances over the years. He has been hospitalized on numerous occasions as a result of venomous snakebites. On one occasion, his leg was amputated during a hospital stay after a six-foot rattlesnake bit him during a show at a hotel in Addison, Texas ("Jackie Bibby: Texas Snakeman"). During his first appearance on *Go-Big Show*, Bibby was zipped up in a sleeping bag filled with venomous snakes and, after a moment was pulled out by his assistants, emerging unscathed. For his second appearance on the show, Bibby held eight rattlesnakes in his mouth while holding additional snakes in each hand. For good measure, his assistants placed a tarantula on his head.[10]

Onward

It is not simply the act of killing animals for entertainment that has fallen out of favor. As collective public opinions have continued to change over the course of generations, simply utilizing live animals in the context of family entertainment has become controversial and resulted in increased public outrage. Live animals such as elephants, horses, tigers, and camels were once a staple in many circuses. As pressure from animal rights activists has increased along with shifting public opinions and ongoing allegations of abuse, many circuses have been forced to remove this tradition from their shows completely, which has resulted in numerous traditional circus companies going out of business.

Even the Ringling Bros. and Barnum & Bailey Circus, once widely known for its many acts involving large animals, faced obstacles after the turn of the 21st century. In 2000, they were involved in a legal battle that lasted 14 years. It was brought on by

---

10. On his website, Jackie Bibby lists himself as holding the following Guinness World Records: Holding the most rattlesnakes in one's mouth (13 rattlesnakes), laying in a bathtub with the most snakes (195 rattlesnakes), lying in a sleeping bag with the most rattlesnakes (109 rattlesnakes), sacking 10 rattlesnakes in the fastest time (17.11 seconds), and going headfirst into a sleeping bag with the most rattlesnakes (24 rattlesnakes) ("Jackie Bibby: Texas Snakeman"). On December 7, 2021, Guinness World Records posted a photo of Bibby to their Twitter account, noting his achievement of holding snakes in his mouth, but prefaced the post by saying "WE NO LONGER MONITOR THIS RECORD" (@GWR).

animal rights groups that alleged that Ringling Bros. and Barnum & Bailey had been abusing the elephants used in their shows. However, the judge concluded in 2012 that the lawsuit was frivolous and had forced Ringling Bros and Barnum & Bailey's parent company, Feld Entertainment, to pay millions in legal fees. Notably, it was found that an animal rights group paid a former Ringling barn helper $190,000 to help bring about the suit, making him "essentially a paid plaintiff." In 2012, the American Society for the Prevention of Cruelty to Animals was ordered to pay approximately $9 million to the owners of Feld Entertainment. Two years later, in 2014, $15.75 million more was awarded to Feld Entertainment from various other animal rights groups that were involved in the legal battle. The approximate $25 million received by Feld Entertainment equated to roughly the costs they had paid to defend themselves in court (Barakat).

However, Ringling Bros. and Barnum & Bailey was ultimately pushed to remove animals from its company in 2016. The following year, the company announced that, after 146 years, it was closing. The closure was at least in part due to declining ticket sales as a result of being no longer able to feature elephants in their shows (Ellis-Petersen). In 2021, Feld Entertainment announced plans to relaunch Ringling Bros. and Barnum & Bailey Circus in 2023 with a new and completely animal-free format (Zoltak).

Even snake charming in India, which was once a notable form of entertainment and a profession to some, has experienced a sharp decline. Snake charming itself was actually banned in India in 1972 as a part of a wildlife protection act.[11] Law enforcement has been increasingly cracking down on enforcing the law in more recent generations since the early 2000s (Singh).

Despite all of these developments and occurrences, shades of geek-like attitudes are still found in modern entertainment. These attitudes are evident in television shows like *Fear Factor*, where contestants eat insects and other unsanitary things for viewers' amusement. To some degree, this is also evident in competitive eating events, where the audiences

---

11. There is an economic principle called The Cobra Effect that refers to unintended negative consequences of an incentive that was designed to improve society or individual wellbeing. This principle came about during the British rule of India. Delhi was overrun with cobras, so officials began offering a bounty on cobra skins as an incentive to reduce the cobra population. However, soon people began to game the system by setting up snake farms to breed snakes just for their skins. It resulted in high payouts for all the snake skins but no reduction in the natural populace as intended. The bounty was soon withdrawn and the farmed snakes set free in the wild, which increased the number of snakes in the wild (Hartley).

marvel not just at the sheer quantity of food consumed by the competitors, but also the messy and often uncouth spectacle that is created in the process. Elements of geek can even be seen in some niches of pornography, where consuming bodily fluids is fetishized.[12] Some genres such as *gokkun*, where the focus is on the subject swallowing large volumes of semen, take the approach to an extreme. At a point, one wonders when the goal of legitimate sexual arousal has been disregarded in favor of attempting to entice the viewer by pushing boundaries though an extreme orally based spectacle.

As far as where the sideshow geek is headed in the future, it is impossible to predict with certainty. However, an earnest revival of any sort seems unlikely due to today's social and legal standards, though smaller references and simulated tributes may occur at certain niche events. In all likelihood, the term will continue to be used nearly exclusively in its modern context of computer tech and entertainment fandom culture until the sideshow geek is simply a footnote in dictionaries as an archaic definition of an old, forgotten sideshow act. Instead of having context for this reference, future generations may stumble upon the alternate definition and wonder if something so seemingly absurd actually occurred or was merely the result of an urban legend.

Geek shows were not only a very real thing but were culturally significant and quite popular at one point in history. Much like the outsider status that the term represents, it is challenging to come to a definitive conclusion on the matter of where the sideshow geek's relevance stands in the pages of time.

For some, geek shows were an in-demand attraction that not only gave work to those with minimal skillsets but also generated money and entertained a willing public. To others, they were disgusting displays of blatant exploitation and abuse. Whatever your own opinion, the sideshow geeks occupied a unique niche they carved into entertainment history.

---

12. Incidentally, a pornographic film was released in 1971 called "The Geek," which features a group of adults hiking through the woods – which are inhabited by a part-animal, part-human creature known simply as "The Geek". Unsurprisingly, The Geek ends up engaging in coitus with a couple of the female characters toward the film's climax.

Appendix 1 - NOTICE ON JACQUES DE FALAISE, His habits, his foods, and how he stays safe

English translation of *NOTICE SUR JACQUES DE FALAISE, ses habitudes, sa nourriture et sa santé (NOTICE ON JACQUES DE FALAISE, His habits, his foods, and how he stays safe)*. Originally published by the BAILLARD printing house in 1820. Translation by Jean Albiges.

***

Jacques Simon, also known as Jacques De Falaise, was born on the edge of the Ante in 1754. He spent a good portion of his life in the quarries of Montmartre, near Paris, where he worked on the most obscure and tiring jobs. For the longest time, he ignored an astonishing ability that nature had given him. When he did, he shouted like the Francaleu in the Metromania:

« In my stomach, one day, this talent should be found,

And I was sixty years old when it happened »

Only fate itself allowed him to discover this talent, a few years ago. Jacques attended one of his colleague's weddings and thanks to his cheerful mood, he was sought out by a group of young villagers, with whom he was forced to leave the table to partake in candid games. After having played the main-chaude and the Colin-maillard, they moved on to a game consisting of hiding one of the player's boxes or a piece of jewelry that another player had to find. Jacques, in charge of hiding a chain and a locket that the bride had just taken off her neck, had foolishly hidden these in his mouth. The grimace on his face was quick to betray him. After having designated him, one of the players, who was starting to catch on as to why Jacques was staying silent, finally asked him to admit if he had the jewelry or not. Jacques, a bit surprised to have been so quickly discovered, wanted to make it hard for his opponent. Without thinking, he swallowed the chain and the locket, then opened his mouth wide to say: "You see that I don't have it." The public's surprise was quickly followed by fear when they realized that Jacques had swallowed the groom's gifts. Everyone ran toward him, begging him to reveal what he had done with the objects, but Jacques, bothered by all the sudden accusations and with what seemed to be not a worry in the world concerning the foreign object in his stomach, broke away from his friends and said, "Walk away, walk away; I'll bring it back to you tomorrow." This adventure astonished onlookers even more when Jacques came back to work the next day, as healthy as ever. Since that time, he has often repeated this number, and always to great success. Objects like keys, crosses, and rings were given to him to swallow. His experiments with swallowing only inanimate objects soon gave way to testing with living animals which were swallowed with just as much ease. Finally, for almost a year, his talent was put to use as entertainment for all the workers in the quarries. Having convinced itself that he was perfectly safe, Jacques accepted the offer from one of his bosses to let the crowd enjoy this extraordinary phenomenon.

Several doctors and surgeons from the capital had scrupulously examined Jacques and were unable to explain this singular phenomenon from the results. They even admitted that there were no differences between his organs and those of a normal person, with the exception that Jacques's throat was a little bit wider than ordinary. They came to the conclusion that Jacques was capable of expanding his throat much farther than usual. This feature, which people in the industry have written off as being without any interest, does not take anything away from his amazing skill, forcing them to think about how he actually manages to accomplish these feats.

It's hardly noticeable that Jacques, despite performing his number numerous times the same day, is never tired or bothered, which is made even more surprising by the fact that everyone knows that the insertion of a smaller foreign body in the esophagus is enough to cause mortal injury. There are many examples of these types of injuries throughout history. Anacreon died by suffocation with a raisin seed lodged in his pharynx. The poet Gilbert suffocated with the keys to his safe, swallowed in a fit of madness. Finally, the sultan Selim was one day with his favorite sultana, who was cheekily catching with her mouth the cherries that her master was throwing. One of the cherries unfortunately got lodged in her throat, causing deadly spasms and convulsions.

Jacques's experiments seem, at first, just as dangerous as these stories. However, the knowledge that he has already been successful in accomplishing so many of these tricks is absolutely vital to reassuring onlookers as they see him put a 20" sword down his throat, all the way to his torso. We would expect, at least, that the removed sword would come out stained with blood, but to our great surprise, the sword is removed with only the slightest hint of the humidity of his breath on the blade.

The number where Jacques swallows nuts does not provoke the same level of fear, as it is quite common to swallow cherry or apricot pits. However, one must admit that there is a big difference between the pit of a fruit, which is smooth and moist, and the shell of a large nut, dry and rough. The fact that he can ingurgitate these confirms his great ability to expand his throat as well as a unique sensibility of the internal membranes.

The number in which Jacques swallows a stovepipe goes against all laws of physiology; we cannot comprehend how the fragile membranes inside his organs aren't ripped up by the passing of an object that is so rough and has so many sharp angles.

Swallowing a rose along with all its needles is even less fathomable. Anyone who has picked up a rose knows how sensitive and harrowing their needles are. How is it possible that these sharp needles are able to find a way through? One explanation naturally comes to the mind of the spectators, as these experiments were performed in the very same place where crowds would often come to witness great feats of strength and agility. We are therefore tempted to believe that their minds are still fascinated by some of these wonderful illusions, which have become so familiar to the enthusiasts of the Hotels des fermes theatre. However, all it takes is a little deductive thinking to confirm the existence of this phenomenon. Jacques is not a wizard. He performs alone, surrounded on all sides by the crowd, for everyone to see any and all of his moves. After he has finished, even the most dubious onlookers will easily be convinced that the means required to create this illusion would be even more inconceivable than the reality before them.

When it comes to cards, the public can see that Jacques swallows them without shrinking or destroying them with his teeth in the slightest. The trick does not even last long enough for the cards to be wet with his saliva.

The white mouse is from Africa. This little quadruped, which is similar in appearance to a squirrel, is prized for its flexibility. However, despite its tiny size, it has formidably corrosive teeth and sharpened claws which can cause great pain. It is once again impossible to explain how those same teeth, capable of cutting into the hardest of surfaces, are able to traverse Jacques's intestinal membranes without causing any damage. As of this day, he has only ever complained of a few bites on his lips.

The sparrow is armed with a strong beak and vigorous talons. He is covered in feathers, a fact that by itself should make the swallowing of this bird nearly impossible. The ingestion of a live eel and crayfish is seemingly even worse than a grass snake. The eel is more agile and persistent than its reptilian counterpart and, what's more, 15 months after swallowing, Jacques often felt his stomach unsettled. Whenever the animals that he had ingurgitated were too active for too long, Jacques simply had to drink a few drops of rum and eau-de-vie to stop them. That is all it took for the cycle of digestion to restart and continue as usual.

The nickname Polyphagia is all wrong for Jacques, since according to the Greek etymology, it means "great eater." These words do not qualify Jacques, as he does not eat great quantities; quite the opposite. It would be easy to say that he does not eat a lot for a man who spent the majority of this time laboring in the fields.

It may take much longer and many more scientific studies to be able to physically explain Jacques's astonishing experiments. Although there must be a logical explanation, it has not yet been found. This talent for ingestion is far from the ordinary laws of nature, so we have to consider it a rare exception, which has been perfected, over time, with practice. Jacques's experiments have been proven safe for him. Even if he wanted to, he can no longer bring back all of the living things from his stomach, animals that often represented disgust and fear. This gift is truly an anomaly of nature. Individuals who believe that those performing these types of experiments are actively searching for their death are wrong. We can say for sure that this trepidation is unfounded. This number does not constitute an act of suicide; it is simply a game with nature, an anomaly, which happens throughout time and space. Because of this anomaly, Jacques had to take certain precautions in order to maintain his strength and health, resulting in a sober, active lifestyle, allowing him to continue ignoring the living beings inside his body. To conclude this notice, we will recount the tale of two adventurers who, like us, firmly believe that Jacques has a gift, the gift of swallowing any objects that can possibly fit in one's stomach.

On the 20th of August 1815, Jacques was doing his experiments in front of a great number of spectators, some of whom were English. One of them challenged Jacques to swallow his watch, so Jacques asked for the man's watch to inspect its size. The watch was barely in his hands before he swallowed it, along with the chain. This action causes fear as much as surprise. The silence in the room was broken by sounds of disgust made by some women and several "very well" proclamations from the English section. The lucky spectators spoke far and wide to his friends and family, of which there were many in Paris. Each and every one of them would vouch for the authenticity of this seemingly tall tale. Mr. Comte's theatre was full every night from then on. Jacques offered to repeat this experiment; however, people wisely stopped bringing their watches to shows. Finally, after a few days, a nobleman challenged him to swallow coins, which Jacques accepted. Thirty coins were swallowed with great ease, making the crowd laugh repeatedly in the process. The game eventually stopped when the gentleman said that he had run out of money.

Appendix 2 - Biographical Sketch of Serpentina the Serpent Lady

Biographical Sketch of Serpentina the Serpent Lady. From the author's private collection.

BIOGRAPHICAL SKETCH
OF
SERPENTINA
THE SERPENT LADY

BIOGRAPHICAL SKETCH

OF

SERPENTINA

THE SERPENT LADY

Of all the many great curiosities of nature that have been presented to the public from time to time, positively not one of them can equal in anatomical and physical peculiarities the subject of the present sketch.

The Eighth Wonder of the World, the Despair of Doctors, the Puzzle of Scientists are only a few of the many appellations that have been bestowed upon this interesting lady.

FIG. 1—SERPENTINA'S ORDINARY POSITION

In her we are confronted with the unusual sight of a prepossessing young lady, 37 years of age. She was born in Douglas, Ontario, Canada, and is one of a family of children, but the father, the mother, the brother and the sisters are ordinary in ap-

pearance; nothing unusual in their personal appearance or physical characteristics. The peculiarity of Serpentina consists of the
fact that she possesses no bones in her body below the shoulders,
i. e., no spinal column, vertebrae, or backbone, but in every respect she is exactly the same as any normal young woman of
the same age.

Looking at Serpentina for the first time, visitors will feel
inclined to pity her, but the writer can assure them that Serpentina needs neither pity nor sympathy. She does not know what
an ache or pain means, and she has never needed the services
of a physician since she was a small child.

Yet she has been examined by hundreds, not because she
ever needed their services, but simply because she was good
enough to submit to examinations for their benefit and instruc-
tion.

FIG. 2—SERPENTINA'S SLEEPING POSITION

And yet Serpentina is one of life's tragedies, for wherever
she is placed, there she must stay until some one goes for her.
She must always have someone within call, and consequently
she can never know the real meaning of an individual life.

Just imagine, if you can, how you would feel for thirty-seven

years you had never straightened out the lower limbs, never once
stood upon your feet, and consequently never taken one step of
walking exercise.

In all those years Serpentina has only been able to assume,
or be placed in three different positions. The first one (Fig. 1)
her ordinary reclining position. That position is to her the same
that sitting in a chair is to you. In that position she passes the
greater part of her time. When she sleeps she is placed in the
position illustrated in Fig. 2. Each night for thirty-seven years
she has slept in that position.

Exercise of some kind is a necessity in order to prevent the
internal organs from becoming congested. So the only exercise
Serpentina can take is for her to be placed in the position illustrated in Fig. 3.

FIG. 3—SERPENTINA'S ONLY EXERCISE

THE CAUSE . . .

Serpentina's condition, in the opinion expressed by the leading physicians, is described as being a case of "Arrested Ossification," caused by a lack of developing power of the mother, probably due to overwork before the child was born.

Appendix 3 - On the Subject of Geek Shows with Clarence Samuels

Transcript of interview on the subject of Geek Shows
Clarence Samuels
May 08, 1980
Transcript courtesy of Rhett Bryson
Rhett Bryson would like to thank Dr. Jim Pitts for all of the introductions to showfolk over the years in his geek research. They proved to be invaluable resources to primary research information on the fascinating subject of geeks and geek shows.

***

This is the transcript of a taped interview with Clarence Samuels made on the lot of a touring circus in Travelers Rest, SC. Rhett Bryson and Jim Pitts were talking with Mr. Samuels, who had some years ago run a geek show with a performer named Ali Boo.

Rhett: How long ago was it that you worked with Ali Boo?

Samuels: Five years ago. He's been dead now three years. He was about the best.

Rhett: How many years did you work with him?

Samuels: Huh...fourteen. He was something.

Rhett: Could you describe the way the show looked from the front?

Samuels: Well, he was the type of person that would change the front. Like he wanted to put up a banner line...the next week he might want to go into the jungle and cut down trees. You know...It's true, and build a front like a wild man and make it like a cave, you know...he was something.

Rhett: So he had some control with the way it looked? He had some ideas about how he wanted to present the act?

Samuels: Right, he'd have different ideas and he would change it. Kept the valance though, you know, used the valance....like fairs, he would use it at fairs, but on still dates he would do anything to attract attention.

Rhett: Did you have a taped bally out front or did you have a front talker?

Samuels: Oh, you had a talker on the front. You couldn't put a tape on it then. Tape wouldn't have done any good. Because this week he would do one type of show and the next week he would change it and the next night he might change.

Rhett: What did the inside look like? What was the situation? Did you have a cage or a pit?

Samuels: You had a pit. And when he did a wild man...We went to New York and got this man on the make-up- staff from NBC...CBS, I'm sorry...on the fourth floor of the NBC building. He give us this whole long string, you know...hair...and at night he would always put the hair on his arms...and he would look like a wild man.

Rhett: What other types of costumes did he wear?

Samuels: We put overalls on him...and a bandana..with the teeth, you know...put the teeth in...with fangs coming out. Now when he would do this, we could put him in a cage.

Rhett: You had a cage at the end of the pit?

Samuels: No, no...We would have the cage and the pit...two different things. When you wanted to do wild man, at the jungle land...we'd put the cage in...work in the cage. When we would do the geek, he would work in the pit. Some places you couldn't do the geek, so you would do the wild man.

Rhett: Tell me about the wild man. You would get the crowd in, and the wild man, he was out of sight...or just sitting in the cage?

Samuels: He'd walk around the cage...see, the cage would be in the middle of the tent. So he would walk all around there.

Rhett: They stood, there were no seats or anything?

Samuels: Right. And when he got so many in there and he wanted them out...he would bust out. And everybody would leave.

Rhett: He didn't do anything except act wild, shake the cage?

Samuels: He would do nothing. They would just watch him.

Rhett: And when he had a big enough crowd, he would break out and run them out?

Samuels: Right. He would look at everybody and...right in the eye, you know...and walk around and look, you know...like a wild man would really do. And when they got too many in there, he would chase them out.

Rhett: And then build the crowd up again?

Samuels: Yes. But Ali Boo, there's never been anybody else like him.

Rhett: When he did the geek act, then...did he have the same costume?

Samuels: No, no.

Rhett: How did he dress for that?

Samuels: He had all of his hair cut off, just a little peak at the top of his head, like an Indian, you know. And hot pants, cut the pants off. And nothing else, that's all.

Rhett: And it was a wooden pit? A wooden sided pit?

Samuels: We'd have canvas. And we would have a door, like at the back. And he'd, you know, come out the door. He'd run them out. Anything he did would run them out.

Rhett: That was always his finish?

Samuels: It's a thrill, it's always a thrill, that's all. You don't chase much or it don't mean nothing, you know. There was a chain, you know.

Rhett: You had him chained to a post?

Samuels: You know, like a chain and a bar. And he would be shaking the chain.

Rhett: He'd make noise, but he would never talk?

Samuels: Never say a word. He would shake the chain, he had a microphone there, you know, shaking the chain and the noise be on the midway...and he get ready to bust out, you know...and hit that door, and everybody would hear it on the midway, you know.

Rhett: Was there somebody else in there with him? Who would turn the animals loose?

Samuels: No, no...he had boxes. He kept them all in boxes. Now this guy would take the pig and bite the pig.

Rhett: Was it a small pig? How big was it?

Samuels: Yea...it would be a small pig.

Rhett: Would he kill them, would he kill every animal that he used? Or he just bit on them?

Samuels: He just bit on them. He bite on them...when he bite on them, they would squeal, you know.

Rhett: Didn't you tell me about the frogs?

Samuels: Oh yes...The frogs there. He would swallow the frogs. He would open his mouth and you see no frog, right...then he would close his mouth...and spit the frog out.

Rhett: The frog would hop on off, right.

Samuels: Right.

Rhett: So, he would wait for the crowd to build up, and he would do a couple of those things, and chase the crowd out?

Samuels: Yeah, that's right...Do you remember Pongo? There was this one guy called Pongo. He was crippled, peg leg. He would also bite the snakes, you know...peel the snake, you know...hold them in his mouth, peel the snake.

Rhett: Peel them with his mouth.

Samuels: And roaches, whatever you give him, he would eat. Anything you would bring him.

Rhett: It was a challenge act? He would eat whatever they would bring him?

Samuels: Right, light bulbs, he'd take light bulbs...he did everything. He wasn't as good as Ali Boo, though. Ali Boo, he was more of a producer. He knew what he wanted to produce and he knew how to act it, you see, and that makes a difference.

Pitts: Where is he now?

Samuels: Ali Boo, he's dead now.

Rhett: Was Ali Boo an independent, or did he sign on with some shows?

Samuels: He was always independent, always. We were friends, you know...form way back. When I had the review, and we would play on midways where the different freaks would be, they would always come to talk to me, sit around the review and shoot the bull, you know. And they would always ask..."Why don't you get into grind shows?" And I wasn't interested in them. That is how I could get it. How I got so many acts. Because when I did go into, everybody wanted to come in.

Rhett: It helps you to have several attractions, to get people to come in with you?

Samuels: Yeah, it would. The only thing wrong with it, you don't make as much money with it as with the reviews, there is no comparison. The review would do...say like we had four shows here. These little shows, like. When we would come on the bally...the band would play...we would start selling tickets then, while the band's playing, while the talker is talking, right. We all go back, the band go back to the stage. We got 500 people, paying $2.50. How you going to catch that when you got 12 people who going to stand there 15 minutes, talking? You can't. There is no way. There is no comparison. Course, it's a passe thing now.

Rhett: The small shows don't go well anymore? The big shows even don't pull as well as they used to?

Samuels: Because it's been so many bad shows, you know....fake shows...so when people get bit...five or six times in a row...if something did come that was decent, they wouldn't believe it.

Rhett: Has there ever been any sort of policing in you industry to stop those bad shows, to get them off?

Samuels: The owner of the carnival wants the back end shows, something back there.

Rhett: Was the freak show always on the back end?

Samuels: Always.

Rhett: Did you see other geek shows besides the Ali Boo show, that were different in some way?

Samuels: Yes, but not as good. There were quite a few, but they weren't nothing near as what were Mango and Pango which was (unintelligible), which you know...he died last year. He was good. He would go up on the show and do the tricks with the sand, you know with the water and the sand, put his hand in and come up with the dry sand. You know, he did a lot of magical things. He was all right. But, uh, those two guys were the best.

Rhett: Did some of the shows pick up a local person and put him in the geek show? Just get some wino from town or something?

Samuels: (Name uninteligiable), he would do that. Come right here. He wouldn't care.

Rhett: He just carried his physical show, the joint, and pick up somebody?

Samuels: That's right, that's the worst thing you can do.

Rhett: Do you think the audiences knew, when they were seeing Ali Boo's show that they were seeing a good show?

Samuels: Sure, sure...Any midway that he was on, after the first night, word of mouth brought them in. I don't care what you were doing on the midway, you couldn't get the crowd to leave there. They wanted to stay around to see who is going to run out and who is going to fall, who was going to get excited, you know, who was going to talk about it.

Rhett: Would Ali Boo ever come out on the bally platform?

Samuels: Oh no. No, he wouldn't. During the day you wouldn't know where he was. He was an entertainer.

Pitts: Do you remember any of the spiel that they used?

Samuels: I can't remember. Let me see, now. The talker would say: "Ladies and gentlemen, you see what just happened? This little man is wild. He doesn't speak English, he doesn't understand. He is stronger than an ox, he was two sets of teeth. And his teeth are perfect. Could it be the food that he eats? Why? Ladies and gentlemen, when you see this little man, you will understand why we say that he is so wild, because when you talk to him...he wears no clothes, he might tear them off of himself. But we will protect you, don't worry."

Rhett: You have got to make them feel safe?

Samuels: Oh, yeah.

Rhett: When you say little man, was he actually physically a small person?

Samuels: No, no. Ali Boo was a big man, big man. He was good size.

Rhett: Had he been that all of his life in the carnivals and shows? Or did he do other things as well?

Samuels: That was all, he was an actor, a producer.

Rhett: Where did he live when he wasn't with the show?

Samuels: There wasn't any time that he wasn't with a show. Because, the shows...when the season closed, on the East Coast, well, the fairs are starting in California.

Rhett: So, he always had dates?

Samuels: Always. He booked himself.

Rhett: How did he travel? What sort of an outfit did he have?

Samuels: A trailer, he had a little trailer he pulled. He lived out of the trailer, pulling the show behind it.

Rhett: How old was he when he died?

Samuels: 74. And he looked like he was about your age (37). When I read that he was 74 years of age, I couldn't believe it. I didn't know it. Because we never discussed age. To see him, his actions, his talk, it was nothing like someone 74 years old.

Rhett: What kinds of animals did he use in his act besides pigs and frogs? Did he use chickens?

Samuels: Snakes, chickens, everything he could find. He'd be walking along, grasshoppers, whatever he could find. Anything.

Rhett: He seemed to enjoy his work, from what you have said.

Samuels: He did. He did. The next day, be talking about the different things that he did. Little new things that he would do.

Rhett: It seems like that was rare, that he would add to his act, have the intelligence to think of new things to do.

Samuels: That's right, he was a producer. The average one was an illiterate. You take them and say do so and so, and they say "Ok, I'll do it."

Rhett: He was obviously respected on the lot?

Samuels: He was like, like he was the operator. He was treated as if he was the operator, not an employee.

Rhett: I appreciate you sharing with me your remembrances of the act and that part of the carnival that is gone now.

Samuels: There will never be another.

Rhett: You told me before that there are no more geek acts on the road and there are not likely to be because of the protection of the animals...

Samuels: Oh, you won't ever see it again...now in Miami, we play Miami, with Sonny Dixon, who played with Amusement of America, with Jack Royal, with (?) Shelton, with these shows. But with the youth fair in Miami, you can't put a freak show in there...If you could get one person, one person who could really do an act...with insects only, it would work...but you can't be cruel to animals. But to find somebody who would take a fly, you know...or anything, just take anything...if a guy would do that, today it wouldn't put him out of business.

Appendix 4 - What We Know About Waino and Plutano, Wild Men of Borneo

What We Know About Waino and Plutano, Wild Men of Borneo, Vaudeville, Music Halls, Revues, Cabarets, and Variety Shows Collection, SPEC.TRI.0063, Jerome Lawrence and Robert E. Lee Theatre Research Institute, Ohio State University Libraries.

PRICE FIVE CENTS.

WHAT WE KNOW ABOUT

WAINO and PLUTANO,

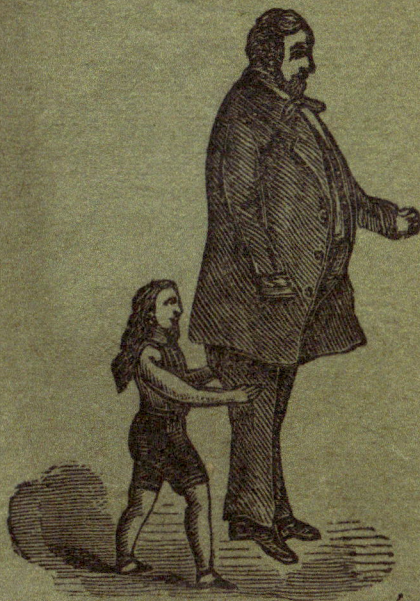

WILD MEN OF BORNEO.

WITH POEMS DEDICATED TO THEM.

WAINO AND PLUTANO,

Age, about 50 years.   Weight, 45 lbs.

The Wild Men of Borneo !

CAPTURE.

CHAPTER 1.

With a few facts to serve as a basis we might construct a plausible and interesting narrative of the life and adventures of these little men previous to their capture, but such is not our intention ; we will give facts as we have them and leave speculation to the imaginative reader.

After many years of associations with these singular little beings their origin remains as much a mystery as it was the day we first set eyes on them, and no doubt it will remain so to the end of time.

When captured by Capt. Hammond on the rocky coast of the Island of Borneo they were, without doubt, men grown—that was in the year 1848. We now judge them by their features to be at least fifty years old. If they had not at that time attained full growth and strength, they could not have resisted, long and violently, the force of four stout seamen. When made prisoners at last, after one had been separated from the other outside their cave, they still refused to be pacified, and remained for many months unsubdued. Even after landing in the United States the savage nature of both asserted itself, and it was only by degrees that they were reconciled to the habits of civilized life. Human they were, however, though rude and restive; and in the course of time, under patient kindness, humanity subdued savageism. To compare these quiet, amiable beings, at middle age, with the "animals" they were once like is surprising and interesting, and recalls to our mind a couple of verses which seem quite applicable to the present case :

There is no earthly gauge
    To limit or confine
The soul of child and sage,
    Whose progress is divine.

There is no human heart
    To smallest mortal given,
But it may claim its part
    In God's Eternal Heaven.

CHAPTER II.

Borneo is an Island so large that England, Ireland and Scotland might be set down in the middle of it. The interior of this vast Island is a dense forest, inhabited by a race of humanity, very little different from the animal creation, which is known to travelers as *Negritos.* Yellowish in color, and undersized, they hold no intercourse with semi-civilized tribes, such as their neighbors, the *Dyaks*, or the *Bugis*, who both differ from Malays of Borneo. They dwell in impenetrable obscurity. No stranger seeks their villages, for traffic or from curiosity. No missionary has instructed them. They are strange to us, as a people ; and all we can learn, from the books of travelers in Borneo, is to the effect that they live in caverns, or make nesting places like birds, upon the boughs of trees.*

Whatever may have been the ancestry of our two little "Wild Men" their characteristics are as much a problem in natural science now as on the day they were landed from a vessel on our shores. They were then, literally, "wild animals," full of monkey antics, ugly in temper, and hard to manage. Thirty years of "development" under kind, educative treatment, have made these rude crea-

*Alfred Russell Wallace, in his book on the Malays, says the Negritos are dwarfs, about four feet six inches in stature. Their names mean "little negroes,"

tures—now become middle-aged men—what
the "image of God" was created to be—intelligent, amiable and self-possessed human beings. Though so diminitive in person, the
compact *form* of each is "the human form divine ;" and for symmetry of proportions, it
might serve as a model for sculpture. The
tenacity of their muscular and bony structure
endows them with greater physical power
than is commonly possessed by full-grown
men. Either Waino, by his own strength, or
Plutano, unaided, can lift a weight of several
hundred pounds, and if you observe the play
of their well-knit sinews, you may judge that
without an ounce of superfluous flesh on
either body, they can exert force to an extraordinary degree. Mentally, our little
"Wild Men" have steadily progressed ; although some laxity of membrane in their
throats denies them the blessing of speech
beyond a few tones not pleasant to hear ; but
their natures, from year to year have im-
proved in mutual kindness, general courtesy
and the desire to please. Time has marked
lines of age on their faces, but their hearts
are still youthful ; even as their glossy, silken
head covering continues soft and beautiful.

It is a matter of regret, indeed, that speech
was not among the gifts bestowed upon these
little men by nature ; or that some cause, in
their infancy, prevented its proper exercise.
Discovered as they were, in a wild condition,
with no covering on their bodies, and wandering over a savage district, no clue could
be gained to their prior history by communi-

cation through any language spoken where they were found, or through subsequent intercourse, when they had, after some years, been made to understand a few English words. Their real organs may have been perfect at birth, and afterward reduced to feebleness from lack of exercise in any utterance except gutteral tones or witd cries. Be that as it may, no satisfactory information concerning their habits or whereabouts, before capture in that forest wilderness, has ever been obtained, and from the few fragments of memory they retained, only a brief statement of their early life would be warranted. They may have been *lost* or abandoned, in childhood, before they articulated any language; and if so they may have been born in another savage country, because we have accounts of fishermen belonging to the mainland of India being blown to sea, or carried by ocean currents in their frail boats, to the Islands of Oceanica, eight hundred miles away. Captain Cook found on the Island of Wateoo, in Polynesia, three inhabitants of Otabetta who had been drifted between the two Islands a distance of 550 miles.

CHAPTER III.

A Spanish traveler † in the Philippine Isles, north of Borneo, found the *Tagals*, a tribe of Indians, living as he says, "in a state of plenty, tranquility and innocence, resembling the golden age." A chain of Islands extends from Borneo toward the coast of India, near the Burman Empire, and not a great distance from Siam ; and we know that Siamese and Burmese — especially their females — are lighter skinned than Hindoos, besides being more or less refined in their customs. If a small vessel, carrying a Burmese or Siamese family, were cast away on the Island of Borneo, that supposition might account for our two little "wild men" being left to wander in the condition they were in when first seen. But as before remarked, no definite recollection could be awakened in the minds of those roving children or men ; whatever age they may have reached when discovered by the New England captain. If they were offspring of those *Negritos* of Borneo, who dwell in tree-habitations, we may surmise some of their antecedents ; but, if they were brought to that Malay island from the mainland, we can only trace their origin by seeking a resemblance in their natural features, to the lighter skinned tribes of India, some of whom are descended, without mixture, from the same Caucassian race which gave birth to Hebrews and Grecians of ancient time.

Impressions of their past existence remained in the minds of both, we may suppose, for a number of years ; because they carried about brains and eyes, in their small heads, which were neither dull nor unobservant. But before they were able to comprehend the meaning of English words, it is quite likely that the earlier memories and associa-

had faded away, under the impress of new and changing scenes, as they journeyed from place to place. In nearly thirty years of intimate relations with their companions and protectors, they have never given any coherant account of their experience in a state of wild nature ; and we are left to conjecture what manner of life they could have led.

When first brought before the public Waino and Plutano were hardly more elevated in social standing than ourang-outangs of a like size; but no ourang-outang could climb a tree with more agility than they displayed. Even in middle age, they are experts in all such exercises. If you examine their little fingers, you will find the conformation such as to afford them astonishing prehensile powers, enabling them to *grip* an object, and retain their hold. Either of them can lift his entire body by his little finger, and so swing, to and fro, in the manner of a Borneo gorilla.

During the years that they have been before the public they have exhibited their wonderful strength by lifting one or two men, selected from the audiences in the manner shown in the cut. Impossible as it may seem to those who have never witnessed their feats of strength we have known them to lift, individually, as much as 450 pounds. Formerly, Waino was the strongest of the two, but about twelve years ago while in the act of lifting two heavy men, the temporary stage upon which they were exhibiting gave way and in the fall the weight of the two men came upon the little fellow in such a way as to crush his hip which has caused the permanent lameness now so noticeable. How such minute forms can contain such remarkable strength is a mystery to all. Their great activity and rapidity of motion is also a source

FEATS OF STRENGTH.

of wonder and surprise. As you may have observed Plutano is almost constantly in motion, pacing up and down the platform in a

quick, restless manner, while his keen eye
takes in every surrounding object. Previous
to his injury Waino was equally as active.
A little incident which occured some years
ago will illustrate their wonderful speed.
While exhibiting at a fair in Kentucky, Plutano became much enraged by the tantilizing
conduct of a drunken man in the audience,
and seizing a horse whip from the hand of a
bystander he struck the fellow a sharp cut
across the face. The man caught Plutano
by his long hair and dragged him from the
platform, when quite a desperate fight ensued. Many present would like to have seen
which would come off victorious, but fearing
injury to the "little man" they were separated, and Mr. W—— undertook to correct
Plutano for his hasty exhibitions of temper ;
but our little hero was too much enraged to
listen to reason or be controlled by moderate
force. He eluded the grasp of his master
and escaping from the tent, sped with the
fleetness of a "wild animal," through the
crowd and out on the main road towards
S——. Several persons started in pursuit,
but so swiftly did the little light form skim
over the ground that in a few minutes it was
entirely lost to view. Seeing the necessity
of the case his pursuers returned and after
securing some of the fleetest horses in the
neighborhood started again in pursuit. For
some time they tracked him by the small
footprints in the dust ; then the trail was
lost, he having evidently chosen the soft,
grassy roadside. Some turned into the

woods and searched in every direction, thinking he might have sought a hiding place in
the trees. After traversing a distance of
12 miles the foremost horseman was stopped
by a signal from a resident by the way, who
asked him if he was looking for anything,
and upon being informed of the case in hand,
stated that the "queer little being" they were
in search of had reached his house about an
hour previous and was then in the back yard
amusing himself with the dogs. When the
rest of the pursuers came up and they approached the little fellow, he made no effort
to evade them, and appeared perfectly willing
to return. Calculating from the time he
started to the time of his arrival at the farm
house, he must have traveled at the rate of a
mile in five minutes.

CHAPTER IV.

In disposition our "little men" differ widely; and in consideration of this dissimilarity
of this disposition, Capt. Hammond gave
them the peculiar Spanish names of Waino
and Plutano—Waino signifying good and
Plutano bad. The former was much more
easy to subdue than the latter, and has ever
since exhibited a gentle, passive nature,
greatly at variance with that of Plutano, who
is bold, reckless and daring, quick tempered
and always hard to control. But kindness
and perseverence has accomplished more than
was ever hoped for. If we should recall

their mental and moral progress during all the years since they came to us as "wild animals" to be nurtured and developed into manliness of character and disposition, it would show their souls unfolding, page after page, of intelligence like the leaves of a copy book. It would interpret the way of nature, under influences of social care and affection, gradually but surely informing their minds and hearts. God, our Heavenly Father rescued, through human means, these two children of the wilderness, from their savage surroundings, and out of all exposures and dangers, to lead them into our civilization and point out for them the path toward eternal happiness in a better world to come. He has watched over their lives with the same Divine Providence that oversees all human lives, whether they are lowly or exalted. Though orphans here, on earth, and claiming relationship with no familiar race of mankind, these little beings, we are assured, will find, through Heavenly mercy, an immortal kindred of souls in their life to come; if they continue to live blamelessly, and as brothers to all men, perform their human duties; so that, when called away—as we must all be summoned, sooner or later—our "wild men of Borneo," Waino and Plutano, may be as well prepared to enjoy Eternal Life, in the "image of God," as are the highest and wisest of our sacred teachers; whatever be their religion, or however they may seek to worship the God who made them.

14   WAINO AND PLUTANO.

As a poetic description of wild savage life,
and of the wild men" themselves, we may
here introduce some verses written to Waino
and Plutano, by a friend of theirs :

WORDS DEDICATED TO

WAINO AND PLUTANO,

WILD MEN OF BORNEO.

In the Island of Borneo, beneath an Eastern sky,
Just under the Equator, with mountains towering
    high,
Where roves the wild Ourang-Outang, Gorilla and
    Malay,
And beasts of fiercest nature are watching for their
    prey,—

The huntsman with his dog and gun, undaunted,
    undismayed,
Walked forth into the forest to prosecute his trade;
When looking up in search of game, perchance his
    eye did see,
Two little men of infant size suspended in a tree.

These little men made off with speed, and ran their
    lives to save,
And, like David, when pursued by Saul, took shelter
    in a cave.

But here their folly soon was proved, for the hunter
stopped their way,
And then contrived to capture them and carry them
away.

And now as little prisoners, for twenty years or
more,
The land of North America they've nearly traveled
oe'r;
And thousands have beheld them, and wondered at
their size,
And the feats of strength they perform doth every
one surprise.

For these men, though very small indeed, are of
great strength possessed,
With bone and sinew small but firm, and full developed chest;
Their heads are small, their features thin, com-
plexion very fair;
And down their backs flow gracefully their soft and
silken hair.

Here we behold the matchless power, the wisdom
and the skill
Of Him who made these little men according to
his will;
But more admire the wondrous love, the goodness
and the grace
Of Him who died the soul to save of Adam's fallen
race.

16 WAINO AND PLUTANO,

For out of every nation that dwells beneath the sky,
There shall be some that will be saved to dwell with
  God on high ;
Then the little men of Borneo may share the Sa-
  viour's love,
For all who serve Him here below shall reign with
  Him above.

Appendix 5 - Life & History of Alfonso, the Human Ostrich: with Barnum and Bailey's Greatest Show on Earth, European Tour

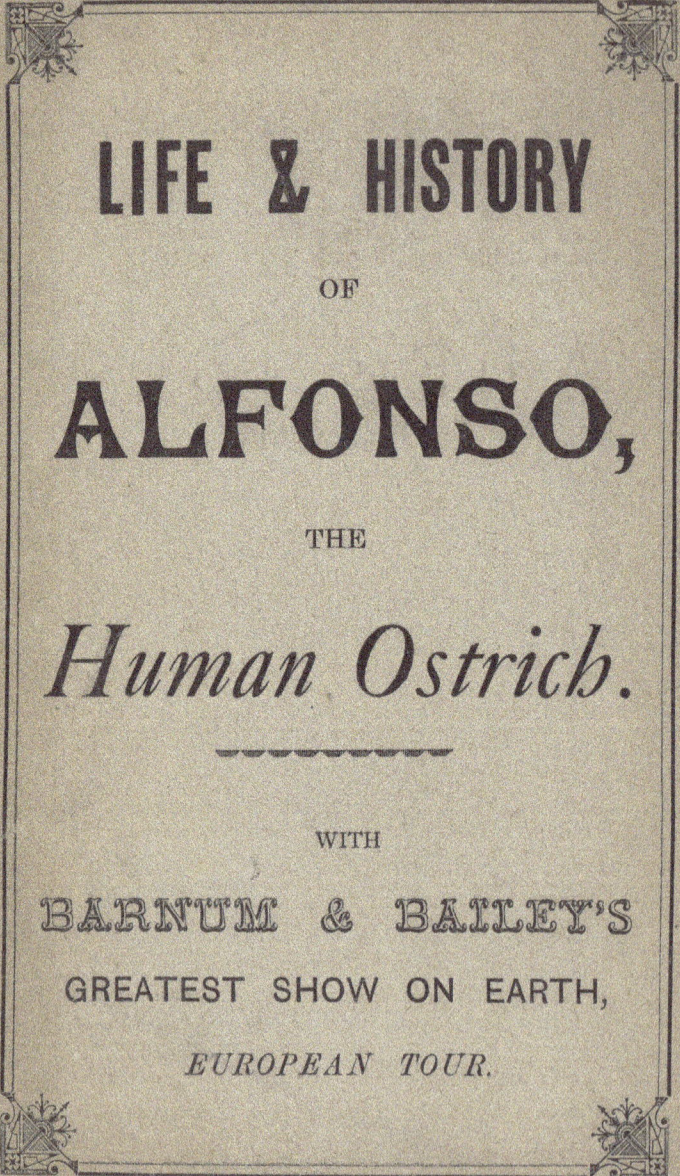

LIFE & HISTORY

OF

ALFONSO,

THE

Human Ostrich.

WITH

BARNUM & BAILEY'S

GREATEST SHOW ON EARTH,

EUROPEAN TOUR.

E. ARNOLD, Printer, 30, Blythe Road, Kensington, W

LIFE & HISTORY
OF
ALFONSO,
The Human Ostrich.

THE Human Ostrich is so called because his digestive organs are different from those of any man yet brought before physiologists or showmen.

Digestion signifies the act of separating or distributing, hence its application to the process by which food is made available for nutrition purposes.

The ostrich is known to eat continually and to swallow, most differently from all other birds, gravel, rags, nails, and what not; and without such substance the bird grows weak and its plumage fades.

ALFONSO does daily, and many times a day, swallow Poisoned Beans, Cork, Glass, Cotton Wool, Paraffin, &c., and retains good health with it; but without these foreign substances he is dispepsic.

The X-Rays plainly show the foreign substances dissolve in the Duodenum and intestinal tract, acids of the first stomach having no effect.

As his errand life shows, ALFONSO was born in the British West Indies on December 8th, 1862. When but a boy he left home on a sailing vessel as a vallet for Captain Briggam.

As his duties were continuous he had but little time for thought after himself, and he always had plenty to do. The ship was well provided with such food as is admitted for young and strong men, but ALFONSO was noticed to lose his vigour and it was generally supposed that he was homesick.

Inquiries on this supposition gave no light. They were now twenty-eight days from his home. Landing at Portland, Maine, U.S.A., he went ashore, and true to instinct, began to nibble broken glass, gravel, and some sand, to the astonishment of all his many friends, who were much interested in his welfare, he being a jolly fellow.

It required some artfulness to dodge and evade his friends long enough to get his " Pastry," but a great improvement in his health was noticed at once, and gradually he acknowledged that he had always fed on such food as far back as he could remember.

It is not customary for the inhabitants of these isles to do this.

Just his particular taste, which no one could understand, so was quite annoying to him wherever he wished to book as seaman. He then sought employment at a hotel as a bell boy. So well was the proprietor pleased with ALFONSO, that he was gradually promoted to dining room and kitchen stewart.

In such employment he travelled from Maine to California, and in December 1886 we find him in Chicago, Illinois, the Museums of that town then paying large salary for almost anything strong or uncommon. Soon after his friends prevailed on him until he consented to to allow himself to be exhibited as the Human Ostrich for Kohl & Middleton, of 150 Clark Street, under very enterprising management.

Being well started he has not been allowed to stop this line of work since, and he has featured with many large Circuses in the U.S.A.

Last fall Mr. James A. Bailey, Agent, prevailed on him to join the Barnum and Bailey Greatest Show on earth. As in all his previous trips he is giving entire satisfaction both to Mr. Bailey and the British public.

Yours respectfully,

ALFONSO.

OLYMPIA, LONDON.

Appendix 6 - What Doctors Say of Mac Norton

English translation of the medical pamphlet *Ce Que Disent Les Médecins De Mac Norton (What Doctors Say of Mac Norton)*. Translated by Olivier Palmer and Gary Varney. Facsimile of the original pamphlet follows the translated text. From the author's private collection.

***

Doctor Louis Pares

June 24, 1922

Institute of Physiotherapy - Radium - X-Rays - Hot Air Electricity - Phototherapy Mechanotherapy

RADIOLOGICAL EXAMINATION

Name: Mac Norton

Region: Stomach

Process Used: Radiography and Fluoroscopy

Image: #4181 and 4182 Position

First, Mr. Mac Norton shows us the various exercises that made him appreciated by the audience. He ingests large quantities of water, then he renders it in jets of various sizes without any effort; if he encounters any resistance, he waits and after a while renders a new jet. He doesn't force his stomach, he says. He swallows live frogs and renders them at will; he swallows bank notes of various values and renders the one asked, etc.

Direct radiological exam

The subject is of strong corpulence; a direct exam doesn't show the gastric pocket full of water or with the living frogs. As he renders the frogs, we may have seen the retrocardiac space (in a 3/4 position), but this impression was a glimpse and may be wrong.

Radiological exam with opaques objects

1. The subject, with his stomach holding water, swallowed solid, opaque masses composed of bismuth carbonate contained in a tied goldbeater's skin. Three packs of various volumes were swallowed. They were swallowed one after the other. They go down slowly in the esophagus, and the biggest object goes up and down several times before getting in the stomach.

Inside the stomach they keep at the surface, it seems, of the liquid. As the subject wants to render them, a string contraction projects the objects in the esophagus through the cardia and makes them go up very fast, a second or so.

2. Water being rejected by the usual way, the subject swallows an opaque liquid. It shows a perfectly toned stomach, not lowered, not expanded, that molds on the swallowed liquid as he drinks it, the stomach has a socket form, and for two glasses of bismuth, it doesn't go below the ombilic; for a greater quantity, it grows longer while keeping full in a horizontal and vertical manner. The peristaltic contractions are intense and lead to a gradual discharge through the pylore, which is normal.

As the liquid is rejected the pylore shuts, the lower part goes up, and the liquid is pushed away with strength through the cardia.

Louis Pares.

References

International Hospital, 180 Vaugirard St. [Paris]
June 15, 1911
Palace of Learned Societies
Conference by Dr. Paul Fares
December 19, 1911
Society of Medicine
December 23, 1911
Doctor Desterne, Hospital Beaujon
December 26, 1911

***

English translation of the promotional text found on the back cover:

I SAY I am an extraordinary scientific phenomenon in/on the order of quadruped mammals with 4 stomachs.

I DRINK 1 - 220 liters in 2h30min, 2 - 100 glasses in 10 minutes.

I EAT 52 dry breads of 4 pounds in 48h.

I SWALLOW, fishes, water tortoises, frogs, water snakes alive and by the dozens.

I KEEP THEM in the compartments of my stomach for at most 2 hours, like Jonas in the whale, then I restore them in broad daylight more "alive and kicking" than ever.

CE QUE DISENT
LES
MÉDECINS
DE
Mac NORTON

Docteur LOUIS PARÈS

INSTITUT DE PHYSIOTHÉRAPIE
——— RADIUM ———
RAYONS X — ÉLECTRICITÉ
AIR CHAUD — PHOTOTHÉRAPIE
MÉCANOTHÉRAPIE

Montpellier, le 24 Juin 1922

1, RUE DU CARRÉ-DU-ROI

TÉLÉPHONE N° 7-02

EXAMEN RADIOLOGIQUE

Nom : **Monsieur Mac NORTON**

Région : **Estomac**

Procédé utilisé : Radiographie et Radioscopie

Cliché N° **4181 et 4182**   Position

Monsieur **Mac NORTON** nous montre d'abord les divers exercices qui l'ont fait apprécier du public. Il ingurgite de grandes quantités d'eau, puis il la rejette en jets de divers diamètres sans aucun effort apparent ; si il éprouve une résistance quelconque, il attend et au bout d'un instant il émet un nouveau jet. « **Il ne force pas, dit-il, son estomac.** » Il avale des grenouilles vivantes, puis les rend au commandement, il avale des billets de banque de diverses valeurs et envoie celui qu'on lui demande, etc.

Examen radiologique direct. — Le sujet est de forte corpulence, l'examen direct de l'estomac ne permet pas de voir la poche gastrique remplie d'eau ou contenant les grenouilles. Lors du rejet des grenouilles, il nous a paru voir s'assombrir l'espace rétrocardiaque (en position de 3/4), mais cette impression très fugace peut être sujette à caution.

Examen radiologique par corps opaques. — 1°) L'estomac contenant de l'eau, le sujet a avalé des **corps solides opaques** constitués par du Carbonate de Bismuth renfermé dans de la baudruche ficelée. Il y avait ainsi 3 paquets de volume différent.

Ceux-ci ont été avalés successivement. Ils descendent lentement dans l'œsophage, et le plus volumineux des paquets monte et descend plusieurs fois avant de pénétrer dans l'estomac.

Une fois dans l'estomac, ils se maintiennent à la partie supérieure, à la surface du liquide, semble-t-il. Lorsque le sujet veut les rejeter, il se produit une forte contraction qui projette les paquets dans l'œsophage à travers le cardia et les fait remonter avec une vitesse considérable, une seconde peut-être seulement.

2°) L'eau étant rejetée par le procédé qui lui est familier, le sujet ingère le liquide opaque (émulsion de gélobarine). Celle-ci nous permet de constater que nous avons affaire à un **estomac parfaitement tonique, non abaissé, non dilaté,** qui se moule sur le liquide ingéré au fur et à mesure de l'absorption, l'estomac a la forme en chaussette et pour deux verres de bismuth, il ne descend pas au-dessous de l'ombilic ; pour une plus grande quantité, il s'étale et s'allonge légèrement, mais en restant constamment rempli dans ses portions horizontale et verticale. Les contractions péristaltiques sont intenses et aboutissent à une évacuation graduelle par le pylore qui est normal.

Lors du rejet du liquide, le pylore se ferme, le bas-fond remonte et le liquide est chassé avec force à travers le cardia.

Louis PARES.

Références

Hôpital International, 180, Rue de Vaugirard
15 Juin 1911

Palais des Sociétés Savantes
Conférence par le Docteur Paul FARÈS
19 Décembre 1911

Société de Médecine
23 Décembre 1911

Docteur DESTERNE, Hôpital Beaujon
26 Décembre 1911

THE HUMAN AQUARIUM
MAC NORTON
JE DIS.. Etre un phénomène scientifique extraordinaire de l'ordre des quadrupèdes mammifères à 4 estomacs.
JE BOIS.. 1° une pièce d'eau de 220 Litres en 2 Heures 30 minutes.
2° 100 Bocks en 10 minutes.
JE MANGE.. 52 pains secs de 4 livres en 48 Heures.
J'AVALE.. Poissons, Tortues d'eau, grenouilles. Water Snackes Vivants et par douzaines
JE LES GARDE.. Au plus longtemps 2 heures dans les poches de l'estomac,
Tel Jonas dans la baleine
puis je les restitue au grand jour tout vivants et plus frétillants que jamais
l'AQUARIUM HUMAIN
I. D. M. 1726 — 54, Faubourg Saint-Denis - Paris-10e

Appendix 7 – The Wild Man of the Prairies; or "What is It?"

Promotional pamphlet regarding a wild man attraction known as "The Wild Man of the Prairies; or 'What is It?'" *The [[Wild Man]] of the Prairies or "What is It?"* 1846. [Pamphlet]. At: Place: National Fairground Archive, University of Sheffield. Available through: Adam Matthew, Marlborough, Victorian Popular Culture, http://www.victorianpopularculture.amdigital.co.uk.libproxy.wustl.edu/Documents/Details/NFA_178T1.001

NOW EXHIBITING

AT THE EGYPTIAN HALL, PICCADILLY,

THE WILD MAN OF THE PRAIRIES;

OR,

"WHAT IS IT?"

Is it Human? Is it an Animal? Is it an extraordinary freak of Nature? or, is it a legitimate member of Nature's works? Is it not the long sought for LINK between Man and the OURANG-OUTANG, which Naturalists have for years decided does exist, but which has as yet been undiscovered? Its Exhibitors do not pretend to assert what it is, there have been innumerable speculations on this point; some, deciding it to to be the SATYR celebrated among the ancients in their mythologies—indeed its appearance favours the supposition, however wild and romantic it may seem; others have decided it to be a legitimate gendre between Man and some of the Animal races already known and acknowledged as approximating to human nature, which inhabit the vast, untracked wildernesses of India, Africa, and South America. Beings,

2

similar in description, have been seen and taken by adventurous
travellers in all these countries; but none have been secured or even
approached, comparable with this, which in every respect fills the space
so long void between Man and the Brute. Its Exhibitors have not
decided upon its rank in the scale of intelligence, notwithstanding the
balance of humanity in its favor; they have without adopting any
theory or conclusion of the various Naturalists, named it the " WILD
MAN OF THE PRAIRIE; or, " WHAT IS IT," which latter is the
universal exclamation of all who have seen it. It is of the Male species,
and much LARGER than an ordinary sized MAN, though not quite so
tall. Its Features, Hands, Ears, and the entire upper portion of its
Body, are almost perfectly HUMAN; the lower part or Hind Legs
and HAUNCHES decidedly ANIMAL ! Its Body is entirely covered,
except the Face and Hands, with long flowing Hair of various shades.
It is grave and serious in its general disposition, yet can Leap,
Run, and Climb with the agility of a Monkey. It has the intelligence
appertaining to Humanity, is exceedingly quick of Imitation, and can
do whatever it sees done, or whatever Man can do, except Speak, Read,
and Write. Its MEMORY one of the most striking Faculties, is won-
derfully acute; it recollects persons after seeing them once, distinguishes
Colors, remembers what is said to it, and in spite of habits engendered
by its Wild, Animal Life, always strives to imitate Man. It lays the
Cloth, sets the Table, and serves the Dishes to its Keeper, (not forgetting
itself when an opportunity of Sweetmeats occurs,) with the *au fait* of a
finished Waiter; lifts its Hat, shakes Hands, and bows with the grace
of a Master of Ceremonies; shoots with the Bow and Arrow; plays
Ball; beats the Drum; goes through the Military Exercies; and
plays various Games with a skill that would do honour to HOYLE
himself. Its precise age is not known, but judging it by the ordinary
rules it is supposed to be about Sixteen. It was captured, or rather
procured by barter of Guns, Beads, and other Trinkets, from a
TRIBE of COMANCHE INDIANS, by a party of MISSOURI
Hunters and Traders near the GUADALUPE Mountains in MEXICO.
The Indians, with whom it had been upwards of Ten Months, discovered it on an excursion to UPPER CALIFORNIA, hunted it down,
and by partially maiming, captured, and in a great measure domesticated
it to their mode of life. It was not until a long parley had been held,
that they were induced to part with it—they had come to regard it with

3

a degree of veneration, and indulged it to the greatest possible extent.
The first account of it appeared in a letter to the "ST. LOUIS
REPUBLICAN." from one of the party who had taken the prize.

"My dear White, if our TRAPS have failed this time our luck in another
shape has not, we have caught a real Savage Divinity—a regular out and out
Heathen, half Indian, half Bear, a sort of nondescript Demi-God, which the
Indians have been worshiping until they saw our Guns and Beads. I can
hardly describe it. It is like a Man all above its middle, only a "heap" larger,
the rest of its Body is as Animal as you please. It is short and stout as an
Esquimaux, savage as a "Meat Axe" to strangers, but quiet enough among the
Squaws. We first saw it in the "Oak Openings" coming down the Guadulupe
Mountains; one of the party was about shooting it for a Bear. when it scented
us and ran away on all fours, we giving it chase and following at least half a
dozen miles until we came "stock" upon a lot of COMANCHES where we
found it safely huddled in the corner of a Wigwam. The Indians said they
caught it in the PRAIRIES of CALIFORNIA; we at once made them an
offer, and after a long higgling about the "truck," they consented to take two
Guns, some Knives, and a Quart of Beads. We shall take it down to Austin
and let the Texans have a peep at it, then to New Orleans on our way home.
Just make up your mind, "Mi Boy," as the general says, "to see a leetle the
strangest crittur in any diggins!"

Such was the Hoosier description that led the present proprietors to
visit New Orleans to procure it for Exhibition, which they did at an
expense of several Thousand Dollars. It may not be amiss here, to
extract a short notice from one of the New Orleans Prpers respecting
this extraordinary Being. It is from the pen of the talented Editor of
the Picayune.

"We have just seen at the 'Armoury Rooms,' the most remarkable Animal
or Man, and we cannot say which, that has ever been exhibited in this, or we
believe in any other community. We had heard of its capture, its character,
and wonderful conformations, but thought it, like the thousand other advertised
shows, some catchpenny monstrosity; but we were mistaken. Whatever this
may be in the scale of Animal or Human Nature, it is certainly the strangest
Living thing our citizens have ever had the privilege of seeing. It is a Man
above its middle in every feature; below, it is as certainly Animal. Its height
does not exceed Four and a Half Feet, its Legs are very short, its Arms like the
Ourang Outang's, quite long; and its Body is larger than an ordinary sized
Man's. Covered, except its Face and Hands, with long flowing Hair, and

4

bespeaking humanity in all its looks; it stands a wonder among the World's wonders."

This was the general expression of the press, they could not elaborately describe it for they knew not what it was.

It is beyond question the most ASTONISHING LIVING PHENOMENA or NONDESCRIPT ever seen. During its short stay in New Orleans it was visited by an immense number of people, who, with one accord, pronounced it entirely UNPARALELLED. It has been constantly growing more domesticated and reconciled to its new mode of Life. It enjoys good health. It lives principally upon Nuts and Fruit, though, from long habit, it requires now and then a Meal of RAW MEAT. It drinks Milk, Water, Tea, and Coffee, and is partial to Wine, Ale, and Porter. It is not averse to being exhibited, and though sometimes shy and savage when approached too near by strangers, is kind, docile, and obedient to the slightest commands of its Keeper. It is Neat in all its Habits, fond of Ornamenting itself with Dress, and its Exhibition is such as cannot offend the most delicate taste. As a Nondescript, one of the greatest wonders in Nature, which has ever been so fruitful of strange and unaccountable things, its Exhibitors offer it to the Public, who must judge whether this description of the WILD MAN of the PRAIRIES, or "WHAT IS IT" is exaggerated or not.

HOURS OF EXHIBITION:

From half-past 11 *to* 1; *half-past* 3 *to* 5; *and half-past* 7 *to* 9.

Doors Open quarter-of-an-hour previous.

Admission, - ONE SHILLING,

Children under Ten Years, Half-Price.

FRANCIS, PRINTER, 25, MUSEUM STREET, BLOOMSBURY.

Chapter 16
Works Cited

@GWR (Guinness World Records). "WE NO LONGER MONITOR THIS RECORD Jackie Bibby once held 11 rattlesnakes in his mouth at once :o." *Twitter*, 7 Dec. 2021, 10:19 AM. https://twitter.com/GWR/status/1468238620045856769?ref_src=twsrc%5Etfw. Accessed 2 Jan. 2022.

"2,000 See Goldfish Gulping Show On Court House Plaza." *The Gazette and Daily (York, PA)*, 4 Apr. 1939, p. 2.

"A COLORED HEART-BREAKER." *The Saint Paul Globe*, 28 Dec. 1886, p. 4.

"A DYSPEPTIC EDITOR." *Camden Daily Courier*, 17 July 1886, p. 1.

"A Few Fads and Follies of an Earlier Day." *The Des Moines Register*, 24 Mar. 1968, pp. 20-21.

"A Headless Chicken." *The Chatham Record (Pittsboro, North Carolina)*, 19 Aug. 1886, p. 3.

"A Headless Rooster Alive a Year." *The Daily Chronicle (Knoxville, Tennessee)*, 10 Feb. 1884, p. 3.

"A MARKET FOR FREAKS." *The Times (Philadelphia, Pennsylvania)*, 15 Aug. 1883, p. 4.

"A MEAL OFF LAMP CHIMNEYS." *The Buffalo Times*, 17 May 1886, p. 1.

"A Peculiar Professor on Trial." *The San Francisco Examiner*, 13 June 1885, p. 3.

"A STONE EATER." *Asheville News*, 2 Dec. 1858, p. 4.

"Abdullah the Butcher Profile." *Wrestlingdata.com - the World's Largest Wrestling Database*, https://www.wrestlingdata.com/index.php?befehl=bios&wrestler=30 . Accessed 13 Nov. 2021.

"Abnormal Appetites." *The Railroad Brakemen's Journal*, vol. 5, no. 8, Aug. 1888, p. 5-6.

"About Esau." *The Dispatch*, 2 Dec. 1899, p. 5.

"ACID TOSSER HITS SPARTA SHOWMAN." *The Chattanooga Times*, 16 Aug. 1959, p. 2.

"ACTIVITIES AT ATTERBURY." *The Franklin Evening Star*, 9 Feb. 1943, p. 2.

"After Eating Snakes, Glass, Iron, 'Bosco,' 75 Years Old, Desires Christmas Dinner." *The Evening News*, 25 Nov. 1929, p. 1.

"Aged 'Bosco' In Hospital." *Star-Gazette*, 23 July 1929, p. 19.

"Albert E. Hayes, Jr. '42, Crowned New Champion Of Intercollegiate Goldfish Swallowers Yesterday." *The Tech (Cambridge, MA)*, 31 Mar. 1939, p. 1.

"Albert Still Leading." *The San Francisco Examiner*, 12 May 1889, p. 2.

"ALL SORTS." *The Saint Paul Globe*, 17 June 1888, p. 11.

"Alonzo Gill (1902-1979)." *AncientFaces*, www.ancientfaces.com/person/alonzo-gill/5 7239149. Accessed 9 Aug. 2021.

Anderson, Harry. "Hello, Sucker! (TV Special)." *Showtime*, 1986.

Antill, Bill. "Mentally Ill Need Facilities." *The Palm Beach Post*, 29 Aug. 1962, p. 1.

Apel, Therese. "Teen Who Bit Head off Hamster Withdrawn from Ole Miss." *USA Today*, Gannett Satellite Information Network, 31 Mar. 2015, www.usatoday.com/ story/news/nation/2015/03/31/teen-who-bit-head-off-hamster/70745284/. Accessed 9 Aug. 2021.

"ARRESTED SNAKE EATER TELLS OF HIS PROFESSION." *The Atlanta Constitution*, 10 July 1904, p. 10.

"ATTERBURY HAS EATING WONDER." *The Republic (Columbus, IN)*, 23 Dec. 1942, p. 8.

Austin & Stone's Museum Advertisement, *The Boston Globe*, 3 Oct. 1886, p. 11.

B.W. "'Cooch Dancer' Season's Low." *Dayton Daily News*, 30 July 1975, p. 38.

Ballantine, Bill. "Carny an Afternoon with Cynthia Paulsen, Who Kept the Wonder City Alive." *Florida Magazine*, 30 Sept. 1984, p. 9.

Barakat, Matthew. "Animal Groups Agree to Pay Nearly $16M to Ringling." *The Washington Times*, 15 May 2014, www.washingtontimes.com/news/2014/may/15/animal-g roups-agree-to-pay-nearly-16m-to-ringling/. Accessed 9 Aug. 2021.

Barker, Eddie. "He Saw the Geek Eat the Bird Feathers and All - Or Did He?" *The Atlanta Constitution*, 28 Sept. 1960, p. 5.

Baron, Percy. "Collection of Rare and Interesting Cases." *The London Medical and Physical Journal*, XLII, pp. 203–205. July to December, 1819.

Bayle, Frank. "Thousands Converge On Winter Shows." *The Tampa Times*, 7 Feb. 1959, pp. 1-10.

"Bee Combo's Ky. Trek a Winner; Spending Is Up." *The Billboard*, 7 Aug. 1943, p. 30.

"Beno, The Snake Eater." *The Billboard*, 6 Oct. 1900, p. 5.

BIOGRAPHICAL SKETCH OF SERPENTINA THE SERPENT LADY

Blassie, Fred, and Keith Elliot. Greenberg. "Classy" *Freddie Blassie: Listen, You Pencil Neck Geeks*. Pocket Books, 2003, p. 17.

Blau, Andy. "Re: Geeks..." Received by Nathan Wakefield, 23 Sept. 2021. Email.

Bloodgood, David. Interview. By Nathan Wakefield. 1 June 2022.

Bodhi, Sinn. Interview. By Nathan Wakefield. 7 August 2020.

Boles, Don. *The Midway Showman*. The Pinchpenny Press, 1967.

"Bosco Is Better." *The Pittsburg Daily Headlight*, 8 Sept. 1900, p. 4.

"Bosco Original 'Eat-Em-Alive.'" *The Pittsburg Headlight*, 31 Aug. 1911, p. 5.

"Bosco Wants Snake Money." *The Coffeyville Weekly Journal*, 26 Oct. 1900, p. 3.

"Bosco Will Be Here." *People's Voice*, 22 Aug. 1901, p. 3.

"'Bosco' Dead." *The Akron Beacon Journal*, 2 Dec. 1899, p. 1.

"'Bosco' Is Dying from a Snake Bite." *The Leavenworth Weekly Times*, 6 Sept. 1900, p. 1.

"'Bosco' Left Town." *The Pittsburg Headlight*, 4 July 1901, p. 1.

"'Boscos' Hard on Rattlers." *The Washington Post*, 11 Oct. 1908, p. M4.

Bosworth, Patricia. *Diane Arbus: A Biography*. W. W. Norton Company, 2005.

Braden, Frank. "The 'Wonders' Of A Circus Side Show." *Illustrated World*, Jan. 1922, pp. 1-13.

Bragg, Rick. "Jazzy Final Sendoff for Chicken Man." *The New York Times*, 1 Feb. 1999, p. 17.

Brian, Magic. "RE: Geek Act Questions." Received by Nathan Wakefield, 1 Mar. 2019. Email.

Brubaker, Jack. "Goldfish Gulping." *Lancaster New Era*, 10 Jan. 1984, p. 10.

Brunn, George Le. *The Wild Man of Borneo Has Just Come to Town*, Francis, Day, & Hunter, 1890. Sheet music print.

Bryson, Rhett. Interview. By Nathan Wakefield. 6 March 2023.

Bryson, Rhett. Notes from Joe McKennon interview. 19 Sept. 1982. Personal collection of Rhett Bryson.

Buckholder, Alfred. "Some Wonders From the West." *Strand Magazine, Volume 21*, edited by George Newnes, 1901, pp. 465-471.

Bügmüncher, Reggie. Interview. By Nathan Wakefield. 14 May 2020.

Burdette, Dick. "They'll Charm You Wittily At Fun Fair." *The Orlando Sentinel*, 18 Nov. 1976, p. 1.

"CAN PLAYING THE MONKEY MAKE A MAN A BRUTE." *The Spokane Press*, 18 Mar. 1910, p. 13.

"CARGO OF SNAKES." *The Chatham Record (Pittsboro, NC)*, 27 June 1895, p. 1.

"Carnival Act Here Brings Complaints." *Hope Star*, 30 Sept. 1977, p. 1.

"Carnival 'Snake Lady' at Hanazono Shrine in Shinjuku." *Tokyo Reporter*, 21 Nov. 2010, . Accessed 9 Aug. 2021.

"Carnival, n." *OED Online*, Oxford University Press, June 2021, www.oed.com/view/ Entry/28104. Accessed 30 July 2021.

Casal, Tom "Mike the Headless Chicken Festival" Received by Nathan Wakefield. 4 Sept. 2019. Email.

"Case of Polyphagia." *The London Medical Repository and Review, Section II. - - Abstracts of Practical Facts, British, and Foreign, with Remarks*, III, no. 15, 1826, pp. 265-266.

Caulfield, James. *Portraits, Memoirs, and Characters, of Remarkable Persons, from the Reign of Edward the Third, to the Revolution*. Vol. 1, R. S. Kirby, 11, London-House-Yard, Paternoster-Row, 1813.

Caveney, Mike, and William V. Rauscher. *Servais Le Roy: Monarch of Mystery*. Mike Caveney's Magic Words, 1999.

"Cecum." *Encyclopædia Britannica*, Encyclopædia Britannica, Inc.

"Chaz Chase Diet A Lighted Cigar For Lunch." *Tyler Morning Telegraph*, 24 July 1981, p. 15.

"Chaz Is The Name, Says Chaz Chase; So 'Chaz' It Is!" *The Cincinnati Enquirer*, 17 Jan. 1932, p. 5.

"Cheer Leader At N. M. College Challenges Mines Fish Gulpers." *El Paso Herald-Post*, 3 Apr. 1939, pp. 1, 7.

"Chicken Man Makes Magic for the GOP." *The Daily Spectrum (Saint George, UT)*, 16 Aug. 1988, p. 11.

"Chickens Now Safe From Prince." *The Atlanta Constitution*, 7 Oct. 1973, p. 6.

Christ, C.M. Interview. By Nathan Wakefield. 17 September 2020.

Christopher, Milbourne. *Magic, a Picture History*. Dover Publications, 1991.

"Circus and Carnival Advertisements Section." *The Billboard*, 25 Oct. 1919, p. 74.

Claude Louis Delair, Aka Mac Norton." *Université De Napierville*, www.udenap.org/personnalites/mac_norton.htm. Accessed 21 May 2020.

"Coal Heaver's Capacity." *The Star Press (Muncie, Indiana)*, 22 Feb. 1925, p. 13.

Cohen, Howard. "Florida High School Student Bites Head off a Live Chicken." *Miami Herald*, 4 Apr. 2018, www.miamiherald.com/news/state/florida/article207874479.html. Accessed 11 May 2020.

Coleman, Joe. Interview. By Nathan Wakefield. 4 June 2019.

"Collegiate Goldfish Eaters." *St. Louis Post-Dispatch*, 9 Apr. 1939, p. 10.

Collis, Helen. "Contestant in Arabic Version of Britain's Got Talent Bites Head off Snake." *Daily Mail Online*, Associated Newspapers, 9 Oct. 2013, www.dailymail.co.uk/news/article-2449865/Contestant-Arabic-version-Britains-Got-Talent-bites-head-snake.html. Accessed 9 Aug. 2021.

Condon, Tom. "Sick Sideshow of Drug Addict Has Got to Go." *Hartford Courant*, 5 May 1988, p. C1.

Cooper, Frank. "City Youth Claims Fish Gulping Mark." *The Daily Times (Salisbury, MD)*, 15 Apr. 1973, p. 1.

Corsaro, David. "Todd Robbins: Dead End and Scrambling." M-U-M, vol. 112, no. 5,

October 2022, pp. 37-38.

Crawford, Byron. "Former Sideshow 'Wild Man' Has His Day in the Center Ring." *The Courier-Journal*, 6 Apr. 1979, p. B1.

Cullen, Frank. *Vaudeville, Old & New: an Encyclopedia of Variety Performers in America*. Routledge, 2007.

"Curiosity Of Nature Will Be Displayed." *The Brownsville Herald*, 4 Feb. 1937, p. 11.

"Cyrus Gingrich Dies From Heart Attack Saturday Evening." *The Daily News (Lebanon, PA)*, 23 Apr. 1951, pp. 1-5.

Dante, Georgette. Interview. By Nathan Wakefield. 7 March 2023.

"Dark Horse Co-Ed Grabs Goldfish Swallowing Title." *The Austin American*, 6 Apr. 1939, p. 1.

Devault, Russ. "Harry Anderson, True or False." *The Atlanta Constitution*, 7 June 1986, p. 29.

"DIGESTION IS FAST, THAT'S WHY HE CAN SWALLOW GOLDFISH." *The Oshkosh Northwestern*, 8 Apr. 1939, p. 18.

Dimuro, Gina. "'No Other Life Than That Of A Freak': The Story Of Annie Jones, P.T. Barnum's Bearded Lady." *All That's Interesting*, 2 May 2019, allthatsinteresting.com/annie-jones-bearded-lady.

"DIVORCES 'MONKEY-MAN.'" *The Hutchinson Gazette*, 4 Feb. 1910, p. 1.

"Does Tricks Before Staff." *Star-Gazette (Elmira, NY)*, 30 Apr. 1928, p. 19.

Eastman, Tom. "Best of The Ear: English Jack, Hermit of Crawford Notch." *The Mountain Ear*, 5 Feb. 1982, www.conwaydailysun.com/news/best-of-the-ear-english-jack

-hermit-of-crawford-notch/article_90d9e9f5-8f31-5a3b-a946-ba7d7b9306a4.html. Accessed 9 Aug. 2021.

"Eats Garter Snake When He Finds His Socks Coming Down." *The Tampa Tribune*, 21 Feb. 1919, p. 7.

"ECCENTRIC SWALLOWERS." *St. Louis Globe-Democrat*, 24 Nov. 1889, p. 11.

"Eden Musee." *The Nebraska State Journal*, 3 Dec. 1889, p. 5.

Ellis-Petersen, Hannah. "The Big Stop: Ringling Bros Circus Closes after 146 Years." *The Guardian*, Guardian News and Media, 15 Jan. 2017, www.theguardian.com/us-new s/2017/jan/15/ringling-bros-circus-closes-animalrights-barnum-bailey-peta. Accessed 9 Aug. 2021.

"Emporia, Kan., Events" *The Billboard*, 13 Oct. 1900, p. 2.

"ESAU LIKES SNAKES." *The Salina Daily Union*, 27 Sept. 1900, p. 1.

"'Esau' Is Dead." *The Coffeyville Weekly Journal*, 7 Sept. 1900, p. 7.

"Event and Comment." *The Michigan Alumnus*, June 1905, pp. 401-402. *HathiTrust*, Michizupo.

"Exit of Oofty Goofty." *The San Francisco Examiner*, 28 June 1885, p. 4.

"F. & M. Wrestler Downs Six Live Goldfish And Becomes New Champion Of Gulpers." *Intelligencer Journal*, 23 Mar. 1939, p. 1.

"Facts About Freaks and Fakes." *Rapid City Journal*, 16 Dec. 1925, p. 6.

"Facts about Microcephaly." *Centers for Disease Control and Prevention*, 23 Oct. 2020, www.cdc.gov/ncbddd/birthdefects/microcephaly.html. Accessed 21 July 2021.

"FAMOUS FOR OSTRICH STOMACHS." *Harrisburg Daily Independent*, 18 June 1890, p. 3.

"Famous Freak, Zip, 83, Dying." *The Evening News (Harrisburg, Pennsylvania)*, 9 Apr. 1926, p. 22.

"Farm Security Administration/Office of War Information Black-and-White Negatives." *Library of Congress*, www.loc.gov/pictures/search/?q=russell%20lee%20snake%20sides how&co=fsa. Accessed 9 Aug. 2021.

"FATE PLAYS HAVOC WITH 'HUMAN OSTRICH'." *The Pittsburgh Press*, 10 Apr. 1901, p. 12.

Fellner, Chris. "Ward Hall Talks about Geeks." *Freaks*, Nov. 1998, p. 14.

Fiedler, Leslie A. *Freaks: Myths and Images of the Secret Self.* Anchor Books Edition, 1993.

Filan, Kenaz. *The New Orleans Voodoo Handbook*. Destiny Books, 2011.

"FIRE EATING REQUIRES ONLY NERVE, SAYS KI KI." *The Los Angeles Record*, 15 Apr. 1907, p. 4.

FitzGerald, William G. "SIDE-SHOWS." *Strand Magazine, Volume 13*, edited by George Newnes, 1897, pp. 407-416.

Flintoff, Corey. "In India, Snake Charmers Are Losing Their Sway." *NPR*, 8 Aug. 2011, www.npr.org/2011/08/08/139086119/in-india-snake-charmers-are-losing-their -sway. Accessed 9 Aug. 2021.

Frank, Priscilla. "Artist Joe Coleman Paints Serial Killers And Celebrities." *HuffPost*, 23 Nov. 2015, www.huffpost.com/entry/joe-coleman-paintings_n_564cafe6e4b08c74b73 3963a?guccounter=1. Accessed 9 Aug. 2021.

"Freddie Blassie, Pro Wrestler Popular as Villain, Dies at 85." *The New York Times*, The

Associated Press, 8 June 2003, www.nytimes.com/2003/06/08/sports/freddie-blassie-p
ro-wrestler-popular-as-villain-dies-at-85.html. Accessed 9 Aug. 2021.

Friday, Jon. Letter to Rhett Bryson. 11 Dec. 1986. Personal collection of Rhett Bryson.

Gartner, Michael. "Geek's Hobby Is Not for the Faint of Heart." *Hartford Courant*, 30
Mar. 1987, p. C2.

"Geck, n.1." *OED Online*, Oxford University Press, June 2021, www.oed.com/view/E
ntry/77280. Accessed 30 July 2021.

"Geek, n." *OED Online*, Oxford University Press, March 2020, www.oed.com/view/E
ntry/77307. Accessed 30 July 2021.

"Geek, v." *OED Online*, Oxford University Press, March 2020, www.oed.com/view/En
try/257679. Accessed 30 July 2021.

"Geek." *Dictionary.com*, www.dictionary.com/browse/geek. Accessed 9 Aug. 2021.

"geek." *Merriam-Webster*, www.merriam-webster.com/dictionary/geek. Accessed 9 Aug.
2021.

"Geek." *Online Etymology Dictionary*, www.etymonline.com/word/geek. Accessed 9
Aug. 2021.

Gervais, Marty. *My Town: Faces of Windsor*. Biblioasis, 2006.

"Glom, v." *OED Online*, Oxford University Press, June 2021, www.oed.com/view/Ent
ry/79071. Accessed 30 July 2021.

"'Gobbler' Recalls Goldfish Swallowing." *Fairbanks Daily News-Miner*, 9 Mar. 1974, p.
10.

"Gold Fish Eating Athlete Sets New Gulping Record." *The Hammond Times*, 3 Apr.

1939, p. 1.

"Goldfish Eating Record Set By DePaul Student." *The Jacksonville Daily Journal*, 8 Apr. 1972, p. 8.

"Goldfish Gulper's Condition Fair; College Head Denies Suspensions." *Intelligencer Journal*, 5 Apr. 1939, p. 1.

"GOLDFISH GULPERS SUSPENDED BY SCHOOL." *The Gazette and Daily (York, PA)*, 4 Apr. 1939, p. 2.

"GOLDFISH GULPING TITLE NOW AT 74." *Standard-Speaker (Hazleton, PA)*, 1 Apr. 1939, p. 1.

"Goldfish Supply Wiped Out By Swallowing Contestants." *Alabama Journal*, 3 May 1968, p. 16.

"Goldfish Swallowing 'Goes Pro,' Night Club Performer Gulps 127." *The Boston Globe*, 12 Apr. 1939, p. 2.

"Goldfish, Angleworms, Now It's White Rats." *The Paducah Sun-Democrat*, 13 Apr. 1939, p. 1.

"Goldfish-Gulping Professional Now." *Lansing State Journal*, 12 Apr. 1939, p. 16.

"Good Old Goldfish Swallowing Revived." *The Daily Item (Sunbury, PA)*, 7 Feb. 1969, p. 7.

"Good Program Last Night." *The Daily Telegram (Long Beach, CA)*, 4 May 1907, p. 4.

"Great Waldo Is Dead By His Own Hand, Love Sick." *The Daily American (Somerset, Pennsylvania)*, 21 Aug. 1952, p. 5.

Gresham, William Lindsay. *Monster Midway; an Uninhibited Look at the Glittering*

World of the Carny. Rinehart, 1953.

Grow, Doug. "Carny-Turned-Priest Hawks Life on the Midway." *Star Tribune*, 16 Jan. 1994, p. 3B.

Guinness World Records. "RE: United States | /contact/record-enquiry" Received by Nathan Wakefield, 2 Dec. 2019. Email.

"'HABA HABA' MAN BURNED BY GASOLINE." *The Oregon Daily Journal*, 12 Mar. 1910, p. 12.

"Hadji Ali, Miracle Man, Coming Here." *The Capital Times (Madison, WI)*, 1 Oct. 1928, p. 4.

"Hadji Ali, the "Human Camel". 1935. *Sherman Grinberg Library*, www.gettyimages.com/detail/video/los-angeles-superimposed-over-members-of-the-los -angeles-news-footage/539738054. Accessed 9 Aug. 2021.

"Hadji Goes Whale One Better." *The Charlotte Observer*, 11 Feb. 1927, p. 2.

Hall, Ward. "King of the Sideshows". Interview by James Taylor. *James Taylor's shocked and amazed!: on and off the midway*. Taylor & Kotcher, Dolphin-Moon Press, 2018.

"Harry Blitz, Original 'Haba-Haba' Man, Dead." *The Minneapolis Morning Tribune*, 8 June 1915, p. 8.

"Harry Tucker On Main Street." *Richmond Times-Dispatch*, 24 Sept. 1936, p. 11.

Hartley, Dale. "The Cobra Effect: No Loophole Goes Unexploited." *Psychology To-day*, Sussex Publishers, 14 Oct. 2020, www.psychologytoday.com/us/blog/machiavellia ns-gulling-the-rubes/202010/the-cobra-effect-no-loophole-goes-unexploited. Accessed 9 Aug. 2021.

Hartzman, Marc. "A Touch of Knowledge: Pregnant Snake Charmer for Hire." *Huff-*

Post, 7 Dec. 2017, www.huffpost.com/entry/a-touch-of-knowledge-preg_b_4938739 . Accessed 9 Aug. 2021.

Hartzman, Marc. *American Sideshow: an Encyclopedia of History's Most Wondrous and Curiously Strange Performers.* Jeremy P. Tarcher/Penguin, 2005.

"Harvard Student Quits Goldfish-Gulping Race." *The Boston Globe*, 22 Mar. 1939, p. 12.

"Haunted House Facts." *America Haunts*, 31 Aug. 2019, www.americahaunts.com/ah /facts/. Accessed 9 Aug. 2021.

"He Found Snakes." *Topeka State Journal*, 26 Feb. 1902, p. 6.

"HE LIVED ON METAL." *Harrisburg Telegraph*, 27 Feb. 1900, p. 3.

"HE SWALOWED LIVE GOLDFISH." *The Indiana Gazette*, 4 Mar. 1939, p. 2.

"Headless Chickens." *The San Francisco Examiner*, 30 Sept. 1879, p. 1.

"HEADLESS ROOSTER STRUTS HIS STUFF." *Spokane Chronicle*, 19 Sept. 1945, p. 2.

"'HEADLESS WOMAN' ILLUSION EXPOSED; POLICE CLOSE SHOW." *St. Louis Post-Dispatch*, 29 Apr. 1939, p. 1.

"HEADLESS, YET ALIVE AND WELL." *The Columbian (Bloomsburg, Pennsylvania)*, 19 June 1868, p. 1.

Heinke, Ed. "'Wild Men Of Borneo' Home At Mount Vernon." *The Tribune (Coshocton, Ohio)*, 1 Apr. 1973, p. 2.

"HERE'S ANOTHER! YOUTH SAYS HE'LL EAT 25 ROACHES." *The Gazette and Daily (York, PA)*, 21 Apr. 1939, p. 1.

Hester, Matthew. "The History of Pro Wrestling in The U.S (Part 1)." *Bleacher Report*, Turner Sports Network, 11 Aug. 2010, www.bleacherreport.com/articles/433611-the -history-of-pro-wrestling-in-the-us-part-1. Accessed 1 Aug. 2021.

Hezekiah Trambles (1898 - 1979)." AncientFaces, www.ancientfaces.com/person/heze kiah-trambles-birth-1898-death-1979/90651421. Accessed 9 Aug. 2021.

Hicks, Jack. "Hermit Finds All He Needs Are Memories." *The Cincinnati Enquirer*, 16 Mar. 1987, p. A9.

Hill, David. "Remembering Harry Anderson: A Magician Hiding in Plain Sight." *The Ringer*, 17 Apr. 2018, www.theringer.com/tv/2018/4/17/17248358/harry-anderson-o bituary-night-court-magic. Accessed 9 Aug. 2021.

"Hiram and Barney - WILD MEN OF BORNEO." *The Human Marvels*, 11 July 2017, www.thehumanmarvels.com/wild-men-of-borneo/. Accessed 9 Aug. 2021.

"History - American Museum of Magic." *American Museum of Magic*, www.american museumofmagic.com/history/. Accessed 9 Aug. 2021.

Houdini, Harry. "Houdini's Entertaining Chat." *The New York Dramatic Mirror*, 8 Nov. 1902, p. 18.

Houdini, Harry. "Reading and Rubbish." *The Conjurers' Monthly Magazine*, Oct. 1906, p. 49.

Houdini, Harry. "Unknown Facts Concerning Robert Houdin." *Conjurers' Monthly Magazine*, 15 Sept. 1906, pp. 6-9.

Houdini, Harry. *Miracle Mongers and Their Methods A Complete Expose*. E.P. Dutton & Company, 1920.

Houdini, Harry. *The Unmasking of Robert-Houdin*. The Publishers Printing Co., 1908.

Hudson, Walt. "I Was a Teenage Blockhead!" *Sideshow World*, . Accessed 9 Aug. 2021.

"HUMAN OSTRICH DINES TOO FAST ON HARDWARE." *The New York Times*, 13 Apr. 1904, p. 9.

"'HUMAN OSTRICH' DEAD." *Wilson County Citizen*, 18 June 1897, p. 1.

"Human Ostrich's New Diet." *The Times-Democrat* (New Orleans, LA), 22 Nov. 1908, p. 2.

"Humane Society Missed Good Chance to Relieve Bosco's Suffering." *The Minneapolis Tribune*, 2 July 1901, p. 7.

Hunniford, John. "Recollections of a Veteran Magician." *Linking Ring*, Oct. 1956, pp. 27-29.

Hutsell, James K. "Missouri Manuscript." *Tri-County News* (King City, MO), 21 Apr. 1939, p. 2.

"IN GENERAL." *Chicago Tribune*, 14 Jan. 1887, p. 8.

"In Our Last Issue' Section." *The Billboard*, 3 Aug. 1935, p. 57.

"IRON DID NOT DIGEST." *Muscatine Semi-Weekly News Tribune*, 6 May 1904, p. 3.

"IS SWALLOWING SAME AS EATING?" *Fort Scott Tribune and The Fort Scott Monitor*, 16 May 1911, p. 3.

Isay, David, and Harvey Wang. *Holding On*. W.W. Norton & Company, Inc., 1996.

"It Was Bosco, Not Esau." *The Coffeyville Weekly Journal*, 14 Sept. 1900, p. 7.

Ives, Mike. "The Midway Just Ain't What It Used to Be." *Arizona Republic*, 10 Nov. 1980, p. C11.

Jackie Bibby: Texas Snakeman." *Jackie Bibby: Texas Snakeman*, http://www.texsnakem an.com/. Accessed 2 Jan. 2022.

Jackson, Kimberly L. "LCCC Student Takes '89 Title." *The Morning Call*, 30 Aug. 1989, p. B3.

Japenga, Ann. "*SHOWSTOPPERS.*" The Los Angeles Times, 1 Sept. 1992, pp. E1-E8.

"JOHN FASEL, HUMAN OSTRICH." *Times Union*, 2 May 1904, p. 7.

Johnny's United Shows Advertisement, *The Billboard*, 17 June 1957, p. 92.

Jones, Jack. "Vaudeville Comic Chaz Chase Dies at 82." *The Los Angeles Times*, 6 Aug. 1983, p. 7.

"JONES, The GLASS-EATER." *Hagerstown Exponent*, 7 Apr. 1886, p. 2.

Kahn, Max. "Mad Riot of Fun." *Detroit Free Press*, 19 Apr. 1908, p. 6.

Kalver, Bruce. "Dorothy Dietrich - A Great Escape." *M-U-M*, Apr. 2016, pp. 36-43.

Karr, Todd. "Soirees Fantastiques The Magic of Robert-Houdin ." *MAGIC Magazine*, Oct. 2006, pp. 46-50.

Kellock, Harold, and Beatrice Houdini. *Houdini, His Life Story: from the Recollections and Documents of Beatrice Houdini*. Heinemann, 1928.

Keyser, Wayne. "Carny Lingo." *On the Midway*, 2008.

King Jr., W. A. *Rattling Yours...Snake King*. W.A. King, Jr., 1964.

"KNIFE BLADES FOUND IN 'HUMAN OSTRICH.'" *The Ellensburg Dawn*, 7 Apr. 1908, p. 1.

Laroche, Stephen. "Breaking Kayfabe with Kamala." *SLAM! Wrestling*, CANOE Network, www.canoe.ca/SlamWrestlingBiosK/kamala_jul01-can.html. Accessed 1 June 2021.

"Last Joke of The Campaign." *The Times (Richmond, Virginia)*, 6 Nov. 1900, p. 4.

Lewis, Arthur H. *Carnival*. Trident Press, 1970.

"Litho-, comb. form." OED Online, Oxford University Press, June 2021, www.oed.com/view/Entry/109136. Accessed 30 July 2021.

Littlechild, Chris. "The Man Who Ate An Airplane Piece By Piece." *Ripley's Believe It or Not!*, 2 Apr. 2019, www.ripleys.com/weird-news/mangetout/. Accessed 9 Aug. 2021.

"Live Headless Chickens." *The Weekly Marysville Tribune*, 31 Dec. 1879.

"Local Brevities." *The San Francisco Examiner*, 10 Sept. 1890, p. 6.

"Looking Backward." *The Waxahachie Daily Light*, 13 Jan. 1912, p. 5.

"Looks Like The Press Ate A Lot More That Day Than Deliberato." *The Paducah Sun-Democrat*, 4 Apr. 1939, p. 1.

"Lubbock police determine touring side show too freaky." *Austin American-Statesman*, 23 Feb. 1997, p. B3.

Lucy The Geek, *Mezco Toyz*, www.livingdeaddolls.com/lddarchive/30_01.html. Accessed 9 Aug. 2021.

"MADE HIS STOMACH SELF-SUPPORTING." *The Washington Standard*, 1 May 1908, p. 2.

Mank, Gregory William. "Afterward." *Censored Screams: The British Ban on Hollywood*

Horror in the Thirties, McFarland & Company, Inc., 1997, p. 165.

Mannix, Daniel P. *Freaks We Who Are Not as Others*. Juno, 2000.

Mannix, Daniel P. *Memoirs of a Sword Swallower*. V. Vale, 1996.

Mansfield, Brian. "Ozzy Osbourne Bit the Head off a Bat 33 Years Ago Tonight." *USA Today*, Gannett Satellite Information Network, 21 Jan. 2015, www.usatoday.com/story/life/entertainthis/2015/01/20/ozzy-osbourne-bit-the-head-of f-a-bat-33-years-ago-tonight/77604434/. Accessed 9 Aug. 2021.

"Many Snake Eaters." *The Billboard*, 8 Dec. 1900, p. 10.

Marcelliee, Rhadolph. "The Black Magician." *The Success Book - Volume Two*, edited by Jay and Frances Marshall, Magic, Inc., 1975, p. 323-332.

Marshall, Steve. "Donba Jutsu." *MAGIC Magazine*, Jan. 2010, pp. 48-51.

Massachusetts General Laws. Section 33. General Law - Part IV, Title I, Chapter 272, Section 33, www.malegislature.gov/Laws/GeneralLaws/PartIV/TitleI/Chapter272/Se ction33. Accessed 1 Aug. 2021.

Matsuyama, Mitsunobu. "The Legend of Donba-Jutsu." *Gibecière*, Winter 2015, pp. 9-52.

Maurer, David W. "Carnival Cant: A Glossary of Circus and Carnival Slang." *American Speech*, 5th ed., vol. 6, Duke University Press, 1931, p. 331.

McCardell, Roy. "Step Up and Hear Roy McCardell." *The Nebraska State Journal*, 6 Nov. 1921, p. 13.

McHarry, Charles. "From Goldfish to Panties and Back..." *Daily News (New York, NY)*, 25 May 1952, p. 64.

McKennon, Joe. *Circus Lingo*. Carnival Publishers of Sarasota, 1980.

McKennon, Joe. Letter to Rhett Bryson. 18 Feb. 1987. Personal collection of Rhett Bryson.

McNamara, Brooks. "Talking." *The Drama Review* 31.2 (1987): pp. 39-56.

Meah, Johnny. "Notes on Geeks." *Freaks, Geeks & Strange Girls*, Last Gasp, 2004, p. 138.

Metrowebukmetro. "Man Bites off Snake's Head Live on TV." *MetroUK*, Associated Newspapers Limited, 23 Feb. 2010, www.metro.co.uk/2010/02/23/man-bites-off-sna kes-head-live-on-tv-123851/. Accessed 9 Aug. 2021.

Michigan Legislature. Section 750.347, 1931 - Am. 2015. www.legislature.mi.gov/(S(l 2lqtrecl4yl01xinzvlp5jn))/mileg.aspx?page=getObject&objectName=mcl-750-347. Accessed 1 Aug. 2021.

Mieg, Juan. "Curious Notices on the Spectacle of Mr. Robinson." *Gibecière*, edited by Noah Levine, Winter 2014 ed., Conjuring Arts Research Center, 2014, pp. 105-169.

"Minstrels and Vaudevillers." *The Brooklyn Citizen*, 5 May 1889, p. 6.

Mitchell, James E. *The Story of Jack, The Hermit of The White Mountains*. 1891.

"More Knocks." *The Rockland County Journal News*, 11 Aug. 1951, p. 4.

"MUNCIE MAN, BITTEN THOUSANDS OF TIMES BY THE MOST POISO-NOUS OF SNAKES, DIES." *Muncie Evening Press*, 13 Feb. 1939, p. 1.

Murphy, Ray. "Inside Look at Fairs." *The Boston Globe*, 3 Feb. 1983, p. 60.

Murray, Jeffrey. Letter to Rhett Bryson. Feb 1987. Personal collection of Rhett Bryson.

Neutert, Natias. "Bottom's Up!" *Genii*, Mar. 1993, p. 320.

Nickell, Joe. *Secrets of the Sideshows*. The Univ. Press of Kentucky, 2008.

"NO PROSECUTION FOR THROWING A SNAKE." *Norwich Bulletin*, 19 May 1911, p. 1.

Notice Sur Jacques De Falaise, Ses Habitudes, Sa Nourriture Et Les Moyens Qu'il Emploie Pour Conserver Sa Santé. Impr. De Ballard (Paris), 1820.

"Odd Characters in Houston (No. 4.)." *The Houston Post*, 10 Aug. 1900, p. 8.

"Oddball Olympians Perform." *The Tampa Tribune*, 30 Apr. 1974, p. 7D.

Oliver, Mark. "The Story Of Tarrare, The Insatiable Glutton Who Ate Everything From Human Flesh To Live Eels." *All That's Interesting*, All That's Interesting, 8 Aug. 2018, allthatsinteresting.com/Tarrare. Accessed 9 Aug. 2021.

Onion, Rebecca. "The Snake-Eaters and the Yards." *Slate Magazine*, Slate, 27 Nov. 2013, www.slate.com/news-and-politics/2013/11/the-green-berets-and-the-montagnards-ho w-an-indigenous-tribe-won-the-admiration-of-green-berets-and-lost-everything.html. Accessed 9 Aug. 2021.

"Oofty Goofty - He Goes to the Wrong Place to Sell His Wares." *San Francisco Chronicle*, 1 Nov. 1887, p. 5.

"Oofty Goofty in Helena." *The Independent-Record*, 20 Jan. 1893, p. 1.

"Opening of the Six-Day Walking Match." *San Francisco Chronicle*, 10 May 1889, p. 6.

"Orphans Doubt If Elephant Can Duplicate Feats of Hadji Ali." *Reading Times*, 27 Feb. 1926, p. 3.

"Osco The Snake Eater Is Out of the Business." *Davenport Morning Star*, 28 June 1902, p. 8.

"Ostrich Stomachs." *The Daily Palladium (Benton Harbor, Michigan)* 16 Aug. 1890, p. 3.

"Ostriches Out of Picture As Hadji Ali Eats." *Wisconsin State Journal*, 5 Oct. 1928, p. 4.

Pares, Louis. *Ce Que Disent Les Medecins De Mac Norton*, Institut De Physiotherapie, 1922.

Parsons, Neil. *Clicko: The Wild Dancing Bushman*. University of Chicago Press, 2010.

Patrin, Nate. "Punks, Geeks, Kings, And Men: Listening To 'Classy' Freddie Blassie's Discography." *VICE Sports*, VICE Media, 6 May 2016,www.vice.com/en/article/3dgq9 w/punks-geeks-kings-and-men-listening-to-classy-freddie-blassies-discography. Accessed 9 Aug. 2021.

"PETE WILL SHAVE THE LION TAMER." *The Brainerd Daily Dispatch*, 12 July 1912, p. 3.

"Phrase 'Pencil Necked Geek' Is Devised." *History TV*, AETN UK, www.history.co.uk/ this-day-in-history/27-april/phrase-pencil-necked-geek-is-devised. Accessed 9 Aug. 2021.

"Police Stop Two Carnival Exhibits." *Henryetta Daily Free-Lance*, 25 May 1951, p. 1.

Polidoro, Massimo. "Blind Alley: The Sad and 'Geeky' Life of William Lindsay Gresham." *Skeptical Inquirer*, July / August 2003, pp. 14-17.

"Polyphagy, n." *OED Online*, Oxford University Press, June 2021, www.oed.com/view /Entry/236718. Accessed 30 July 2021.

"Prefers a Diet of Snakes." *The Dispatch*, 20 Sept. 1900, p. 1.

"Pugilistic." *The San Francisco Examiner*, 16 May 1887, p. 3.

"Pure Clean Grit." *The Capital Journal*, 29 June 1903, p. 7.

Putnam, Dave. "Where Are Those Geeks and Freaks?" *Indiana Gazette*, 22 May 1996, p. 9.

"Queen' Accused of Assault." *The Victoria Daily Times*, 10 May 1911, p. 1.

Rankin, Allen. "Rankin File D'ja Ever See Anything Free At A Carnival?" *The Montgomery Advertiser*, 17 Oct. 1948, pp. Three-B.

"Rattle Snakes Ran Rampant After Esau Left Town." *The Daily Herald*, 28 June 1901, p. 3.

"Relatives of 'Bosco' Circus Freak, Are Sought." *The Bridgeport Telegram*, 29 Oct. 1927, p. 10.

"REMARKABLE MEN." *The Courier (Butler, Alabama)*, 4 Oct. 1883, p. 2.

"Remember?" *Carlsbad Current-Argus*, 24 Oct. 1940, pp. 1, 6.

"Ringling Railroad Owner, Art Collector." *The Capital Times (Madison, WI)*, 2 Dec. 1936, p. 6.

"Ripley's Outrageous Oddities." *PBS*, WGBH Educational Foundation, https://www.pbs.org/wgbh/americanexperience/features/ripley-oddities/. Accessed 9 April 2023.

Robert-Houdin, Jean-Eugène. *Memoirs of Robert-Houdin: Ambassador, Author, and Conjurer*, Geo. G. Evans, 1860, pp. 184-191.

Roberts, Jack W. "South Florida Fair Opens At Homestead." *The Miami News*, 2 Feb. 1957, p. 1.

Robinson Jr, George "Re: Contact Us Form Submitted on Viking Mfg. Co." Received by Nathan Wakefield. 23 Feb. 2020. Email.

Rogan, Joe, host. *Joe Rogan Experience #1527 - David Blaine.* YouTube, 18 Aug. 2020, https://youtu.be/NY3Zg37nIHo. Accessed 30 July 2021.

"Rolling Off the Miles." *The San Francisco Examiner*, 2 Jan. 1891, p. 4.

Rosenberg, David. "Shedding Light on Voodoo Rituals in Haiti." *Slate Magazine*, Slate, 6 Nov. 2013, .

Ryan. "'Classy' Freddie Blassie - Dead at 85." *Wrestler Deaths*, Ten Bell Salute, 5 Dec. 2015, www.wrestlerdeaths.com/freddie-blassie-death/. Accessed 9 Aug. 2021.

Rydell, Wendy, and George Gilbert. *The Great Book of Magic.* Plenary Publications International, Inc., 1976.

S.D., Trav. "Hubert's: Last Dime Museum in the Old Times Square." *Travalanche*, 17 July 2018, www.travsd.wordpress.com/2018/07/17/huberts-last-dime-museum-in-the-old-times-square/. Accessed 9 Aug. 2021.

Sabrina. "The True Sideshow Origins Of Freaks And Geeks." *Ripley's Believe It or Not!*, 7 Sept. 2018, www.ripleys.com/weird-news/freaks-and-geeks/. Accessed 9 Aug. 2021.

"SAM HELMS' $40 BEAR." *The Catholic Union and Times (Buffalo, NY)*, 11 Mar. 1886, p. 2.

Samuels, Clarence. Interview. By Rhett Bryson and Jim Pitts. 9 May 1980.

Sann, Paul. "Not Too Tasty, But Oh You Kid, How They Tickle." *The Indianapolis News*, 17 Apr. 1968, p. 42.

"Saturday Night Live - February 9th, 1985." *Saturday Night Live*, Season 10, Episode 13, NBC, 9 Feb. 1985.

"SAYS IGNORANCE ABOUT SNAKES COSTS COUNTRY $220,000,000 AN-

NUALLY." The News-Chronicle (Shippensburg, PA), 9 Dec. 1927, p. 1.

Schiffman, Nathaniel. *Abracadabra!: Secret Methods Magicians & Others Use to Deceive Their Audience*. Prometheus Books, 1997.

Scott, Mary. "'Appalachian Phenomenon' of Snake Handling Explained." *USA Today*, Gannett Satellite Information Network, 18 Feb. 2014, www.usatoday.com/story/news /nation/2014/02/17/snake-handling-phenomenon/5571403/. Accessed 9 Aug. 2021.

Seay, Clara Callaway. "Why Should I Worry?" *The Selma Times-Journal*, 31 Mar. 1922, p. 3.

"Seek Legislative Probe For Goldfish Protection." *The Indianapolis Star*, 31 Mar. 1939, p. 1.

"Serpentina Displayed." *Valley Morning Star (Harlingen, TX)*, 3 Feb. 1937, p. 6.

"Serpentina of the Sideshow, Pet of Circus Freaks, Finds It's a Good World After All." *The St. Louis Star*, 9 Sept. 1922, p. 3.

"Serpentina, A Real Living Mermaid?" *The Plain Speaker (Hazleton, PA)*, 25 Sept. 1937, p. 8.

Shaw, Scott. "Brother Power, The Geek." *Scott Shaw!'s Oddball Comics*, 28 Sept. 2003, https://web.archive.org/web/20120502021207/http://www.oddball-comics.co m/article.php?story=archive2003-09-29&query=Brother%2BPower. Accessed 11 March 2023.

"Shed A Tear For Wild Man Of Boreno." *The Fresno Bee The Republican*, 15 Oct. 1970, p. 1-C.

Sherman, Gene. "Mice and Man." *The Los Angeles Times*, 1 Sept. 1952, p. Part 2, 1.

Shores, Matthew W. "Interlude Misemono and Rakugo : Sideshows and Storytelling."

A History of Japanese Theatre, edited by Jonah Salz, Cambridge University Press, Cambridge, 2016, pp. 184-189.

"Side Show Halted In Aliquippa." *Pittsburgh Sun-Telegraph*, 21 June 1941, p. 3.

"Sideshow Performers Enjoy Jobs." *The Newark Advocate*, 19 Aug. 1987, p. 2.

"Signor Blitz." *The Sun and the Erie County Independent*, 15 Feb. 1889, p. 3.

Singh, Gurvinder. "Inside the Village Defying India's 40-Year-Old Ban on Snake Charming to Keep the Dying Tradition Alive." *Insider*, 30 Oct. 2019, www.insider.com/photos-snake-charmers-in-india-defy-local-laws-2019-10. Accessed 9 Aug. 2021.

Skoyles, John. *Secret Frequencies: A New York Education*. University of Nebraska Press, 2007.

"Snake Eater Bitten Again." *St. Joseph Gazette-Herald*, 25 July 1901, p. 4.

"Snake Eater Bitten by Moccasin." *The Rice Belt Journal*, 30 Oct. 1903, p. 1.

"SNAKE EATER WAS SATISFIED." *The Long Beach Press*, 31 Jan. 1907, p. 1.

"Snake Eating in Kansas." *Washington Palladium*, 21 Mar. 1903, p. 1.

"Snake Nearly Ate Snake Eater." *The St. Louis Republic*, 24 Oct. 1900, p. 9.

"Snake-Oid in Toils of Law." *The Fort Scott Republican*, 14 May 1911, p. 1.

"SNAKEOID' IS READY TO QUIT." *The Tampa Tribune*, 10 Feb. 1921, p. 5.

Snyder, Susan. "Kids Day Draws 87,000 to Fair for Fun, Games." *The Morning Call*, 31 Aug. 1990, p. B3.

Soboleski, Hank. "Hadji Ali, the Weirdest Person to Have Ever Visited Kaua'i." *The*

Garden Island, 29 Mar. 2020,
www.thegardenisland.com/2020/03/29/lifestyles/hadji-ali-the-weirdest-person-to-have
-ever-visited-kauai/?fbclid=IwAR0rL5wWmRgN-3EIQG1EK0xW4KAksY94UiPL0_
gWJptDnkZFomvUDNQqcbw. Accessed 9 Aug. 2021.

Southeast Missouri District Fair Advertisement, *The Billboard*, 10 Sept. 1955, p. 64.

"SPAINIARD EMULATES OSTRICH." *Birmingham Gazette*, 15 Nov. 1932, p. 5.

Statutes of Pennsylvania. Title 18, Chapter 59, Sec. 5904. December 6, 1972,
www.legis.state.pa.us/cfdocs/legis/LI/consCheck.cfm?txtType=HTM&ttl=18&div=0
&chpt=59. Accessed 1 Aug. 2021.

Stegner, Bentley. "My Nite Out." *The Cincinnati Enquirer*, 8 Jan. 1941, p. 6.

Stencell, A. W. *Seeing Is Believing: America's Sideshows.* ECW Press, 2002.

Still on the Road: 1978 World Tour: US December. 7 Nov. 2016, www.bjorner.com/DS
N04890%201978%20US%20Tour%20December.pdf. Accessed 9 Aug. 2021.

"Strangest Diet." *Guinness World Records*,
www.guinnessworldrecords.com/world-records/67621-strangest-diet?fb_comment_id
=719387731513128_954646514653914. Accessed 9 Aug. 2021.

Stuart, John. Interview. By Nathan Wakefield. 5 September 2019.

"Supermensch: Alice Cooper and the Infamous Chicken." *YouTube*, A&E IndieFilms,
https://youtu.be/VpSRweIT_YU. Accessed 9 Aug. 2021.

"Swallowing Live Goldfish Wins $10 Bet at Harvard." *The Boston Globe*, 4 Mar. 1939, pp.
1-16.

Swiss, Jamy Ian. "Presto: A Grand Master." *Genii*, Dec. 2010, pp. 64-70.

Taylor, James. "(After Tonight's about) Geek Shows." Received by Nathan Wakefield, 17 Feb. 2019. Email.

Taylor, John. *Works of John Taylor the Water-Poet Comprised in the Folio Edition of 1630*. S.n., 1869.

"Teacher Inspired Fad of Gulping Goldfish." *The Los Angeles Times*, 7 Sept. 1969, p. 12.

Terrell, Alex. "Horrific Moment French Sports Champion Bites Head off a Live Rooster and Smiles at the Camera." *The Sun*, 14 Aug. 2019, www.thesun.co.uk/sport/9720126 /french-sports-bites-head-live-rooster-camera/. Accessed 9 Aug. 2021.

"The Bella Union." *Star Tribune*, 7 Jan. 1934, p. 51.

"THE BOY OSTRICH." *The Philadelphia Inquirer*, 11 Nov. 1894, p. 24.

"The Chicken That Lived for 18 Months without a Head." *BBC News*, BBC, 10 Sept. 2015, www.bbc.com/news/magazine-34198390. Accessed 9 Aug. 2021.

"THE END OF ESAU." *Daily Advocate (Victoria, TX)*, 5 Sept. 1900, p. 3.

"The First Headless Chicken." *Santa Cruz Sentinel*, 2 Aug. 1885, p. 2.

"THE GLASS-EATER." *The Inter Ocean (Chicago, IL)*, 31 Mar. 1886, p. 8.

"'The Great Waldo' Found Dead of Gas." *The Courier-News (Bridgewater, New Jersey)*, 21 Sept. 1952, p. 28.

"The Headless Chicken Mania." *The Pantagraph (Bloomington, Illinois)*, 26 Sept. 1879, p. 3.

"The Human Ostrich." *Vermont Phoenix*, 2 July 1897, p. 8.

"The Jim Rose Circus vs. Jake the Snake Roberts." *Thrillist*, 9 July 2009, www.thrillist

.com/contest-sweepstakes/jim-rose-circus-vs-jake-snake-roberts. Accessed 9 Aug. 2021.

"The Original Bosco---The Famous Italian Magician." *M-U-M*, Mar. 1918, pp. 1-3.

"The ORIGINAL STONE EATER." *The Times (London, Greater London, England)*, 22 Dec. 1788, p. 1.

"The Rise of The Geek." *Unnatural Selection: Why the Geeks Will Inherit the Earth*, by Mark Roeder, Arcade Publishing, 2014.

"THE ROYAL AQUARIUM." *The Standard (London)*, 3 Oct. 1893, p. 2.

"The Snake-Eating Game." *The Pittsburgh Press*, 26 May 1903, p. 20.

"The Wild Samoans." *WWE*, https://www.wwe.com/superstars/wildsamoans. Accessed 28 March 2023.

"This 'Nut' Ate a Waterbed to Get His Name Recorded for Posterity." *The Billings Gazette*, 15 Oct. 1981, p. 2.

Thomas, Gordon. *Bed of Nails: the Story of the Amazing Blondini with Experiences: an Autobiographical Introduction*. O'Brien Press, 1981.

Thomas-Lester, Avis. "Drug Addict Sideshow Raises Ruckus at Prince William Fair." *The Washington Post*, 13 Aug. 1991, www.washingtonpost.com/archive/local/1991/08/13/drug-addict-sideshow-raises-ruckus-at-prince-william-fair/acd8238e-32ad-4047-8417-4be985e62d88/?utm_term=.a6c0a8026f12. Accessed 9 Aug. 2021.

Thompson, John. "It Wasn't Funny at the Time." *MAGIC Magazine*, Apr. 2008, p. 88.

Thring, Oliver. "Should the RSPCA Have Pursued the Man Who Ate a Live Goldfish?" *The Guardian*, Guardian News and Media, 21 Dec. 2012, https://www.theguardian.com/lifeandstyle/wordofmouth/2012/dec/21/louis-cole-ate-goldfish-rspca. Accessed 1

Dec. 2021.

Tiede, Tom. "Prodigies Bag Big Bucks by Going Pro." *Abbeville Meridional*, 26 Feb. 1980, p. 6.

Torch Glossary of Insider Terms." *Pro Wrestling Torch*, TDH Communications Inc., 2008, www.pwtorch.com/insiderglossary.shtml. Accessed 9 Aug. 2021.

Tregembo, George. Letter to Rhett Bryson. 8 Jan. 1988. Personal collection of Rhett Bryson.

Trota, Michi. "The Bizarre Origins of the Words Nerd and Geek." *Encyclopedia Britannica*, www.britannica.com/story/where-do-the-terms-nerd-and-geek-come-from?fbclid=IwAR3j-cjFbm6H-_jr1kSRjnz4cU_8c1-apG0G0qV2Wau3MgkdWahQeu3-Tss. Accessed 1 Aug. 2021.

"Two Hundred Live Rattlesnakes." *Rutland Weekly Herald*, 29 July 1886, p. 3.

Underwood, Mitya. "Hadji Ali's in a Tough Act to Swallow – Just Ask David Blaine." *The National*, 14 Aug. 2014, www.thenational.ae/arts-culture/hadji-ali-s-in-a-tough-act-to-swallow-just-ask-david-blaine-1.264533?videoId=5587698090001. Accessed 9 Aug. 2021.

"Unemployed WPA Worker' Swallows 142 Fish at Lebanon." *Elizabethtown Chronicle*, 14 Apr. 1939, p. 1.

Uno. "Coney Island, N.Y." *The Billboard*, 30 May 1953, pp. 59, 75.

"Untitled Bill Jones Act Description." *The Republic (Columbus, IN)*, 7 Sept. 1891, p. 4.

"Untitled Walter L. Main Circus Paragraph." *The Ogden Standard-Examiner*, 8 Aug. 1937, p. 12A.

Urban, Sylvanus, editor. *The Gentleman's Magazine*. Vol. 298, Chatto & Windus,

1905.

Usher, William T. *Endangered Species*. Midway Publications, 1999.

Valleau, Henry, and Walt Hudson. "Magical Whirligig." *New Tops*, Mar. 1982, pp. 32-33.

"Volstead Rum Ruins Bosco, Snake Eater." *Detroit Free Press*, 26 July 1929, p. 1.

"W.G. Wade Chalks 207G First 6 Days At Mich. State Fair." *The Billboard*, 17 Sept. 1955, pp. 70-77.

"Wade Grosses 210G AT Mich. State Fair." *The Billboard*, 25 Sept. 1954, p. 71.

Wall, Kim, and Caterina Clerici. "Welcome to Gibtown, the Last 'Freakshow' Town in America." *The Guardian*, Guardian News and Media, 26 Feb. 2015, www.theguardian.com/us-news/2015/feb/26/welcome-to-gibtown-the-last-freakshow -town-in-america. Accessed 9 Aug. 2021.

"Warrant Out for Snake-Eater." *The Evening Transcript*, 18 Dec. 1902, p. 9.

Waugh, Dexter. "501 Goldfish - A New Record." *The San Francisco Examiner*, 13 Oct. 1975, p. 5.

Webb, Sam. "Woman Bites Head off Live SNAKE and Devours It in Front of Horrified Audience on Chinese Version of Britain's Got Talent." *The Sun*, 5 July 2017, www.theguardian.com/us-news/2015/feb/26/welcome-to-gibtown-the-last-freakshow -town-in-america. Accessed 9 Aug. 2021.

West, John H. "Bosco's Experiences - Continued from Last Week." *Baxter Springs News*, 29 Sept. 1900, p. 4.

West, John H. "Bosco's Experiences." *Baxter Springs News*, 22 Sept. 1900, p. 4.

"Westcar Papyrus: Khufu and the Magician." *Ancient Egypt Online*, https://ancientegy

ptonline.co.uk/khufumag/. Accessed 14 Nov. 2021.

"Where the Freaks Go in Winter." *Hamilton Daily News*, 11 Oct. 1930, pp. 12-13.

"Wild Man of Borneo." *The Seattle Post-Intelligencer*, 20 June 1892, p. 3.

Wilder, Paul. "In Our Town." *The Tampa Tribune*, 23 Sept. 1948, p. 9.

Windley, Charles. *From Fleas to Floating Girls*. From the collection of Robert Baxt.

Winter, Sarah Kate Istra. *The Secret History of Carnival Talk*. Faer Press, 2014.

"Wleklinski Takes Blame For Carnival." *The Hammond Times*, 10 Aug. 1950, p. 1.

Wood, Graeme. "Wrestlemaniac." *The Atlantic*, Atlantic Media Company, 2012, www.theatlantic.com/magazine/archive/2012/07/wrestlemaniac/309010/. Accessed 9 Aug. 2021.

Wood, Dallas E. "The Prowler." *Redwood City Tribune*, 25 July 1940, p. 12.

"WOODBURY DOTS." *Camden Daily Courier*, 12 Mar. 1886, p. 1.

Wright, Tolly. "David Blaine Went on an Epic Quest to Learn How to Regurgitate Frogs." *Vulture*, New York Media, 19 Jan. 2017, https://www.vulture.com/2017/01/how-david-blaine-learned-to-regurgitate-frogs.html. Accessed 9 Aug. 2021.

"Wyckoff Benevolent Meets." *Times Union (Brooklyn, NY)*, 2 Mar. 1912, p. 12.

"Yorker To Try For Goldfish Eating Title." *The Gazette and Daily (York, PA)*, 31 Mar. 1939, p. 2.

"Zip The 'What Is It?'" *Weird NJ*, weirdnj.com/stories/local-heroes-and-villains/zip-the-what-is-it/. Accessed 24 Aug. 2022.

Zoltak, James. "Feld Entertainment Is Bringing Ringling Bros. and Barnum & Bailey Circus Back." *VenuesNow*, 21 Oct. 2021, https://venuesnow.com/feld-entertainment-is-bringing-the-circus-back/. Accessed 24 Aug. 2022.

Index

Special Thanks

The author would like to thank the following for their support and contributions to this book.

Jean Albiges
The American Museum of Magic
Robert Baxt
Bentley Historical Library
Andy Blau
Jay Bliznick
David Bloodgood
Sinn Bodhi
Magic Brian
Reggie Bügmüncher
Rhett Bryson
The Conjuring Arts Research Center
C.M. Christ
Joe Coleman
Georgette Dante
City of Fruita
David Gilleran
Alan Howard
Houghton Library
Jerome Lawrence and Robert E. Lee Theatre Research Institute
Jim R. Moore
The National Archives
New Hampshire Historical Society

Petra Schweigert Otto
Olivier Palmer
Lisa Marie Pompilio
George Robinson Jr.
Nat Sharpe
Peter Striffolino
John "Red" Lawrence Stuart
Paul Szauter
James Taylor
Gary Varney
Wellcome Collection

About the Author

Nathan Wakefield is a writer, juggler, actor, musician, and marketer from southeast Michigan. He has a bachelor's degree in marketing from Ferris State University. When he is not busy working on projects, he enjoys practicing martial arts, attending rock concerts, and seeking out various forms of weird entertainment.

www.ingramcontent.com/pod-product-compliance
Lightning Source LLC
Chambersburg PA
CBHW040828300326
41914CB00059B/1288